The Many Faces of Political Islam

The Many Faces

— OF —

Political Islam

Religion and Politics
in the Muslim World

MOHAMMED AYOOB

The University of Michigan Press

— Ann Arbor —

2011   2010   2009   2008   4   3

A CIP catalog record for this book is available from the British Library.

Library of Congress Cataloging-in-Publication Data

Ayoob, Mohammed, 1942–
    The many faces of political Islam : religion and politics in the
Muslim world / Mohammed Ayoob.
        p.   cm.
    Includes bibliographical references and index.
    ISBN-13: 978-0-472-09971-9 (cloth : alk. paper)
    ISBN-10: 0-472-09971-X (cloth : alk. paper)
    ISBN-13: 978-0-472-06971-2 (pbk. : alk. paper)
    ISBN-10: 0-472-06971-3 (pbk. : alk. paper)
    1. Islam and politics.   2. Islam and politics—Islamic countries.
    3. Islamic countries—Politics and government.   4. Islam—21st century.   I. Title.

BP173.7.A875   2008
320.5'57—dc22   2007030970

For Salma—
intellectual companion, best friend

Contents

Preface

This book is a work of synthesis that aspires to fill a major gap in the literature on political Islam—namely, the need for an introductory text that is readily intelligible to the nonspecialist reader while simultaneously highlighting the complexity of the subject and avoiding oversimplification. The book is written both for students and for general readers interested in the subject. The idea of the book emerged from my own experience over the past several years of teaching an upper-division undergraduate course on political Islam to students majoring in political science, international relations, history, and sociology. It became apparent to me that an overarching text written within a comparative framework was necessary to introduce undergraduates to the subject before they proceeded to study more detailed material specific to particular themes, regions, or countries.

There is no dearth of high-quality specialist literature on various aspects of the interaction of religion and politics in Islam. However, much of it is very dense, highly specialized, country specific, and not easily ingested by students without adequate background in the study of Islam and/or of the Muslim world. Above all, there is no single text that analyzes comparatively the various forms of political activity undertaken in the name of Islam and presents them in a way that would make the multifaceted phenomenon intelligible to students and general readers alike. The book that I have written will, I believe, be able to perform this task. It aims not only at providing students and lay readers a comprehensive and comprehensible introduction to the subject of political Islam but also at directing them to further readings to which they can turn for additional and detailed information on individual themes and case studies. I believe that the greatest value of the book lies in its capacity to perform this dual function.

I reckon that the very same qualities of this book that are likely to appeal to students will attract the general reader genuinely interested in understanding the relationship between religion and politics in the Muslim world. The book will therefore help to dispel many of the misconceptions and stereotypes about political Islam—and, indeed, about Islam itself—among the general public, while still encouraging its readers to maintain a critical and analytical approach toward the subject. This, I believe, is an essential task given the distortions, whether deliberate or unwitting, apparent in a great deal of the writing on the political manifestations of Islam.

"Political Islam" has become a growth industry in the West in general and the United States in particular following 9/11. This has led to the emergence of a large number of half-baked "experts"—especially among the media and, with a few honorable exceptions, in the policy think tanks—who speak and write about the subject with a degree of confidence and authority that is usually related inversely to the amount of knowledge they possess about it. The situation in academia is, thankfully, much better. However, much of the scholarly literature on the subject is written by academics for each other, is highly specialized, and is not widely read either by the lay public or by students other than those who aspire to become specialists themselves.

This book attempts to bridge the gaps both between gown and town and between academic specialists and the large number of students in the social sciences and humanities interested in gaining an understanding of political Islam but not intending to become specialists in the subject. The large majority of undergraduates in political science, international relations, history, and related disciplines in the English-speaking and English-reading countries do not have adequate background of Islam and political Islam before taking a course on the subject. This book hopes to introduce these students and the general reader to the phenomenon of political Islam lucidly, without jargon, and without taking recourse—as far as possible—to non-English terms. At the same time, this book aims at alerting its readers to the complexities of the subject and its contextually rooted character. It does so by demonstrating, above all, that there are many faces of political Islam and that much of the political activity undertaken in the name of Islam is determined by discrete national contexts. The book therefore attempts to demolish the monolithic image of political Islam that has become standard fare in the West in much popular writing (the genre most read and most influential) regarding this subject.

Some of the major themes of the book were presented in seminars and/or lectures at a number of institutions, including the Center for Strategic and

International Studies (CSIS) and the Carnegie Endowment for International Peace, both in Washington, D.C.; the Council on Foreign Relations and the International Peace Academy in New York; the International Institute for Strategic Studies, the Royal Institute of International Affairs, University College, the London School of Economics, and the Institute of Ismaili Studies, all in London; the Department of International Relations at Bilkent University, Ankara; the Foundation for Sciences and Arts (Bilim ve Sanat Vakfý) in Istanbul; the American University of Kuwait; the School of International Studies at Jawaharlal Nehru University, New Delhi; the Centre for Security Analysis in Chennai; and the Institute for Defence and Strategic Studies at Nanyang Technological University, Singapore. The feedback I received to many of these presentations helped me to refine my arguments and sharpen my conclusions.

I am very grateful to Mustapha Tlili, founder and director of *Dialogues: Islamic World—U.S.—The West,* a program currently based at New York University and earlier at the New School University in New York, for inviting me to coauthor the background paper "Who Speaks for Islam?" for the project "Who Speaks for Islam? Who Speaks for the West?" and present it at a workshop hosted by Prince Hassan bin Talal in Amman. Chapter 2 of this book, "Islam's Multiple Voices," was inspired by the work I did on the background paper for the project, and Mustapha deserves much of the credit for focusing my attention on this very important topic. I am also grateful to Shireen Hunter, formerly director of the Islam Program of the CSIS and currently director of the Carnegie Project on Reformist Islam at the Prince Alwaleed bin Talal Center for Muslim-Christian Understanding at Georgetown University, for inviting me to participate in a CSIS project called "Barriers to Modernization and Democratization in the Muslim World." The paper that I presented on the interplay of internal and external factors obstructing the democratization of Muslim countries in the Middle East as part of that project helped to clarify much of my thinking on the prospects for democratization in the Muslim world. Several of the ideas first presented in that paper are reflected in parts of this book in more mature fashion.

This book would not have been completed but for a generous Capacity Building Grant from the MSU Foundation through the Office of the Provost of Michigan State University. The grant helped me get release time from teaching and funded research travel undertaken in connection with this project. Dean Sherman Garnett and Associate Dean Norman Graham of James Madison College, the school of public affairs at Michigan State University, supported my endeavors and facilitated the completion of the book in multiple ways, for which I owe them a huge debt of gratitude. Hasan Kosebalaban, Gamze Cavdar, and Matthew Zierler, three of the brightest and most promising young scholars of international relations I have come across in recent years, helped me in several ways in bringing the project to fruition, for which I am deeply grateful. In particular, Hasan spent long hours on the final draft of the manuscript, making substantive comments, checking and formatting endnotes, and making sure that the manuscript conformed to the publishers' specifications. I cannot thank him enough for his assistance, always rendered with a smile and a request for more "work." Jim Reische, my editor at the University of Michigan Press, was an invaluable source of sage advice that helped to keep me on the "straight and narrow" and prevented me from going off on too many tangents.

This book has profited immensely from the fact that, thanks to the vision of current president and former provost Lou Anna Kimsey Simon, Michigan State University has in the past three years assembled a critical mass of faculty interested in diverse aspects and regions of the Muslim world. The presence on campus of my Muslim studies colleagues—young, energetic, highly intelligent, and exceptionally committed to the study of the Muslim world—provided me with an environment very conducive to thinking about and discussing various facets of political Islam. Their input, while often indirect, has been very valuable to my work. MSU has further demonstrated its commitment to the study of the Muslim world by simultaneously establishing a Muslim Studies Program and a Muslim Studies Undergraduate Specialization. Both these ventures have dramatically helped increase MSU students' and faculty's exposure to and understanding of the Muslim world. I am particularly proud of having been chosen to lead these efforts at Michigan State University at this critical juncture.

My wife, Salma, was, as usual, a source of great strength during the period I was working on this book. She has had a long-standing interest in the interaction between religion and politics in countries of the Middle East and South Asia. Her incisive comments about various aspects of this complex subject, based on her readings and her observations as we traveled together several times in the Middle East during the past few years, often helped me sort out in my mind issues that would otherwise have remained unresolved. The book is dedicated to her in gratitude for her support and in recognition of the fact that she is the only person whose ideas I have felt free over the years to appropriate without acknowledgment or attribution.

Abbreviations

AKP   Justice and Development Party
AM   al-Muhajiroun
FIS   Islamic Salvation Front
HT   Hizb ut-Tahrir al-Islamiyya
JI   Jamaat-i-Islami
JUI   Jamiat-ul-Ulema-i-Islam
MB   Muslim Brotherhood
MMA   Muttaheda Majlis-i-Amal
NU   Nahdlatul Ulama
PA   Palestinian Authority
TJ   Tablighi Jamaat

CHAPTER 1

Defining Concepts, Demolishing Myths

Over the last decade and a half, but especially since 9/11, three major assumptions have inspired much of the popular discussion about political Islam. These are, first, that the intermingling of religion and politics is unique to Islam; second, that political Islam, like Islam itself, is monolithic; and third, that political Islam is inherently violent. This book will argue that none of these assertions captures the reality of the multifaceted phenomenon fashionably called "political Islam." It will do so by demonstrating that the Islamic religious tradition is no different from many others in terms of wrestling with the issue of religion in politics and politics in religion. It will also do so by exploring the multiple voices that claim to speak for Islam and the discrete national contexts that give different manifestations of political Islam their distinctive local color. It will do so further by arguing both that mainstream Islamist parties—which form the overwhelming majority of Islamist political formations in terms of numbers, membership, and support bases—by and large abjure violence and that factions that engage in violent activity often do so in response to state repression or foreign occupation. It will also argue that transnational extremist organizations, such as al-Qaeda and Jemaah Islamiyah, are fringe phenomena that are marginal to the primary political struggles going on within predominantly Muslim societies. Finally, it will demonstrate that political Islam does not operate in a vacuum and that variables external to Islamism, principally the nature of domestic regimes and the substance of major powers' foreign policies, have substantial impact on the emergence, popularity, and durability of Islamist movements and parties.

What Is Political Islam?

Before beginning a discussion of issues related to political Islam, one must provide an adequate definition of the terms *political Islam* or *Islamism*—that is, Islam as political ideology rather than religion or theology. At the most general level, adherents of political Islam believe that "Islam as a body of faith has something important to say about how politics and society should be ordered in the contemporary Muslim world and implemented in some fashion."[1] While correct as a broad, sweeping generalization, this is too nebulous a formulation for it to act as an analytical guide capable of explaining political activity undertaken in the name of Islam. Greg Barton points out: "Islamism covers a broad spectrum of convictions. At one extreme are those who would merely like to see Islam accorded proper recognition in national life in terms of national symbols. At the other extreme are those who want to see the radical transformation of society and politics, by whatever means, into an absolute theocracy."[2]

A more precise and analytically more useful definition of Islamism describes it as "a form of instrumentalization of Islam by individuals, groups and organizations that pursue political objectives." According to this definition, Islamism "provides political responses to today's societal challenges by imagining a future, the foundations for which rest on reappropriated, reinvented concepts borrowed from the Islamic tradition."[3] While Islamists do not necessarily agree on the strategies or tactics needed to re-create a future based on their conceptions of the golden age of early Islam, they share the yearning to "go back to the future" by reimagining the past based on their readings of the fundamental scriptural texts.

The reappropriation of the past, the "invention of tradition"[4] in terms of a romanticized notion of a largely mythical golden age, lies at the heart of this instrumentalization of Islam. The invention of tradition provides many Islamists the theoretical tools for dehistoricizing Islam and separating it from the various contexts—in terms of time and space—in which Islam has flourished over the past fourteen hundred years. In theory, this decontextualizing of Islam allows Islamists to ignore the social, economic, and political milieus within which Muslim societies operate. It therefore provides Islamists a powerful ideological tool that they can wield in order to "purge" Muslim societies of "impurities" and "accretions," natural accompaniments of the historical process, which they see as the reason for Muslim decline. However, context has a way of taking its own revenge on abstract theory when attempts are made to put such theory into practice. This is exactly what has happened to Islamism, a topic I will return to later in this book.

The Islamic Conception of the Golden Age

Patricia Crone characterizes the Islamic notion of the golden age, central to Islamist thinking, as a "primitivist utopia, both in the sense that it presented the earliest times as the best and in the sense that it deemed a simple society to be the most virtuous."[5] This notion of a golden age, limited to the time of the Prophet and the first four "righteously guided" caliphs, is not a novel twentieth-century idea.[6] It has existed, with certain variations, from the earliest centuries of Islam. However, what is new is the way it is used by modern Islamists. These Islamists posit that it is possible to re-create that golden age in the here and now and that the political energies of Muslims should be devoted toward achieving this goal by reshaping and reconstructing Muslim polities in the image of Islam's first polity, the city-state of Medina.

In contrast, the classical Muslim notion of the golden age hinged on the assumption that it is unattainable in historical time. This implicitly contextualized it in seventh-century Medina and thus ruled out its re-creation in the present or future. In fact, this continues to be true of the majority traditionalist view of the golden age today. Carl Brown has pointed out: "[M]ainstream Muslim political thought throughout the ages has protected inviolate the idealized early community by resisting the temptation to relate too precisely the pristine model to stubborn reality. The model of the early community remains thus an unsullied norm, but in the terminology of modern political science the maxims derived from the idealized model are not readily operationalized."[7] This idealization but presumed inoperability of the golden age model helped the vast majority of Muslims to reconcile themselves to the reality of imperfect political arrangements, including unjust orders and tyrannical rulers.

Only some small groups no longer politically relevant, such as the Kharijites and the early Ismailis, advocated implementing the golden age model in historical time. But they were either suppressed or unable to capture the imagination of the large majority of Muslims, who remained rooted in reality and suspicious of millenarian movements.[8] The largest minority sect, the Imami, or Twelver Shiites, came to terms with what they considered to be unjust rule through the mechanism of the occultation of the twelfth imam, the Mahdi, whose return is considered essential by them to usher in legitimate rule among Muslims and in the world.[9] Had it been otherwise—that is, had the golden age been generally perceived by a substantial segment of Muslims as a model to emulate in historical time—it would have led to incessant turmoil threatening Muslim societies with recurrent anarchy. The notions of justice and equality, enshrined in the golden age model, would have attained priority over those of order and hierarchy, thus threatening the fragile stability, first, of the Umayyad and Abbasid empires and, subsequently, of the multiple Muslim polities that succeeded them. Moreover, the model of the city-state of Medina would have never worked in the context of huge agricultural and hydraulic empires that emerged out of early Muslim conquests. These needed dynastic rule to provide continuity and stability, thus rendering the quest for the ideal an exercise in futility.[10]

Justifying the Status Quo in Classical Islam

Political quietism, which, despite periodic turbulence, became the norm among Muslim masses living under Muslim rulers for a thousand years, was the product in part of the indefinite postponement into the far future of any attempt at replicating the imagined model of perfect justice and equality that were presumed to reign supreme during the time of the Prophet and his immediate successors. The Shiites, as pointed out earlier, achieved this by sending their twelfth imam into occultation and postponing the creation of a just order until his return. The majority Sunnis achieved the same result partly by accepting the notion of the return of their own *mahdi* toward the end of time. In greater part, however, political quietism was justified by the Sunni *ulama,* the religious scholars, with the help of two interrelated arguments.

First, they argued that the alternative to tyranny would be anarchy that could lead to the dissolution of the *umma,* the community of believers, thus throwing out the baby with the bathwater. This argument was buttressed by selectively quoting from the Quran, especially the verse "O ye who believe! Obey Allah and obey the messenger and those of you who are in authority."[11] It was reinforced by reference to the maxim, often attributed to the Prophet, that "sixty years of tyranny is better than one day's anarchy." Carl Brown points out: "Rather than a divine right of rule, Islam came to recognize a divinely sanctioned need for rule . . . The Islamic tradition asserted, in effect, that mankind's need for government was so overwhelming as to make the quality of that government decidedly secondary."[12] It would not be wrong to assert that Thomas Hobbes must have been familiar with this classical Islamic argument. His social contract theory mirrors it quite faithfully.

The second argument took as its starting point the assumption that a Muslim ruler, however corrupt and unjust, was essential to preserve and defend the land of Islam against infidels and to ensure that Muslims in the realm could practice their religion freely. The existence of less-than-perfect political orders was also justified with reference to the belief that Muslims could not perform their religious obligations unless they had an imam or caliph presiding over the community, in whose name the Friday sermons could be read and who could be deemed the leader of the caravan (the metaphor used by Patricia Crone for the Muslim *umma*),[13] leading the community to salvation. Again, the character of the imam/caliph was deemed secondary, and Muslim theologians went to great extents to legitimize rule by caliphs who were visibly unjust, cruel, and corrupt.

Sunni theologians of Islam's classical period turned the defense of the status quo into a fine art. When the Abbasid caliph became a mere handmaiden of Turkic warrior-rulers from the ninth to the thirteenth centuries, leading *ulama* devised ways to bestow legitimacy on him even though he no longer exercised power in any real sense of the term. For example, in a novel interpretation of the caliph's role, the famous theologian Al-Ghazali of the eleventh and twelfth centuries advocated a division of labor between the sultan and the caliph, with the former exercising power on the latter's behalf while the latter continued to symbolize the religious unity of the *umma*. He went to the extent of justifying usurpation of power by Turkic dynasts, who constantly overthrew and replaced each other in different parts of the nominal caliph's domain, by ex post facto investiture by the caliph of their right to rule over territories they had acquired by force.[14] In fact, this practice became common in the later Abbasid period in a desperate attempt by the caliph and his advisors to make theory conform to reality. Writing two hundred years later, the Hanbali theologian Ibn Taymiyya, commonly considered to be the forebear of Ibn Abd al-Wahhab and his puritanical interpretation of Islam, argued: "The essence of government . . . was the power of coercion, which was necessary if men were to live in society and their solidarity was not to be destroyed by natural human egoism. Since it was a natural necessity, it arose by a natural process of seizure, legitimized by contract of association. The ruler as such could demand obedience from his subjects, for even an unjust ruler was better than strife and the dissolution of society; 'give what is due *from* you and ask God for what is due *to* you.'"[15]

Despite the contemporary Islamists' admiration for Ibn Taymiyya, they have in theory radically reversed the traditional orientation of Islamic theological interpretation. Their position that the golden age of pure and pristine Islam can be re-created in the contemporary era has had the opposite effect of that of political quietism and stable political orders so dear, for good reasons, to the hearts of most Islamic scholars of the classical period. The Islamists' current rhetoric mobilizing popular opinion in support of their vision has capitalized on the increasingly democratic and participatory sensibilities of the modern age. It has thus helped to mobilize large segments of the population in many Muslim countries that may otherwise have remained politically apathetic. This has certainly had destabilizing effects; but, at the same time, it has contributed in substantial measure to democratizing the political culture of several Muslim countries because of the high value it places on political activism and participation. I will return to this theme when I discuss the impact of political Islam on important Muslim countries later in this book. However, it is clear that leading theologians of the classical period of Islam would not have approved the use of political Islam for objectives against the status quo.

Colonialism and the Emergence of Islamism

As we know it today, Islamism, or political activity and popular mobilization in the name of Islam, emerged in response to a set of factors that were introduced into the Muslim world as a result of the latter's encounter with the West from the eighteenth century onward, when the West became increasingly powerful and the lands of Islam became progressively weak. This, in Muslim perceptions, was a reversal of the normal and presumably divinely ordained order of things, at least as it had persisted for a thousand years before the beginning of European ascendancy. Thus it needed both explanation and remedy. One of the most powerful explanations of Muslim degeneration was provided by those who came to be known as Salafis (meaning emulators of the *salaf al-salih,* the "righteous ancestors"). They argued that the primary reason for Muslim decline lay in the fact that Muslims—rulers and subjects alike—had deviated from the model set out for them by their righteous ancestors. The Salafis advocated that the remedy for Muslim degeneration lay in their return to the original path of Islam and in the re-creation of the model that had prevailed in the presumed golden age of the Prophet and the first four caliphs.

To be fair to the original proponents of the idea of returning to the pristine Islam of the earliest centuries, leading figures among them, such as the nineteenth-century theologian and jurist Muhammad Abduh of Egypt, advocated such a course because they believed the original teachings of Islam to be in total accord with the scientific positivism and rationality that underpinned modernity. Eminent historian Albert Hourani explains things from Abduh's point of view: "[T]he mark of the ideal Muslim society is not law only, it is also reason. The true Muslim is he who uses his reason in affairs of the world and of religion; the only real infidel (*kafir*) is he who closes his eyes to the light of truth and refuses to examine rational proofs."[16] Abduh's aim and that of his peers who thought on similar lines was to rescue Muslim societies from backwardness and superstition, which they saw as consequences of un-Islamic accretions introduced in the later centuries of Islam.

However, this modernist interpretation of the golden age was overshadowed by those among the revivalists, such as Abduh's Syrian disciple Rashid Rida, who interpreted the return to the golden age in literal terms and advocated the creation of an authentic Islamic polity based on their imagined model of the Islamic society at the time of the Prophet and his immediate successors in seventh-century Arabia. Paradoxically, Abduh himself was responsible for opening the way for such a revivalist interpretation. Malcolm Kerr has argued convincingly: "[B]y asserting that Muslims must look back to their earliest history to discover the principles of their faith, he encouraged others to reexamine traditional institutions of government and law as they had presumably existed in the great days of the Rashidun [the righteously guided] and to explain in what respects they had become corrupted. 'Abduh's stimulus thus made the almost forgotten classical theory of the Caliphate and the resurrection of the Shari'a as a comprehensive legal system live options for such men as Rashid Rida."[17]

Abduh's ideas, therefore, not only generated much of the modernist thinking in the Arab world but also inspired what came to be known as the Salafi movements in the early decades of the twentieth century. H. A. R. Gibb has pointed out: "In the matter of doctrine he [Abduh] had made a stand against uncritical acceptance of authority, or *taqlid* [imitation] . . . [But] his theological followers, led by a Syrian disciple, Shaikh Rashid Rida, continued the process with a characteristic glide toward extremism. By carrying the rejection of *taqlid* back beyond the founders of the schools [of jurisprudence] to the primitive community of the *salaf*, the 'great ancestors,' and combining with this the quasi-rationalism of scholastic logic, but without Muhammad Abduh's ballast of catholicity, they naturally gravitated toward the exclusivism and rigidity of the Hanbali outlook."[18] Scriptural fundamentalism and the rejection of accumulated tradition emerged out of this rigid literalist and decontextual-ized version of Salafism that has spawned much of contemporary Islamist thinking. Thus Abduh's prescription about returning to pristine Islam to redis-cover the rational roots of the Islamic faith turned out to be a double-edged sword. It inspired both modernist and rationalist discourse within Islam as well as a more literal call to return to Islam's golden age and re-create it in the mod-ern world.

The replacement of Muslim rulers by European colonial powers also reopened the whole question of legitimate authority in the Muslim world. As long as Muslim potentates ruled over Muslim subjects, the fiction of religious legitimacy for such rule could be maintained even if the rulers did not measure up to the original yardstick set up by the Prophet and his immediate successors. Colonialism, by replacing Muslim rulers with infidel ones, changed the entire paradigm on which authority was based in the Muslim world. Fundamental religio-political questions, including whether Muslim countries under Euro-pean rule were any longer *dar al-Islam,* "the abode of Islam," began to be raised. It was argued that if they were not, then it was the right of all Muslims, collectively and individually, to restore them to their Islamic status. If they were, then it was by definition illegal under Islamic law for them to be ruled by infidels, and it became the duty of all Muslims, individually and collectively, to strive to overthrow colonial regimes.

Therefore, out of the colonial experience emerged the equation of the Islamic concept of jihad with "striving" and "struggle" for freedom and inde-pendence in the modern political sense. Jihad, in this sense, provided the motive and the justification for many anticolonial wars and uprisings from British India, through the Anglo-Egyptian Sudan and Italian Libya, to French Algeria. Consequently, the defense of the homeland and the religious obliga-tion to defend *dar al-Islam* became inextricably enmeshed with each other in the popular Muslim imagination.[19] Resistance against non-Muslim foreign domination and encroachment, whether direct or indirect, thus became the paradigmatic jihad of modern times. The use of the term *jihad* today by Islamists denoting resistance not merely against direct foreign occupation, as in Iraq, but more generally against an iniquitous international order domi-nated by the United States and its allies has emerged as a logical corollary of the jihads waged against European colonialism in the nineteenth and twentieth centuries. Today, political Islam as a major vehicle for resistance against occu-pation and domination receives its legitimacy and credibility to a large extent from this equation of the term *jihad* with resistance to foreign domination of Muslim lands and peoples.

However, while it would be extremely difficult for common Muslims to disentangle the political and religious dimensions of resistance to foreign domination, there was and continues to be a clear distinction for hard-core Islamists between merely throwing out the foreign occupier and the creation of a state based on their imagined model of the pure and pristine age of Islam. The former was perceived as but the first step toward attaining the latter. Earliest instances of anticolonial jihad, such as those in Algeria, India, Sudan, and Libya, also witnessed attempts by the leaders of the premodern Islamist resistance movements to establish Islamic polities based on their conceptions of sharia law on territories liberated from colonial powers.[20] Contemporary Islamist political formations, such as the Muslim Brotherhood in Egypt and the Jamaat-i-Islami in Pakistan, are heirs both to the Salafi intellectual tradition and to the practical endeavors on the part of those nineteenth-century anticolonial leaders in the Muslim world who strove to create Islamic polities (as opposed to merely independent Muslim ones) in zones liberated from colonial occupation.

Contemporary Islamism

As the preceding discussion suggests, political Islam as we know it today is a relatively modern phenomenon, although not a very recent one. Its roots lie in the nineteenth-century Muslim encounter with European domination and in Muslim reactions to subjugation by infidel powers. It is no wonder, then, that political Islam speaks the language of resistance to foreign domination not only in the political but in the cultural and economic spheres as well. This is true of most manifestations of this religio-political ideology and of the movements that represent it. The Islamic Republic of Iran, despite its Shia heritage that sets it somewhat apart from the Sunni majority, has best epitomized this phenomenon in recent times.

It is also clear that the Islamists' totalistic bent betrays a very modern sensibility. Robert Hefner has pointed out: "Rather than fidelity to prophetic precedents . . . , the Islamist dream of an all-encompassing religious governance bespeaks a modern bias, one all too familiar in the twentieth-century West. It is the dream of using the leviathan powers of the modern state to push citizens toward a pristine political purity."[21] The twentieth-century concept of the "Islamic state," which has become the central focus for Islamist energies, emerged out of this preoccupation with capturing the state in order to change society. This emphasis on the importance of the state as the instrument of God's (and the Islamists') will sets the Islamists apart from Muslim traditionalists, who are usually wary of too much state interference in matters of religion.

The use of religious vocabulary as the vehicle for resistance against oppressive rule has given contemporary Islamists (as it did their nineteenth-century precursors) a powerful tool for bonding with and, thus, successfully mobilizing Muslim masses. Islamists speak the language of the people by using religious idioms that the common Muslim can relate to because he or she has been socialized in it since childhood. This is one of the major reasons why Islamism has garnered so much emotive appeal in the current era and is able to capture the imagination of ordinary Muslims suffering under foreign domination or oppressive and autocratic rule.

Moreover, as stated earlier, Islamists argue that Muslim societies declined the more they moved away from the model of the golden age that can be found in their romanticized version of the early years of Islam. Their prescription is to return to the primitive utopia of early Islam. The model of the "strangers" having failed, there is a strong tendency to revert to a highly romanticized model of the "ancestors," despite such warnings as Fouad Ajami's that the "people who surrender to the ancestors are, strictly speaking, surrendering to strangers" and that "[a]uthenticity can be as much an escape as dependence and mimicry can be."[22]

Religion and Politics in Islam

Does the conception of a religiously inspired golden age and the striving on the part of some groups to turn this imagined model into reality mean that politics and religion are inextricably intertwined in Islam? Furthermore, does it mean that the politicization of religion is unique to Islam and that other religious traditions are immune to this "malady"? These two questions, while closely interrelated, are analytically distinct and therefore need to be answered separately from one another.

In much of the popular analysis and even in a substantial portion of academic discourse, it is frequently assumed that there is no separation between the religious and political spheres in Islam. This is a myth to which Islamist rhetoric has contributed in considerable measure, especially by making constant reference to the sharia and the concept of the "Islamic state." Consequently, an image has been created not merely of the indivisibility of religion and state but of religion being in the driver's seat determining the political trajectory of Muslim societies, including their inability to accept the notion of popular sovereignty and implement democratic reforms. Nothing could be farther from the truth.

Anyone familiar with the historical record of Muslim polities would realize that, in practice, the religious and the political spheres began to be demarcated very soon after the death of the Prophet in 632 CE. This was inevitable because, according to Muslim belief, revelation ended with the Prophet's death. His immediate temporal successors, the first four "righteously guided" caliphs, while respected for their piety and closeness to the Prophet, could not claim that their decrees were divinely ordained. Several of their actions and interpretations were openly challenged, and religious and/or political dissenters assassinated three of the first four caliphs. Civil war often loomed on the horizon, and two major intra-Muslim battles were fought during the reign of the fourth caliph, Ali, largely as a result of intertribal rivalry. Intra-Muslim strife culminated in the massacre at Karbala in 680 CE of Ali's son and the Prophet's grandson Hussein (himself a claimant to the caliphate) and his seventy-odd companions, by forces loyal to the newly established Umayyad dynasty. The religious schism between Sunni and Shia dates back to this supremely political event, a war for the throne. Politics was clearly in the driver's seat.

The fiction of the indivisibility between religion and state was, however, maintained, primarily to legitimize dynastic rule so as to uphold the unity of the *umma*—even though, as stated earlier, leading theologians had to incessantly engage in intellectual acrobatics to demonstrate such unity. In short, the fiction of the inseparability between religion and politics provided a veneer to the reality of not merely the chasm between religion and state but, not infrequently, the subservience of the religious establishment to temporal authority. Criteria established by Muslim jurists to determine the legitimacy of temporal rule were minimal. There was a consensus that as long as the ruler could defend the territories of Islam (*dar al-Islam*) and did not prevent his Muslim subjects from practicing their religion, rebellion was forbidden, for *fitna* (anarchy) was worse than tyranny, since it could threaten the disintegration of the *umma*. The lessons of internecine conflict during the early years of Islam were well learned. As stated earlier, political quietism was the rule in most Muslim polities most of the time for a thousand years, from the eighth to the eighteenth centuries.[23]

The distinction between temporal and religious affairs and the temporal authority's de facto primacy over the religious establishment continued throughout the reign of the three great Sunni dynasties—the Umayyad, the Abbasid, and the Ottoman. The Ottomans not only succeeded in combining in the same person the title and functions of both sultan and caliph (which had been divided during the latter part of Abbasid rule) but also institutionalized the subservience of the religious establishment to temporal authority by absorbing the religious functionaries into the imperial bureaucracy. The Sheikh al-Islam (Şeyhül Islam in Turkish), the highest religious authority in the empire, was appointed by the Ottoman sultan and held office at his pleasure. The Turkish Republic became heir to this Ottoman tradition and has continued to exercise authority over a highly bureaucratized religious establishment through the Directorate of Religious Affairs, this time in the name of secularism. The Arab successors to the Ottoman Empire also continued to uphold the tradition of the state's domination over the religious establishment but have not been able to control religious institutions and discourse as effectively as Turkey has been able to do.[24]

The link between religion and state in the Muslim parts of South and Southeast Asia has been more complex as well as even more distant, thanks to the greater prevalence of Sufism and syncretism that have allowed religion to carve a sphere almost completely distinct from the state and autonomous of it in most respects. In the case of the Indian subcontinent, the presence of a large non-Muslim majority over whom Muslim potentates ruled for several centuries created a very special situation. In such a context, statesmanship demanded creative compromises that turned Mughal emperors into near deities for their Hindu subjects and that made the Hindu Rajputs into the sword arm of the nominally Muslim empire. Islam could only act as a periodic brake on this process, but it was certainly never in the driver's seat. Attempts to apply puritanical Islamic precepts in matters of state usually turned out to be extremely shortsighted and counterproductive because they alienated large segments of the Hindu military and civilian elites, whose allegiance and collaboration was critical for the maintenance of an empire already suffering from imperial overstretch.[25]

Muslim polities are therefore heirs to the twin traditions of the separation of the political from the religious arena and, where the two intersect, temporal supremacy over the religious sphere. The history of Saudi Arabia, considered to be the most fundamentalist of Muslim societies, demonstrates that when it comes to the crunch, the balance between the House of Saud and the Wahhabi religious establishment tilts decisively in favor of the former. Abd al-Aziz ibn Saud's suppression of the Ikhwan revolt during the early years of the kingdom provides overwhelming evidence of the primacy of the state over religious ideology in this most puritanical Muslim polity.[26] I will return to this topic in chapter 3.

In essence, therefore, the historical trajectory of religion-state relations in Islam, in terms of separation of the two and/or state domination over and instrumental use of religion, has not been very different from that of Western Christianity. However, since there has never been a single locus of religious authority in Islam (unlike in Christianity prior to the Reformation), the religious class did not pose the sort of challenge to temporal authority that the religious hierarchy presided over by the pope did to emperors and kings in medieval and early modern Europe. The dispersal of religious authority in Islam therefore normally prevented a direct clash between temporal and religious power, as happened in medieval Christendom. Simultaneously, given the diffuse nature of religious authority, it prevented the total control, except sporadically, of the religious establishment by temporal rulers. It also helped preclude the establishment of a single orthodoxy that, in alliance with the state, could suppress all dissenting tendencies and oppress their followers, as happened in Christian Europe during the medieval and early modern periods. Wars of religion and persecution of "heretical" sects were therefore infrequent in Islamdom in contrast with Christendom.[27] At the same time, it promoted the creation of distinct religious and political spheres that by and large respected each other's autonomy. This did not mean that the state in classical Islam desisted from using religion to buttress its political legitimacy. Such attempts were made on occasion, particularly under the Sunni caliphates. But the state was never very successful in intruding massively into the religious arena, which largely retained its autonomy from the temporal sphere.

It is interesting to note in this connection that the major schools of Islamic jurisprudence (*fiqh*) that have come to form the basis of what is known as *sharia* originated and evolved outside the sphere of the state and in the arena of theological scholarship. Theologians and jurists interpreted and applied Quranic injunctions and prophetic traditions within the realm of what would now be called civil society. As Wael Hallaq points out, "Islamic law did not emerge out of the machinery of the body politic, but rather arose as a private enterprise initiated and developed by pious men who embarked on the study and elaboration of law as a religious activity."[28] Although the *ulama* and the *fuquha* worked largely in tandem with the state, especially through the offices of the *qadi* (religious judges) appointed by the state, this relationship was not free of tension. This was the case because the codification of Islamic law was in substantial part aimed at formulating rules based upon Islamic teachings that would have the moral and legal capacity to constrain temporal authority in its dealing with its subjects. Sharia, as we know it today, evolved in a Janus-faced fashion, restraining both individual and state behavior. It was not an instrument of the state created by the state to serve the interests of temporal authority. It is ironic that many contemporary Islamists consider the state to be the principal agent for the production and enforcement of the sharia. This reflects the changed role of the state, which has become much more powerful and intrusive in modern times, and the acceptance of this role by the Islamists far more than it follows the practice during the classical era of Islam. It also demonstrates the Islamists' modern sensibility, which is very much at variance with that of the theologians and the jurists of premodern times who were much more wary of state intrusion than the Islamists are today.

Despite the de facto separation of religion and state in classical Islam, the two spheres could not be completely insulated from each other, both because of the initial combination of temporal and religious authority in the person of the Prophet and the righteously guided caliphs and because, as in any society, moral concerns, often couched in religious vocabulary, intruded into the political sphere. Furthermore, political and religious identities often overlapped significantly, thus making religious affiliation a marker of political identity. This provided religion another entry point into politics, and vice versa. Finally, Muslim rulers attempted to use religion and religiously sanctioned titles and institutions as instruments to legitimize their rule.

However, these features are not unique to Islam, even if they manifested themselves in Islamdom in distinctive ways. Islam is no more politicized than Judaism and Christianity, as anyone conversant with the Hebrew Bible and the religious roots of Zionism, on the one hand, and with the Crusades and the political role of the papacy, on the other, will immediately recognize. Examples demonstrating the inextricability of religion and politics abound from non-Judeo-Christian traditions as well. Hindu nationalist organizations in India blatantly use religious terminology to spread their message. The Buddhist Sangha (monastic order) in Sri Lanka has played an important role in defining the national identity of that country in Buddhist and Sinhalese terms. Politics and religion can be a heady mixture; this is demonstrated in all religious traditions, not merely in Islam.

The Myth of the Islamic Monolith

The mixing of religion and politics is no Islamic monopoly. Religion has been used for profane purposes in all religious traditions. This continues to be true in contemporary times as well. The assumption that Islam is unique in this regard is no more than a myth. The same is the case with the assumption that political Islam is a monolith. Despite some similarities in objectives and even more in the rhetoric they employ, no two Islamisms are alike.[29] Political activities undertaken by Islamists are largely determined by the contexts within which they operate. What works in Indonesia will not work in Egypt; what works in Iran will not work in Turkey. Anyone familiar with the diversity of the Muslim world—in terms of socioeconomic characteristics, culture, political system, and trajectories of intellectual development—is bound to realize that the political manifestation of Islam, like the practice of Islam itself, is to a great extent context specific and is the result of the interpenetration of religious precepts and local culture, including political culture. To quote a leading scholar of political Islam, "[I]t is intellectually imprudent and historically misguided to discuss the relationships between Islam and politics as if there were one Islam, timeless and eternal."[30]

It is true that there is an Islamic vocabulary that transcends political boundaries. However, such vocabulary is normally employed to serve objectives specific to discrete settings. In the process, while the Islamic idiom may continue to appear similar to the uninitiated observer, its actual content undergoes substantial transformation. As Eickelman and Piscatori have pointed out, politics becomes "Muslim" by "the invocation of ideas and symbols, which Muslims in different contexts identify as 'Islamic,' in support of . . . organized claims and counterclaims."[31] Since the borders of the sovereign, territorial state normally circumscribe such claims and counterclaims and the contestations that accompany them, much of the politics that goes on in the name of Islam is also confined within those boundaries.

The model of the sovereign territorial state, which had its origins in early modern Europe, was adopted by Muslim countries, as well as by the rest of the Third World, following decolonization. Like the rest of postcolonial societies, Muslim state elites also went about cultivating a sense of territorial nationalism (often a mix of ethnic and religious identities) among their populations, to legitimize the colonially crafted boundaries of their state as well as their right to rule over the state in the name of the nation. In some places—above all, in parts of the Arab world—these attempts at nation building were complicated by the existence of pan-nationalisms.[32] But overall—and including the Arab world—these efforts at nation creation based primarily on territorial criteria have succeeded in large measure, although they have had to often accommodate religious and ethnic loyalties that go beyond the territorial confines of the nation-state.[33]

That the Islamist political imagination is determined in overwhelming measure by the existence of multiple territorial states becomes very clear when one looks at the political discourse of Islamist movements and, even more, their political action. The Jamaat-i-Islami has a Pakistan-specific agenda, just as the Islamic Salvation Front had an Algeria-specific agenda. Even the strategies of the Muslim Brotherhood—which, although founded in Egypt, has branches in various Arab countries—are largely determined by particular contextual characteristics. Thus the branches in Egypt, Jordan, Syria, Kuwait, and Palestine have adopted radically different political strategies in response to specific challenges posed to them within their respective national boundaries. Indeed, as chapter 4 of the present study will demonstrate, the Muslim Brotherhood's parent organization, in Egypt, has itself mutated over time, with its leadership in the early 1980s unequivocally rejecting the more radical and militant ideas associated with Sayyid Qutb, its chief ideologue of the 1960s. Islamist political formations are governed by the same logics of time and space as their more secular counterparts.

If there are several Islamisms operating within discrete political contexts determined by the existence of sovereign, territorial states, why do most pundits, especially in the West, consider political Islam to be a monolithic phenomenon bent on implementing a single grand strategy? This is in part a function of the lack of knowledge of Muslim societies and polities on the part of many analysts in the West, especially those who dominate the media and have made it a habit of expounding their views about political Islam with a degree of self-righteousness that has an inverse relationship to their knowledge of Muslim societies. It is equally a function of the rhetoric employed by Islamists around the world, which appears to most outsiders to be very similar, if not identical.

The various Islamist movements take recourse to similar vocabulary because they draw their inspiration from the same sources and also because this vocabulary is familiar to their audiences. However, once one begins to scrutinize the political objectives and actions of discrete Islamist formations, as will be done throughout the rest of this book, it becomes clear that they are engaged primarily in promoting distinct national agendas, not a single universal agenda. Even the shared preoccupation of various Islamist groups with creating the "Islamic state" makes it very clear that they desire to do so within the territorial confines of existing states. Their objective is to Islamize existing states, not to join them in one single political entity. This demonstrates very clearly that, despite ostensible denials by some of them, Islamists have inter-

nalized the notion that the international system is composed of multiple territorial states—and that it will continue to do so into the indefinite future. It also
implies that they are acutely aware of the ethnic and cultural divisions within
the Muslim world and concede, even if implicitly, that "Islam" is but one—and
not necessarily the most salient—among the numerous identities that peoples
in Muslim countries value. The idea of re-creating a universal caliphate is cher-
ished only by the most fringe elements, such as al-Muhajiroun and Hizb ut-
Tahrir, which are most active among Muslim émigrés in Britain but without
any significant political base within Muslim countries. I will return to a discussion of these groups in chapter 7.

Violence and Political Islam

The assumption that political Islam is inherently violent cannot be farther
from the truth. The extremist transnational organizations that purport to act
politically on behalf of Islam, such as al-Qaeda, are fringe groups, which, while
they capture the West's imagination by their dramatic acts of terror, are marginal to the large majority of Islamist movements and irrelevant to the day-to-
day political struggles within Muslim countries.[34] Most mainstream Islamist
movements operate peacefully within national boundaries and attempt to
influence and transform their societies and polities largely through constitutional means, even when the constitutional and political cards are stacked
against them.[35] In this sense, mainstream Islamist movements, such as the
Muslim Brotherhood and the Jamaat-i-Islami, are reformist, rather than radical, in nature.

The major Islamist political formations, such as the Muslim Brotherhood
(MB) in Egypt, the Jamaat-i-Islami (JI) and the Jamiat-ul-Ulema-i-Islam (JUI)
in Pakistan, the Nahdlatul Ulama (NU) in Indonesia, the Parti Islam se-
Malaysia (PAS) in Malaysia, and the Islamist parties in Turkey (in their various
incarnations) have all played the game by and large according to the rules
established by regimes normally unsympathetic to the Islamist cause. Several of
them have performed credibly in elections, despite the fact that the dice has
usually been loaded against them. Others have learned to function within the
parameters set by authoritarian regimes. Some, such as the JI in Pakistan, have
not shrunk even from collaborating with military dictatorships. Others, such as
the MB in Egypt, lie low when suppressed, then bounce back organizationally
and politically when autocracies liberalize under domestic or international
pressure, but in all cases try to keep their constituencies and organizations

intact as far as possible. I will examine the cases of Islamist political formations in several important Muslim countries in greater detail in subsequent chapters, both to establish their largely nonviolent character and to demonstrate that they are prisoners of their own national contexts and, consequently, that their policies and actions are shaped by the discrete settings in which they operate.

One cannot deny that national Islamist movements have on occasion spawned militant groups that have engaged in violence to attain their objectives. However, these are exceptions rather than the rule. Sometimes, as in Algeria in the 1990s, they have been products of regime policies that have been deliberately provocative from the Islamists' perspective, resulting in armed responses on their part. However, such violent activity has invariably been counterproductive as far as achieving the political objectives of these groups is concerned. Islamist violence has begotten counterviolence on the part of authoritarian regimes whose forces are usually far better equipped and trained than the Islamist groupings. While such recourse to violence and counterviolence has on occasion led to great loss of life and property, it has hardly made a dent in the political status quo that the militant Islamists have sworn to overthrow. Examples ranging from Algeria to Egypt demonstrate the veracity of this assertion.

The most appalling example of violent Islamist activity has been in Algeria, where splinter groups from the Islamic Salvation Front (FIS) launched an armed insurrection in the 1990s following the military-backed regime's decision to cancel the second round of elections in 1992, which the FIS looked set to win. While it is true that the so-called Algerian Afghans returning from fighting the Soviets in Afghanistan contributed to the escalation in violence, the annulment of elections was the key to some Islamists turning to violence, in an act of political desperation. These groups were not able to change the status quo even after more than a decade of violent insurgency. They lost support among the general populace because of their indiscriminate use of violence that led to retaliatory killings, often by vigilante groups acting on behalf of the regime. The insurgency petered out without achieving any of its political objectives.

Militant Egyptian factions, such as the Egyptian Islamic Jihad, have suffered the same fate, although their violence, while sometimes dramatic (as in the assassination of President Sadat), never reached the levels attained by the Algerian insurrection. Some of these factions (notably the Egyptian Islamic Jihad), disillusioned because of their inability to overthrow autocratic and un-Islamic regimes at home, decided to make common cause with transnational groups, such as al-Qaeda, to target the "far enemy"—the West in general and the United States in particular. These groups see the "far enemy" as the principal supporters of un-Islamic and repressive regimes at home, the "near enemy." Therefore, they believe that hitting the United States or the West would undermine support in America and Europe for authoritarian pro-Western regimes in the Arab/Muslim world, leading to the collapse of these regimes. In truth, however, such a shift in the strategy of these groups is an admission of their failure to achieve results where it matters most—namely, at home.[36] I will return to a detailed discussion of this subject in chapter 7.

There are a couple of major cases where Islamist political groupings that can be considered mainstream clearly straddle the violent and nonviolent worlds. The foremost examples of this phenomenon are Hizbullah in Lebanon and Hamas in Israeli-occupied Palestine. However, the violence that both have engaged in is context specific and principally in the nature of national resistance to foreign occupation. Hizbullah was born as a result of the Israeli invasion of Lebanon in 1982 and flourished during the two-decade-long Israeli occupation of predominantly Shia south Lebanon, when it fought a guerrilla campaign against the occupation forces. The end of the civil war in 1990 led to its transformation from a radical, clandestine militia to a mainstream political party with a resistance wing committed to ending the Israeli occupation of Lebanese territory. Hizbullah is represented in Lebanon's parliament as one of the two major Shia parties, the other being Amal. It has become an important player in Lebanon's political game, thanks largely to its vast network of social services that caters to the needs of the most underprivileged and vulnerable sections of Lebanese society.[37]

The withdrawal of Israeli troops from south Lebanon in May 2000 augmented Hizbullah's prestige as the only Arab force capable of compelling Israel to cede conquered Arab territory. Paradoxically, it also made Hizbullah largely redundant as a military force, a factor that may have contributed to its decision to capture two Israeli soldiers in July 2006, which triggered a full-scale Israeli assault on Lebanon. Moreover, the compromises it has had to make in the process of parliamentary participation have diluted its originally stated vision of turning Lebanon into an Islamic polity à la Iran. Nonetheless, Hizbullah continues to be ambivalent regarding its role in the Lebanese polity, refusing to surrender arms, because it sees them as an essential component of its popularity among its constituency, which, while primarily Shia, includes non-Shia elements as well. I will return to this subject in chapter 6.

The Hamas movement is the political wing of the Palestinian Muslim

Brotherhood. Ironically, the Israelis were responsible in part for building up the MB in occupied Palestine in the 1980s, in order to divide Palestinians who, until that time, overwhelmingly supported the Palestine Liberation Organization (PLO). The PLO, dominated by the mainstream nationalist and secular Fatah and led by Yasser Arafat, had been the principal force resisting Israeli occupation. However, with the outbreak of the first Palestinian intifada (uprising) in 1987, the MB, until then engaged primarily in social service and educational and charitable activities, set up its political wing, called Hamas (Islamic Resistance Movement), to participate in the uprising. As the Palestinian resistance became increasingly militant after the 1993 signing of the Oslo Accords, in great part because of Israeli policies of continued Jewish settlement and interminable delays regarding turning over territory to Palestinian control, Hamas gained greater popularity, since it had declared its unequivocal opposition to the Oslo process.[38]

As chapter 6 will demonstrate, Hamas's popularity also resulted in substantial part from the PLO's conversion into the Palestinian Authority (PA) and its role as the intermediary organ of control acting as the buffer between the Israeli occupation and the occupied Palestinian population. The corruption and inefficiency of the PA added to Hamas's appeal. Furthermore, with Israel's policies becoming more oppressive and strangulating the Palestinian economy and with the PA unable to deliver social services, Hamas's network of charitable organizations moved in to fill the void by providing help and succor to the most disadvantaged segments of Palestinian society, especially in the overcrowded refugee camps and shantytowns of Gaza.[39]

At the same time, Hamas developed a military wing (especially in Gaza), which has carried out attacks against Jewish settlers, the occupying Israeli military, and civilians within Israel. During the past few years, Hamas members have undertaken several suicide missions both within Israel and in the occupied territories. However reprehensible, such suicide missions and other violent activities conducted by Hamas—as well as other Palestinian groups, including offshoots of Fatah—cannot be divorced from the fact of Israeli occupation that has generated increasing economic and political desperation among Palestinians in the occupied territories. I will return to a detailed discussion of this subject later in this book.

What distinguishes both Hamas and the Lebanese Hizbullah from al-Qaeda and other transnational Islamist organizations that take recourse to indiscriminate violence is that the violence in which Hamas and Hizbullah engage is restricted territorially and is directed against specific targets that they consider to be obstructing their goals of achieving national independence or freeing occupied territory. Despite America's strong support to Israel, both Hamas and Hizbullah have desisted from attacking American targets during the past two decades. Both Hamas and Hizbullah are organizations that fall well within the logic of the state system and do not have universal visions of a global jihad. In this sense, Hizbullah and Hamas are more similar to the Irish Republican Army or the Basque separatist group ETA than to the al-Qaeda network or Jemaah Islamiyah in Southeast Asia.[40] Their actions are driven more by nationalist considerations than by religious ones, although Islam is a major component of their strategy to mobilize their respective constituencies. This combination of nationalist and religious ideologies has a hoary tradition in the Muslim world, going back to the resistance, often couched in Islamic terms, against European colonial domination from the second half of the nineteenth century onward.[41]

The violence carried out by Hamas and Hizbullah, especially by the former, should not be conflated with the acts of terror committed by al-Qaeda or other groups that share its transnational ideology and strategy. Doing so would be counterproductive because, as the International Crisis Group points out in one of its reports, "[t]o brand all armed struggle by Muslims—even that arising out of opposition to foreign occupation—as terrorism is to strengthen the arguments of al-Qaeda that the problem is the 'further enemy,' i.e., the US and its allies, with whom it is useless to argue or try to negotiate and who only understand the language of brute force."[42] Despite the violence used by Hamas and Hizbullah, most mainstream Islamist political formations have continued to pursue their incremental and peaceful strategies within national confines. In fact, some of them have gone further and have entered what one can call the post-Islamist phase. The Justice and Development Party (AKP) in Turkey, discussed in chapter 5, is the prime example of this phenomenon, having successfully repackaged itself as a conservative democratic party, similar to the Christian Democrats in Western Europe. Hizb al-Wasat (the Center Party) in Egypt is another good example. Several of its founders left the Muslim Brotherhood to establish the organization, in an effort to gain official recognition as a political party in order to openly participate in electoral politics. Official party status has been denied to the brotherhood, although it is well known that it is probably the most popular political formation in Egypt and fields candidates under different labels. Al-Wasat has not been successful so far in getting registered as a political party, although it runs its own nongovernmental organization. The fact that the Muslim Brotherhood leadership has denounced al-

Wasat's founders as having betrayed the brotherhood by leaving the organization and renouncing their Islamist roots demonstrates the organization's post-
Islamist character.[43] Both the Turkish and Egyptian cases will be analyzed in
detail later in this book.

Conclusion

This chapter has attempted to define and disaggregate political Islam as well as
to address the three most popular myths about it in the Western media and
sections of academia. It has demonstrated that the relationship between religion and politics in Islam is not very different from that within several other
Abrahamic and non-Abrahamic religious traditions. It has argued that political
Islam is not a monolith and that Islamist movements in different countries
pursue nation-specific agendas and strategies, despite a superficial similarity in
their rhetoric. It has also shown that the large majority of Islamist movements,
those we term "mainstream," abjure violence and attempt to work within constitutional restraints imposed on them in discrete national settings. While
fringe groups, including breakaway factions and transnational extremist networks, have engaged in violence, they have been unsuccessful in attaining their
ends and, despite their dramatic acts of terror, continue to remain largely irrelevant to the political and social struggles underway in Muslim societies. Several
of these themes will be elaborated in the following chapters.

The next chapter will take up the issue of the multiplicity of Muslim voices
and the consequent cacophony that has led most Western analysts and policy-
makers to focus on the most extreme and violent Islamist formations as the
leading, if not sole, spokespersons for Islam. This is another myth that needs
serious examination.

CHAPTER 2

Islam's Multiple Voices

Despite the presence of substantial evidence to the contrary, some of which has been presented in the first chapter of this book and will be elaborated on in later chapters, many in the West continue to consider Islam to be a monolith. This monolithic perception of Islam often finds expression in articles, commentaries, and editorials that posit a clash between "Islam" and the "West." The latest incarnation of this thesis of a clash of civilizations, inspired by Princeton historian Bernard Lewis and most vividly presented by Harvard political scientist Samuel Huntington,[1] predates the events of 9/11. However, the terrorist attacks on New York and Washington and the later attacks in Madrid and London have given the thesis much greater credibility among the Western public than had been the case earlier.

This thesis is predicated on an essentialist interpretation of Islam as "civilization" (in the singular) rather than as religion and code of ethics that affects and is, in turn, affected by multiple cultural and geographic milieus. Consequently, its popularization has augmented a unitary impression of Islam and Muslims in the West that conceals the enormous diversity not only among Muslim opinion in general but even among those groups characterized as fundamentalists or Islamists. The major impact of the essentialist and monolithic interpretation of Islam on Western perceptions is not merely to paint all Muslims with the same black brush but also to accord the most extremist and violent elements among Islamist activists, who fulminate viciously against the West and on occasion commit dramatic acts of terror, the position of authentic spokespersons for Islam. The latter conclusion is based on the proclivity of the extremist factions to justify their violent actions by quoting selectively from the Quran and the traditions of the Prophet. It is often ignored that they pluck such quotes out of context and stretch their meanings, through very creative interpretations, to absurd limits that include justifying the killing of civilians—Muslims and non-Muslims alike.[2]

According such extremist elements the right to speak for Islam or for the vast majority of Muslims is totally unjustified. As the first chapter has argued and later chapters will substantiate, they are fringe elements in the world of Islam and are almost totally irrelevant to the fundamental issues that most Muslims are busy tackling in their discrete societies. Moreover, just as there is no Islamic monolith, there is no single individual, group, or institution that can rightfully claim to speak for Muslims, let alone on behalf of Islam. As Robert Hefner has pointed out, today "most Muslim societies are marked by deep disagreements over just who is qualified to speak as a religious authority and over just how seriously ordinary Muslims should take the pronouncements of individual scholars."[3]

A Historical Quandary

The question of who speaks for Islam is not a new quandary for most Muslims and has historically been difficult to answer. Islam has neither a pope nor a clearly delineated religious hierarchy. A loose hierarchical structure does exist among the Shia *ulama*, but even in Shia Islam, which is the minority branch, there is currently no single individual or organization that can pronounce authoritatively on theological—let alone political—issues.

In the middle of the nineteenth century, an attempt was made in Iran to establish a single source of religious authority in Shia Islam, with the title *marja-i-taqlid*, meaning "the source of imitation."[4] However, this system broke down after the death of Ayatollah Borujerdi in 1961. Since then, several leading religious figures have enjoyed the prerogative to issue edicts or rulings that become binding, but only on their respective followers—that is, on those who have chosen these particular figures as sources of emulation.[5] These rulings are not considered binding on the followers of other religious figures of equal status. It was therefore no surprise that Ayatollah Khomeini's arrogation of the right to speak on behalf of all of Shia Islam was greatly resented by many leading ayatollahs, both in and outside Iran, several of whom outranked him in the religious hierarchy before the Iranian Islamic revolution inspired by him in 1979.

These divisions of opinion have been very important in the political realm, dividing those among the Shia *ulama* who endorse politically quietist interpretations of Islamic injunctions from those advocating politically activist interpretations of religious doctrines and the various shades of opinion in between. While Ayatollah Borujerdi advocated a quietist line, Ayatollah Khomeini, a student of Borujerdi, expounded an activist position, but only after his mentor's death.[6] Ayatollah al-Sistani, currently the leading *marja* of the Iraqi Shia, falls somewhere in between. While disinclined to intervene in day-to-day political affairs, his "understanding of religious law leaves very little of the world beyond the scrutiny of religious leaders."[7] This has been demonstrated by the various rulings issued by him on unmistakably political matters, such as endorsing participation in elections organized by the occupation authority or approving or disapproving various provisions of the draft interim Iraqi constitution. Such opinions have had binding force on his followers, who form a very substantial proportion of the Shia in Iraq. Al-Sistani may not want the Shia clergy to rule directly, as Khomeini did, but he certainly wants them to have a supervisory or at least an influential advisory role in the future Iraqi political system. This discussion points to the fact that even in the relatively hierarchically delineated clerical system in Shia Islam, there is no single person or institution vested with the authority to issue edicts that are binding on all the faithful. Furthermore, national and ethnic divisions among the Shia, especially between Iranians and Arabs, circumscribe the reach and authority of even the most revered Shia *ulama*.

The problem of locating religious authority becomes much more acute among the majority Sunnis. The term *Sunni* is the shortened form of *ahl al-sunna wa'l-jama'a*, describing those who consider themselves to be the faithful followers of the traditions of the Prophet (*al-sunna*) and the upholders of the integrity of the Muslim community (*al-jama'a*). This nomenclature was adopted by the majority of Muslims, despite theological and jurisprudential differences among them, in order to distinguish themselves from the Shiat-i-Ali, the partisans of Ali, who were perceived as having split from the consensus within the *umma* regarding the succession to the Prophet, thus unleashing discord and dissension among the believers.

Multiple religious voices have historically been the rule, rather than the exception, among the Sunnis, for good reason. The term *Sunni* became a catchall phrase for all those who had not radically broken from the established consensus within Islam, as had been the case first with the Kharijites and then with the various branches of the Shia. The group of people called Sunnis emerged as a result of various compromises among the rest of the believers that had become essential to keep the community united. Therefore, as a matter of pragmatism, multiple interpretations of the Prophet's *hadith* (sayings) and *sunna* (practice) had to be tolerated to keep the community in tact. Consequently, it became the rule among the Sunnis for numerous senior *ulama,* the learned in the law, to exercise the right to issue religious rulings, based on meticulous research of the sources of Islamic law (including the context in which particular revelations occurred) and of accumulated precedents. However, given the multiple centers that can issue such edicts and the multiple sources on which they can base their interpretations, it is not uncommon to find rulings issued by different *ulama* and *fuquha* ("jurists," from the singular *faqih*) to be at variance with each other, depending on the different weight they accord to sources from which they seek guidance and on the different contexts in which they issue their rulings.

The tradition legitimizing several sources of religious authority was institutionalized sometime between the tenth and eleventh century CE, with the consolidation of four major schools of Islamic jurisprudence among the Sunnis— the Hanafi, the Shafi'i, the Hanbali, and the Maliki, named after their most prominent founders.[8] The major Imami Shia school of jurisprudence, called Ja'afri after its founder Ja'afar al-Sadiq (the sixth imam of the Shia), also emerged during this period. Followers of the major schools of Sunni Islam were expected to accord equal status and respect to each one of the four Sunni schools and to consider the decisions of their representative *ulama* as binding on the followers of each of the respective schools. In time, similar respect came to be accorded de facto by the Sunnis to the Ja'afri school of Shia Islam as well.

This policy of live and let live produced several benefits over the centuries. As stated in chapter 1, it helped, above all, to preclude the establishment of a single orthodoxy that, in alliance with the state, could suppress all dissenting tendencies. But it also meant that theological disputations could never be conclusively resolved, because there was no single locus of religious authority that could make binding rulings that would apply to all Sunni Muslims, let alone all Muslims.

Despite this decentralization of religious authority, there was a general consensus among Muslims during the premodern era on the answer to the question of who speaks for Islam. It was commonly recognized that those recognized by their peers as learned in the religious sciences and Islamic jurisprudence had the right to speak for and about Islamic doctrines regarding both moral and societal issues. The *ulama* from different jurisprudential schools and even, for that matter, from within the same school may differ in their interpretations, but their right to interpret the scriptures was recognized based on their mastery of religious texts, both the original scriptures and the accumulated wisdom of authoritative commentaries and Islamic legal precedents.

Colonialism, Modernity, and the Undermining
of the Ulama*'s Authority*

Premodern consensus in the Muslim world about who had the right to speak for Islam lasted until about the first half of the nineteenth century. It was then ruptured by the intrusion of modernity through its various agents—chiefly European colonialism, the print revolution, and mass literacy. The cacophony we experience in the Muslim world today is the culmination of the process that started with the breakdown of this Islamic consensus in the nineteenth century regarding the role of the *ulama* as the sole legitimate interpreters of religion.

European colonial domination reopened the whole question of the nature of authority in Islam by decimating existing political structures and undercutting the legitimacy of the religious authorities. Both the parties to the original contract in *dar al-Islam* between the temporal and the religious—the Muslim potentates who presided over a minimalist state and the largely politically quietist *ulama*—stood discredited. Many lay thinkers and activists in the Muslim world held the religious establishment as responsible as the temporal rulers for Muslim political decline, because of the *ulama*'s perceived collaboration with or at least tolerance of decadent regimes. The *ulama* were inherently conservative because of their knowledge of and emphasis on accumulated tradition and legal precedents and their aversion to innovative interpretation that departed radically from the core of Islamic teachings as understood by the body of religious scholars. They therefore became the target of attack for both the religious revivalists and the increasingly secularized intellectual and political elites, who saw them as practicing and preaching a fossilized form of Islam that had neither answers to contemporary problems nor a vision of the future.

This last conclusion was not completely true, since several *ulama* demonstrated considerable intellectual agility and doctrinal flexibility in an effort to respond to new issues and problems as they arose during the past two centuries. Some creatively reinterpreted earlier jurists' rulings to fit modern circumstances, while others attempted to think through contemporary problems de novo.[9] Nonetheless, the image persisted because the majority of the *ulama*, not trained in the modern sciences, continued to speak a language that appeared arcane, especially to the more modernized sections of Muslim societies. It was no coincidence that this modern stratum was and continues to be responsible for producing many lay Islamist thinkers.

The undermining of the *ulama*'s status as interpreters of the faith was accelerated by the print revolution and the increase in literacy in Muslim countries beginning in the mid-nineteenth century. Thanks to these twin phenomena, the fundamental texts of Islam became available to increasingly large numbers of Muslims, both in their original form in Arabic and, probably more important, in translations in the various vernaculars of the Muslim countries. Consequently, the Muslim world found itself in a situation in the second half of the nineteenth century analogous to that of Western Christendom in the fifteenth and sixteenth centuries, when the printed word and vernacular translations of Christian scriptures became accessible to lay individuals and paved the way for the Reformation in Europe.[10]

Islam's Proto-Reformation

Two ingredients integral to the Reformation—scriptural literalism and the "priesthood of the individual"—also appeared in the Muslim world, with almost the same consequences. Just as Christian fundamentalism, which rejected the accumulated wisdom of religious tradition, was a product of the Reformation, its Islamic counterpart was born out of the proto-Reformation that swept the Muslim world once lay Muslims gained direct access to the fundamental texts of Islam.[11] Religiously inclined individuals, often those educated in nonreligious schools and engaged in secular professions, began exercising their right of individual interpretation of Islamic scriptures, in near total disregard of precedents and interpretations accumulated over centuries by those trained in religion and jurisprudence.

Many among these lay individuals rejected the argument that the four established schools of jurisprudence in Sunni Islam were the sole repositories and conduits of all religious and legal knowledge. Reflecting the phenomenon of the "priesthood of the individual," they exercised their right of *ijtihad* (innovative interpretation to suit changing times and circumstances) and strove to gain the real essence of Islam by going back in history—beyond the time when these schools were founded—to the time of the "venerable" or "pious" ancestors, the first generation of Muslims. They argued that this was necessary because religious scholars who were too obsessed with inconsequential matters of detail, too beholden to temporal rulers, and too fossilized in their approach to religion had distorted the true spirit of Islam in the process of transmission over the centuries.

The print revolution and mass literacy, by providing the laity direct access to the foundational texts of Islam, contributed tremendously to the popularity of revivalist thinking in the Muslim world. Contemporary Islamists are heirs to this revivalist tendency, although, as will be discussed later in this book, many of them have made significant concessions to the contemporary contexts in which they find themselves. These Islamist thinkers, many of whom were not trained in the traditional seminaries that impart religious and legal knowledge, have become the primary challengers, in the scholarly realm, to the *ulama*'s authority to speak for Islam. Consequently, they have contributed significantly to the crisis of religious authority in the Muslim world set off by the twin processes of literacy and the print revolution.

Sunni Islamists and the Ulama

A major difference exists between Sunni and Shia Islamists in their relationship with the *ulama*. The Sunni Islamist formations are largely distinct from and often hostile toward the traditional *ulama*. Several of their leading figures have in the past condemned the *ulama* for practicing and preaching an ossified form of Islam incapable of responding to contemporary challenges. Hasan al-Banna, who founded the Muslim Brotherhood in Egypt in 1928, contrasted the *ulama* of early Islam—who, according to al-Banna, challenged their caliphs, rulers, and governors without fear—to the weakened *ulama* of his time, who were preoccupied with ingratiating themselves with government authorities.[12]

The founder of the Jamaat-i-Islami in the Indian subcontinent, Abul Ala Mawdudi, also held negative views of contemporary religious scholars. Referring to Mawdudi's views on the *ulama*, Seyyed Vali Reza Nasr writes: "His discourse on the Islamic state deliberately sidestepped the *ulama*, depicting them as an anachronistic institution that has no place in a reformed and rationalized Islamic order . . . Mawdudi derided the *ulama* for their moribund scholastic style, servile political attitudes, and ignorance of the modern world."[13] Sayyid Qutb, the chief ideologue of the Egyptian Muslim Brotherhood in the 1950s and 1960s was even more critical of the *ulama*. He denounced the very idea of "'men of religion, who take from religion a profession,' corrupting the Qur'anic message to suit their needs and attributing to God what He did not reveal."[14]

The three thinkers-cum-activists just mentioned were the most important among the Islamist figures of the twentieth century. All of them were trained and engaged in modern professions.[15] Abul Ala Mawdudi began his career as a journalist in the Indian subcontinent, and Hasan al-Banna and Sayyid Qutb, both from Egypt, started their careers in the field of secular education. In 1941, Mawdudi established the Jamaat-i-Islami, which became an intellectual and political force in Pakistan after its creation. Al-Banna established the Muslim

Brotherhood, the premier vehicle for Islamist mobilization in Egypt, in 1928. Sayyid Qutb became the chief ideologue of the brotherhood in the 1950s and 1960s, until he was executed by the Nasser regime in 1966.

Qutb's writings provided much of the basic motivation for Islamist activism after his death. His more extreme interpreters used Qutb's ideas to preach the violent overthrow of the Egyptian regime, which, according to them, had deviated from Islam and could therefore be considered a legitimate target for jihad. Qutb's ideas about jihad being licit against nominally Muslim regimes by the proclamation of *takfir* (excommunication) provided a major departure from traditional Islamic political thought, in which jihad was permitted either for the expansion of *dar al-Islam* or for defensive reasons against non-Muslim opponents and had to be proclaimed by a legitimate Muslim ruler.[16] In this context, the more extreme followers of Sayyid Qutb followed in the footsteps of the Kharijites, an early sect of Islam now virtually extinct, who Patricia Crone identifies as the "first Muslims to engage in *takfir* in a systematic way." Crone explains: "They held themselves to be the only believers. All other alleged Muslims were infidels who could in their opinion be killed and/or enslaved, exposed to random slaughter . . . , and robbed of their possessions, just like the infidels beyond the borders."[17]

There are, however, exceptions to the rule that modern Sunni Islamists are lay intellectuals and activists who look on traditional religious scholars with disdain. Many Saudi radical Islamists are drawn from the ranks of Wahhabi religious scholars, and a nexus that has developed between the radical *ulama* and lay Islamists in Pakistan has produced a form a neo-Wahhabism in parts of that country.[18] Similarly, radical thinkers who share the basic premises of the Islamist worldview have emerged from among the ranks of the *ulama* in Egypt. I will return to these issues later, in chapters that discuss individual countries in greater detail.

The Ulama-*Islamist Relationship in Shia Iran*

The *ulama*-Islamist relationship in Shia Iran has been and continues to be quite different from that prevailing in most Sunni countries. That a group of *ulama* led by Ayatollah Khomeini became the primary vehicle for Islamism and the 1979 Iranian Islamic revolution is a function of the difference between the ways the Shia *ulama* are organized as compared to their Sunni counterparts. The financial independence of the Shia *ulama* from the Iranian state (in contrast to the Sunni *ulama*'s dependence on state patronage) provides a part of the explanation. This independence was achieved to a large extent through the religious laity's payment of *khums* (one-fifth of a person's income) to their chosen *marja* (source of emulation) among the senior clerics. Also, the robust Shia tradition of *ijtihad* allowed a politically activist faction of the Iranian clergy, inspired by Khomeini, to adapt its strategy to the circumstances in which it found itself in the 1960s and 1970s and ride the wave of the broad-based antishah movement to power. The same predilection for innovation provided Khomeini the opportunity to advocate his theory of Islamic govern-ment as one to be guided by the supreme jurist, with the Shia *ulama* acting as the ultimate repositories of both moral and political rectitude.[19]

This did not mean that lay Islamist radicals were totally absent from the Iranian scene. The writings and speeches of lay activists, such as the anticlerical and French-trained Ali Shariati, contributed substantially to the delegitimiza-tion of the shah's regime. However, in the final analysis, they could not com-pete with the *ulama* for the control of postrevolution Iran. The latter had supe-rior organization and much greater financial resources, and the mullahs were able to exploit divisions that existed among the nonclerical forces.[20]

The Shia *ulama* have demonstrated, above all, that their capacity to remain relevant to contemporary issues is much greater than that of many Sunni coun-terparts. This does not mean that the Sunni *ulama* have remained completely fossilized in terms of their interpretation of Islamic doctrines, as many lay Islamists claim to be the case.[21] However, the pace of change has been consid-erably slower among them than among the Shia clerics. As a result, the politi-cal and social roles of the Sunni *ulama* have been overshadowed by those of the college-educated "new religious intellectuals,"[22] the lay Islamists, drawn from the secular professions.

The Nation-State and the Nationalization of Religious Authority

The *ulama*'s authority among both the Sunni and the Shia has been under-mined and circumscribed by another phenomenon in the modern age: the emergence of nation-states in the Muslim world during the twentieth century. The establishment of sovereign states within boundaries largely defined by the European imperial powers effectively put paid to the notion of the universal *umma,* the worldwide community of believers, as a politically relevant cate-gory. While the Muslim world had been de facto divided among several empires, kingdoms, and principalities beginning with the secession of

Umayyad Spain from the Abbasid caliphate in the second half of the eighth century CE, the ideal of the political unity of the *umma* had been maintained, at least among the Sunnis, by, among other things, the continuation of the institution of the caliphate transferred to Istanbul in 1517 following the Ottoman conquest of Egypt. The nominal caliphate was brought to an end in 1924, following the defeat of the Ottoman Empire in World War I and the subsequent proclamation of the Republic of Turkey in 1923.

Nation-states that became the rule in the Muslim world in the twentieth century were conceptually very different from the premodern kingdoms and principalities into which the Muslim world had been traditionally divided. The ideal of nationalism posed a fundamental doctrinal and practical challenge to the concept of the *umma*. It did so by insisting that the nation-state, recognizing no superior and conceived as an organic entity, become the exclusive repository of its citizens' allegiance. This paradigm became dominant despite a fact succinctly pointed out by Carl Brown: "The question not so readily answered . . . was what should be the basis of these presumably natural nation states. Who were 'we' and who 'they' in these nation-building exercises? The answers throughout the Muslim world—just as in the West where nationalism developed—were contradictory."[23]

Despite the lack of total congruity between "nation" and "state," a return to the ideal of a united *umma,* even as a hypothetical scenario, no longer remains a feasible proposition. The sovereign state is here to stay, and most Muslims, including most Islamists, have internalized the values of the sovereign state system and are perfectly at ease working within the parameters of the nation-state.[24] The division of the *umma* into multiple sovereignties is now taken as given. Individual Muslim states may face secessionist challenges, as Turkey, Iraq, and Iran (to name but a few states) have faced from their Kurdish populations. But all these challenges are mounted within the nation-state paradigm. Secessionist groups in the Muslim world are engaged in redefining territorial boundaries based on their preferred definition of the nation. Except for some fringe groups (mentioned in chapter 1 and discussed further in chapter 7), no one seriously raises the issue of reuniting the *umma* within one polity.

The partition of the Muslim world into sovereign nation-states has led to two other major outcomes. First, despite the spread of communication in the twentieth century, the *ulama*'s reach and authority has become restricted within specific national boundaries. For example, edicts issued by the Egyptian *ulama* can be enforced only within Egypt, just as the rulings issued by the Pakistani *ulama* can be applied only in Pakistan. For all practical purposes, the religious authority of the learned in the religious law has been nationalized. Moreover, as the modern state has begun to penetrate society in a way that pre-modern Muslim empires had never done, it has expanded its control of the religious establishment. This has been accomplished, above all, by the state bringing under its control the *awqaf* (plural of *waqf*), the charitable religious endowments created by wealthy and pious Muslims for the subsistence of religious seminaries, mosques, and large numbers of the *ulama*. Mark Sedgwick points out: "In the Sunni world, control of *waqf* is now generally in the hands of the state, the control having been assumed between 1826 and the 1960s as one of various measures aimed at producing strong, centralized states. With control of the *waqf* came the control of the mosques and madrasas they supported."[25]

Bringing religious endowments under state control drastically reduces the financial and, therefore, the intellectual and political autonomy of the religious classes, many of whom have become salaried functionaries of the state, often ruled in the postcolonial period by unrepresentative and authoritarian regimes. This is particularly true of those countries where the Sunnis are preponderant. While the Iranian shah Mohammad Reza Pahlavi attempted a similar policy in Iran as a part of his White Revolution, the strategy boomeranged and was responsible in substantial part for the growing hostility of the Shia clergy that controlled large religious endowments toward the Pahlavi dynasty.

Second, despite the disintegration of the *umma*, Islam continues to be part of the regimes' legitimacy formula in most Muslim countries. This may appear a paradox in the age of nation-states, but justifying policies in the name of Islam and projecting the regime's image as Islamic provides rulers considerable mileage with their populations and an aura of continuity with the rulers of the classical period. Therefore, leaders of Muslim states often portray their national and regime goals as serving the interests of Islam. They use the subservient *ulama* to bolster their image as Islam's spokespersons, thus adding further to the cacophony of ostensibly religious voices in the Muslim world. This is particularly true of self-proclaimed Islamic states (e.g., Saudi Arabia, Iran, and Pakistan) and of Egypt, the seat of the most prestigious Sunni Islamic institution, al-Azhar. However, it is clear to discerning observers that much of the regimes' "Islamic" rhetoric is little more than subterfuge that they utilize to enhance their image. This seems to be as much the case with "revolutionary" Islamic regimes, such as Iran, as with "conservative" ones, such as Saudi Arabia. In the process, however, the rhetoric of these regimes further confuses international audiences as to who really speaks for Islam.

Islamist Political Formations as Spokespersons for Islam

The derogation in the authority of the *ulama* (consequent on their sub-servience to unrepresentative regimes) and the division of the Muslim world into fifty-odd nation-states have provided the opportunity and the space for largely lay Islamist groups of various hues to advance their claims to be considered true representatives of Islam in the public sphere. These groups, such as the Jamaat-i-Islami in Pakistan and the Muslim Brotherhood in Egypt, while they have emerged out of the earlier Salafi movements, are much more modern in their organization and much more in tune with their contemporary political environments. Daniel Brown points out, "While they staunchly defend the theoretical authority of the sunna, the revivalists' commitment to the reintroduction of Islamic law in *relevant* forms makes them pragmatists in practice."[26] This is the case because they are as much products of modernity as they are reactions to it. Their greatest strength lies in their ability to combine their image of the ideal past with a vision that is considered by a substantial number of Muslims as being relevant to the contemporary situation.

Although committed in theory to transforming their polities into Islamic states through the Islamization of society and the eventual enforcement of sharia law, the modern Islamists are adept at making compromises and working within the national frameworks and the constitutional constraints imposed on them.[27] While paying rhetorical obeisance to the concept of the universal *umma,* these political formations do not challenge the existence of the nation-states in which they operate. In essence, they have become exponents of what Olivier Roy has called "Islamo-nationalism."[28] Their basic objectives are to improve the quality of governance in existing states by making such governance conform to Islamic law and to change the moral condition of their societies by making them correspond to Islamic norms. These goals are national, not universal.

These Islamist political formations have succeeded in carving out substantial constituencies within important Muslim states, allowing them to stake a claim to speak for Islam and Muslims within their national boundaries. They have been able to do so primarily because of the nature of many Muslim regimes, especially in the Middle East. Authoritarian and repressive in character, these regimes have been successful in stifling political debate and ruthlessly suppressing political dissent. Their effective decimation of nearly all secular opposition has created a vast political vacuum in their countries, which Islamist formations have moved in to fill. The Islamists have been successful in filling this gap because of the vocabulary they use and the institutions they employ to advance their political objectives. It is very difficult for even the most repressive regimes to outlaw or successfully counter the use of religious idiom for the expression of political dissent. Similarly, it is almost impossible for regimes to wield full control over religious institutions and charitable networks linked to such institutions. These institutions and networks provide the Islamist groups with the organizational base through which they are able to mobilize support.

Consequently, Islamist formations have been able to present themselves as, in many cases, the primary—in some cases, the sole—avenue of opposition to unrepresentative regimes. By suffering for their defiance of dictatorial regimes, they are also able to portray themselves as champions of human rights within their societies. This strategy has bought them a great deal of goodwill from those whom one cannot consider to be Islamists either in religious or political terms. Thus, even while Islamist groups have in many cases become targets of state suppression, they have simultaneously emerged in several instances as the only credible alternative to repressive regimes.[29] As a result, many analysts have concluded that if and when authoritarian and semiauthoritarian regimes in Muslim countries (especially in the Middle East) collapse, they are likely to be replaced by Islamist groups and parties through democratic elections. This has led some commentators, including neoconservative analyst Reuel Gerecht, to deduce that Shiite clerics and Sunni Islamists are the most likely vehicles for the spread of democracy in the Arab world.[30]

Islamic rhetoric that promises to bring Islam back to life and thereby provide solutions to the ills of Muslim societies resonates with large segments of Muslim populations, both because Islam as a solution has not been tried and because other models imported from the West—including secular nationalism, capitalism, and socialism—have largely failed to deliver wealth, power, or dignity to Muslim peoples. Moreover, Islamist groups appear to be paragons of probity when compared to the corrupt regimes that they seek to displace. However, if they come to power, Islamist parties will have to demonstrate the validity of their slogan "Islam is the solution" by addressing the concrete economic and social problems of their societies. Then, their prescription that Islam possesses the solution to all social, economic, and political problems will be severely tested.

The Islamist parties seem to be already in the process of addressing this potential problem. One very credible analysis explains: "Islamist political movements no longer operate with a definite and demanding conception of the

'Islamic state' to be counterposed to existing states in the Muslim world and promoted at their expense . . . As a result, these movements have increasingly explicitly broken with fundamentalist perspectives. Abandoning the revolutionary utopian project of *dawla islamiyya* (Islamic state) has led them to emphasize other themes, most notably the demand for justice (*al-adala*) and freedom (*al-hurriya*) . . . This evolution in political thinking has led Islamist political movements away from theocratic conceptions of the Muslim polity . . . to more or less democratic conceptions which recognise that sovereignty belongs to the people."[31] Such a transformation, although far from complete and unevenly manifested among multiple Islamist formations, adds to their appeal among the Muslim masses, sensitized as they have become to democratic values. One may have doubts whether the Islamists' conception of freedom coincides totally with the liberal notion of individual freedom, and it may contain communitarian, rather than individualist, connotations. But on the whole, this is a healthy development that needs wider recognition than it has received.

Transnational, Militant Islamists

A discussion of Islamism and Islamists' claims to speak on behalf of Islam must tackle the issue of the transnational manifestations of political Islam, including the proclivity of some transnational Islamists to engage in terrorist activities. The recent violent activities of such groups, especially the terrorist attacks of 9/11, have brought militant transnational Islamist groups, especially the al-Qaeda network, to the forefront of Western—indeed, global—concerns. As stated earlier, this has created the image that such groups have become the chief spokespersons for Islam. However, as has been explained in chapter 1, such transnational groups tend to be very marginal to the vast majority of Islamist political activities that are conducted peacefully within the confines of territorial states.

While al-Qaeda and other transnational Islamist organizations will be treated in greater detail in chapter 7, a brief discussion of transnational Islamism is relevant here, since transnational Islamists, especially of the violent kind, make Islam appear threatening to Western eyes. As Wiktorowicz has argued, their "increasingly expansive violence . . . may erode popular support for Al Qaeda, as increased violence did to the GIA in Algeria," but "in the meantime more groups of people will likely find themselves on the jihadi list of legitimate targets," and "attacks may become increasingly deadly as well."[32]

The deadliness of their attacks, however, does not make them Islam's foremost spokespersons. In fact, it discredits them within the Muslim world itself, as does the absence of a realistic political agenda that informs their activities. Their popularity has been exaggerated because of the electronic revolution, which has given them high visibility through audio- and videocassettes and Web sites on the Internet that they use to propagandize their ideology and, sometimes, their violent actions.[33]

Al-Qaeda is not a centralized or structured movement. The term *al-Qaeda* has become a convenient label applied by Western governments and the media to what was and continues to be a broad and diverse "network of networks."[34] Gilles Kepel has pointed out: "Al-Qaeda . . . [is] less a military base of operations than a data base that connected jihadists all over the world via the Internet . . . [U.S. strategists] gave it a vivid, reductionist name—Al-Qaeda—but this served only to reify the network's fluidity, thereby masking its true source of strength. Naming the adversary created the illusion of having identified it."[35] While its nebulous character makes it very difficult to counter al-Qaeda by conventional military means, it also means that it is not in a position to provide a real political option for Muslims engaged in day-to-day struggles within territorially defined political communities. This loosely connected network may continue to engage in dramatic terrorist activity. However, its political impact is likely to be very limited, because of its lack of a well-defined agenda that appeals to a clearly delineated territorial, political, and social base. The only place where it may find such a base is in the part of Iraq dominated by Sunni Arabs, thanks to the anarchical situation created in that country by the American-led invasion and occupation. This is a unique case that cannot be replicated elsewhere, unless what was done to Iraq is repeated in other locations.

As will be discussed further in chapters 7 and 8, it is paradoxical that the U.S. government was largely responsible for creating the Frankenstein's monster that has now turned its guns against America and its allies. It is an irony of history that the "good Muslims" of the 1980s have turned into the "bad Muslims" of today. This is reflected in the vocabulary of Western journalism, which referred to Islamist fighters in the 1980s with the term *mujahedin* and refers to the same elements today with the term *jihadis*. Apparently, it is presumed that while the former term has positive connotations because it is borrowed directly from Islamic vocabulary, the latter term, a corrupted form of the former, is pejorative in its implication. Despite this change in terminology, it is clear that the al-Qaeda network and others of its ilk would have withered on the vine and would certainly never have dared to speak for Islam had they not been encouraged in this venture by those who have now become the militants' primary targets. As Mahmood Mamdani demonstrates so convincingly, Islamist terrorists have a pedigree that has much more to do with American policies of the late cold war years than with Islamic scriptures, which they quote to justify their policies.[36]

The Modernists and Their Intellectual Progeny

At the other end of the political spectrum from the transnational militants stand the Muslim modernists. While less dramatic in their political impact globally, their significance in discrete Muslim countries is likely to be much greater in the long term than that of the transnational jihadis. They therefore deserve mention in this chapter as potential spokespersons for Islam. Chapter 1 referred to the contribution made by the nineteenth-century Egyptian jurist and theologian Muhammad Abduh to reopening the gates of *ijtihad* (independent interpretation) in Sunni Islam and to his attempt to reconcile revelation with reason by going back to the pristine precepts of Islam, which he considered to be in full consonance with rational reasoning. Albert Hourani has argued that Abduh's ideas have had a "lasting influence on the Muslim mind, not only in Egypt but far beyond," and have "become the unacknowledged basis of the religious ideas of the ordinary educated Muslim."[37]

More explicitly and unambiguously modernist thinkers, such as Sir Sayyid Ahmad in India, who was a contemporary of Abduh, made even bolder attempts to demonstrate that Islam, properly understood, was perfectly compatible with reason and did not contravene the laws of nature. Although Sir Sayyid relied almost exclusively on the Quran for his interpretation of Islam, he was no scriptural literalist. As Carl Brown has pointed out, he insisted that Islam was "completely compatible with reason and with 'nature.'" Brown explains: "This meant that any supernatural events in religion, even the Qur'an, could properly be interpreted allegorically or psychologically. In short, [Sayyid] was very much a nineteenth century advocate of science and positivism."[38] Sir Sayyid's ideas ran afoul of the traditional *ulama*, but he made a seminal contribution, at a very crucial time, to the spread of modern education and rationalist thought among the Muslim elite in India, especially by setting up the modern educational institution that eventually became Aligarh Muslim University.[39]

Recent decades have witnessed a renaissance of calls for *ijtihad*, based on rationalist interpretations of Islam in widely varied locales in the Muslim world, ranging from North Africa to Southeast Asia, and among Muslim communities in Europe and North America. A number of Muslim thinkers have approached the issue from different perspectives, but *ijtihad* has been a main point on the agenda of everyone advocating reform of Islamic thought in contemporary times. Knut Vickor explains: "The importance that *ijtihad* has in these modern debates, stems from the possibility it may give to steer a new course for Islam and Islamic Law, a course that stays within the boundary of Islamic tradition, but at the same time avoids the blindness of simply imitating earlier scholars, without consideration of the changing conditions of society. In other words, both for modernists and Islamists, *ijtihad* is a prerequisite for the survival of Islam in a modern world."[40]

The range of reformist views advocating *ijtihad* in one form or another include those propounded by Fazlur Rahman, Abdolkarim Soroush, Abdelmajid Charfi, Mohammed Arkoun, Nurcholish Madjid, Tariq Ramadan, Abdullahi Ahmed An-Na'im, Muhammad Shahrour, and Khaled Abou El-Fadl. Given the diversity of their approaches, interests, and contexts, it is extremely difficult—if not impossible—to synthesize their views into a coherent position. But Suha Taji-Farouki points out: "Their political ideas are often close to the heart of the liberal tradition, based on reason and values of freedom, liberty and democracy. Calling for the detachment of the entire public sphere from the purview of religion, they often project the Qur'an—Islam's foundational text—as a source of general ethical guidelines, rather than the answer to all human issues."[41]

While such such standard-bearers of the new *ijtihad* do not claim to speak on behalf of all Muslims (let alone Islam), their scholarship denotes that contemporary Muslim intellectuals are not averse to accepting rationalist ideas, even if on their own terms. Their views have yet to find adequate resonance among ordinary Muslims, partly because a number of them use rather obscure vocabulary and complex forms of reasoning that make it hard for the lay reader to understand them. Furthermore, several of them are perceived as deviating far too much from mainstream and commonly accepted Islamic ideas to be able to counter the Islamist and traditionalist interpretations of Islamic texts and establish a credible constituency beyond a narrow segment of the intellectual elite. Daniel Brumberg points out: "The problem with the Islamic modernists' arguments is that their project hinges on a complex and often opaque interpretive schema difficult for lay people to grasp. More crucially, many find it difficult to avoid concluding that the core values that modernists' attribute to Islam come from Western political thought . . . [thus leading to the conclusion] that Islamic modernism is a Western project dressed in a thin Islamic garb."[42] Islamic modernists are therefore perceived by some as a fifth column for the West, intent on secularizing the sacred in Islam and carrying out a nefarious Western agenda of undermining the consensus within the Muslim world regarding the fundamental precepts on which the religion is founded.

These modernist and reformist intellectuals ought to be taken seriously, not merely as interlocutors between Muslims and Westerners, but also, in terms of religious and political thought in the Muslim world, as potential alternative foci to the more radical and revivalists interpretations of Islam. However, in order for this potential to be translated into reality, the reformist intellectuals will have to learn to speak the language of the masses and present their arguments in idioms that the common Muslim can understand. While Fazlur Rahman's ideas are possibly the most seminal among the scholars identified in the present discussion, it was his Indonesian student Nurcholish Madjid, popularly known as Cak Nur, who was able to achieve rapport with his people to a substantial extent. He was probably the only one among this group of scholars to have done so.[43] It is unfortunate that both Fazlur Rahman and Nurcholis Madjid passed away while in their most creative phase.

The Swiss-Egyptian scholar Tariq Ramadan has the latent capacity to reach out to a large segment of the Muslim population in Europe but has yet to demonstrate conclusively his success in achieving this goal.[44] His potential appeal to European Muslims lies in the fact, noted by Peter Mandaville, that while he advocates the Muslims' civic responsibility toward states in which they live, "Ramadan's is not an ethics based on sameness." Mandaville explains: "It is quite insistent on the fact that Islam is different, and in some cases, critical of the norms of mainstream Western society . . . The ability to engage in a spirit of civility while maintaining critical distance from certain Western norms is perhaps the greatest strength of Ramadan's approach."[45] Recent events in Europe, including the terrorist bombings in London and Madrid, have demonstrated the high degree of alienation among some segments of the Muslim youth from the societies that they physically inhabit. Ramadan's ideas have become very crucial in this context, because they attempt to bridge the Western-Muslim divide in Europe from a position of intellectual and cultural equality between European and Muslim traditions, without sacrificing the distinctive character of European Muslim populations.

Multiple Voices, Competing Visions

In this chapter, I have tried to demonstrate that there is no individual, group, or tendency in the contemporary era that can speak authoritatively on behalf of Muslims, let alone Islam. Instead, multiple voices express competing visions regarding both the essence of the faith and the optimum relationship between religion and politics within Muslim countries. The Muslim world is too diverse and too divided—along national, jurisprudential, and ideological lines—for a single set of spokespersons to be acceptable to all major components of the worldwide *umma*. Despite attempts by the most extreme elements to usurp the right to speak for Islam, what we have today is a cacophony of different (and often competing) views and opinions in the Muslim world, rather than the deliberate orchestration of a single dominant voice. Furthermore, the extremist voices form but a very small minority within the spectrum of political and religious views expressed in Muslim countries, a fact that will become increasingly clear as this book proceeds.

Islamist articulations, especially those considered mainstream, are no doubt very important among the range of opinions found in the Muslim world. But they are divided primarily along national lines, with Islamist political formations principally preoccupied with issues that matter within the territorial confines of the states in which they operate. Case studies of important, but divergent, Muslim states where Islamist regimes have been in power or where Islamist parties and factions have been politically active in opposition will demonstrate this point more convincingly. The next few chapters will therefore be devoted to scrutinizing several important cases of Islamist governance and/or political activity and the relationship between Islamist political formations and the states and regimes that have set the parameters within which such formations operate.

CHAPTER 3

Self-Proclaimed Islamic States

This inquiry into the relationship between Islam and politics in discrete Muslim countries begins with the analysis of two states, Saudi Arabia and Iran, whose rulers have self-consciously and vociferously proclaimed themselves and their polities to be "Islamic." Their respective claims to be genuinely Islamic are based on two contentions: that their societies and polities are repositories of true Islamic normative values and that their regimes govern their respective societies on the basis of the sharia, the supposedly immutable legal code derived from the Quran and supplemented by the traditions of the prophet Muhammad and the practices of the early generations of Muslims, the *salaf al-salih* (righteous ancestors). However, even a superficial examination of the constitutive principles of the two polities and the policies enforced by their governments in the name of Islam demonstrates such astonishing dissimilarities between them that it is enough to disabuse the observer of the notion that there can be a single, monolithic expression of Islam in the political arena.

These two cases highlight, among other things, the dramatic absence of consensus on the forms and rules of governance that are supposedly derived from the same Islamic teachings and legal precedents. They underline the fact that the fundamental religious texts of Islam do not prescribe any particular model of temporal rule and that the moral principles underlying just governance advocated in the Islamic scriptures can be put into practice through different types of institutions in different times and places. These cases also warn us against accepting at face value claims made by regimes in predominantly Muslim countries that they embody Islamic values or that they are authentic models of Islamic governance. Frequently, such claims are made for self-serving purposes by regimes desperately in need of legitimacy.

This chapter will compare the two self-proclaimed Islamic states in three crucial arenas: the processes of state making and regime legitimation, the internal organization of the two states as reflected in their systems of governance, and the expression of political dissent in the two states as reflected in the rhetoric and activities of movements opposed to existing systems and/or regimes. This comparison is intended to bring out the very different roles played by Islam in these arenas and the extremely divergent interpretations of what is supposed to be "Islamic" where concrete political issues are concerned.

State Making and Regime Legitimation

The Centralization of State Power in Saudi Arabia

One of the best accounts detailing the history of Saudi Arabia begins with the following sentence: "The dominant narrative in the history of Saudi Arabia in the twentieth century is that of state formation, a process that started in the interior of Arabia under the leadership of the Al Sa'ud." The author goes on to state: "The twentieth century witnessed the emergence of a state imposed on people without a historical memory of unity or national heritage which would justify their inclusion in a single entity."[1] One can make the argument, quite convincingly, that it was the absence of a national myth and the near impossibility of creating one amid the diversity in the Arabian Peninsula that in large part necessitated the use of Islam, albeit of the puritanical Wahhabi variety, by the House of Saud as the principal ideological justification for their conquest of the disparate regions that today constitute Saudi Arabia.

The compact between Muhammad ibn Saud, the founder of the Saudi dynasty, and Muhammad ibn Abd al-Wahhab, the founder of the puritanical reformist Wahhabi school that aimed at purging the tribes of Najd of un-Islamic accretions, goes back to 1744 when the latter visited the ibn Saud's capital in Dirriyah and was given protection by the Saudi chieftain. As a quid pro quo, Ibn Abd al-Wahhab declared: "You are the settlement's chief and wise man. I want you to grant me an oath that you will perform *jihad* (holy war) against the unbelievers. In return you will be *imam*, leader of the Muslim community, and I will be leader in religious matters."[2]

Some authors, such as Natana Delong-Bas, have suggested that Ibn Abd al-Wahhab's definition of jihad was defensive and that he did not define non-Wahhabi populations of Arabia as infidels.[3] Others, such as Hamid Algar, have argued that Ibn Abd al-Wahhab and those who adhered to his teachings considered all Muslims who "did not share their understanding of *tauhid* [the unitary nature of God]" to be "guilty of *shirk* [associating others with God] and apostasy," thus justifying the conduct of jihad against them.[4] In light of subsequent developments in the Arabian Peninsula, it is obvious that Algar's depiction of the Wahhabi conception of jihad is closer to the truth. It soon became clear that by offering the religio-political compact to the Saudi chieftain, Ibn Abd al-Wahhab was not just providing religious cover to Muhammad ibn Saud's aspiration for the conquest of other principalities in and around Najd; he was also advancing his own agenda of purifying Islam in the Arabian Peninsula. In the words of Michael Cook, "by bringing the frontier between Islam and polytheism back into the centre of the supposedly Muslim world . . . Wahhabism contrived to be a doctrine of state-formation and conquest."[5]

The contract reached in 1744 laid the foundations for a relationship between the House of Saud and Ibn Abd al-Wahhab's descendants that came to fruition in the twentieth century during the third cycle of Saudi expansion, under Abd al-Aziz ibn Abd al-Rahman al-Saud, commonly known as Ibn Saud in the West.[6] Ibn Saud's conquests in the 1920s—including that of the Hijaz, the cradle of Islam, in 1924–25—laid the foundations of the present kingdom of Saudi Arabia. While the Saudi ruler was busy incorporating the diverse regions of the peninsula into his kingdom, the fiercely Wahhabi tribal levies from Najd, the Ikhwan (Brothers), revolted against him in the late 1920s. They cited, among other reasons for their revolt, his insufficiently Islamic behavior and what they perceived to be his unduly lenient policies toward the non-Wahhabi populations—especially the Shia—of the newly conquered territories.[7] The Ikhwan had formed the backbone of Ibn Saud's conquering forces, but the king did not hesitate to suppress their revolt with great ferocity. In this, he was supported, after some initial hesitation, by the Wahhabi *ulama* and by the British, who used the Royal Air Force against the Ikhwan in areas bordering their mandated territories, thus contributing critically to Ibn Saud's success.[8]

The consolidation of state power and the augmentation of the authority of the al-Saud were essential components of Ibn Saud's struggle against the Ikhwan. Madawi Al-Rasheed reports that this was the case because the latter's rebellion was "not only a religious protest against Ibn Sa'ud" but also "a tribal rebellion that exposed the dissatisfaction of some tribal groups with his increasing powers." Al-Rasheed continues, "The *ikhwan* rebels refused to remain the instruments of Ibn Sa'ud's expansion and expected real participation as governors and local chiefs in the conquered territories."[9] The success of Ibn Saud's state-building strategy was predicated on the diminution of tribal power and clan loyalty that had, paradoxically, helped him to conquer much of the Arabian Peninsula. The suppression of the Ikhwan revolt, by diminishing the influence of tribal forces, considerably helped Ibn Saud to create a supratribal state centered on his family and bearing its name. He needed the support of the leaders of the Wahhabi religious establishment to achieve this goal. The latter, after some initial vacillation, were willing to oblige because they concluded that their corporate interests as well as their objective of purifying Islam in Arabia could be achieved best in alliance with the House of Saud.

The support of the Wahhabi *ulama* against their own protégés, the tribal confederations from whom the Ikhwan had emerged, clearly signaled that the religious establishment had become a partner in state consolidation and—its corollary—the detribalization of the Saudi power structure. One should not, however, confuse detribalization of the Saudi polity with the integration of diverse regional elites into the power structure. Both political and religious power continued to be concentrated in the hands of the Najdi elite. Political power was monopolized by the al-Saud and families related to them by marriage, especially the maternal relatives of Ibn Saud's sons, who numbered several dozen. Religious power was controlled by the al-Shaykh, the descendants of Muhammad ibn Abd al-Wahhab. The cosmopolitan Hijazi elite, which was the product of long association with the Ottoman court and possessed distinct cultural and religious traditions, remained peripheral to the power structure. The Shia living in the oil-rich eastern province of Hasa were and are denied access to political power and influence.[10]

The Wahhabi *ulama*'s endorsement—despite their initial ambivalence—of Ibn Saud's decision to crush the Ikhwan also denoted that they had come to accept their limited role as supervisors of morality and rituals in the unified state and had relinquished the political sphere almost completely to the House of Saud.[11] Consequently, the Wahhabi establishment became an instrument of the state, subservient to the wishes of the ruling family on political matters. However, since the state was constituted in the name of Islam, it was imperative that Islam continue to be used to legitimize its existence as well as Saudi rule over the newly unified polity. Here, the Wahhabi *ulama* played a crucial role in justifying Saudi rule in Islamic terms, by issuing religious edicts endorsing the regime's policies. This was especially important to the regime on controversial issues, such as girls' education, the introduction of television into the kingdom, and the stationing of American troops on Saudi territory. In return, the regime accepted the Wahhabi religious establishment's primacy in matters of religion and social mores and agreed to leave these spheres largely under their supervision, if not in their total control. The religious establishment's role in these arenas was augmented by Saudi state policy following the seizure of the Grand Mosque in Mecca by Islamist radicals in 1979 and its bloody aftermath. I will return to this episode later in this chapter.

The Consolidation of State Authority in Iran

Just as the centralization of state power formed the basic objective of the Saudi regime in the first half of the twentieth century, the consolidation of state authority was the primary motif in the history of Iran in the nineteenth century and much of the first half of the twentieth century. The Persian or Iranian state has been in existence much longer than its Saudi counterpart, more or less within the same boundaries that were bequeathed to it by the Safavid shahs who had unified the domain in the sixteenth century. Despite this fact, Iran's nineteenth-century rulers were consumed by the struggle to maintain a minimum degree of centralized state control over the disparate ethnic and tribal groups inhabiting the country. In nineteenth-century Iran, communal conflicts were the rule, rather than the exception. The weak center was presided over by equally weak Qajar rulers, whose authority was constantly under challenge and who "remained in power by systematically following two concurrent policies: retreating whenever confronted by dangerous opposition; and, more important, . . . manipulating the many communal conflicts within their fragmented society."[12]

However, unlike in the Saudi case, Islam, represented by the Shia *ulama,* was at best an uncertain ally and at worst a hostile force as far as Iran's temporal authorities were concerned. The relationship between Shia Islam (Iran's predominant religion) and Iran's monarchical regimes was highly ambivalent, for reasons embedded in Shia theological doctrines. Nikkie Keddie has explained: "There has always been potential opposition from the Shia *ulama* to the Shah. The latter is, theoretically, regarded a usurper, legitimate succession having passed down through the house of Ali until the last or hidden Imam who will reappear to establish legitimate rule."[13] Despite this injunction, a substantial segment of the Shia *ulama* served the temporal rulers when central authority was strong, under the Safavid monarchs. However, when monarchical authority became weak, the *ulama* became more emboldened in their opposition to temporal power or, at the very least, maintained a respectable distance from it. Such was the case in the nineteenth century, under the Qajar rulers, when "most prominent mujtaheds [senior clerics] remained aloof from the court and interpreted the early texts of Shi'ism to argue that the state was at worst inherently illegitimate and at best a necessary evil to prevent social anarchy."[14]

With certain exceptions, this continued to be the case in the twentieth century, under Pahlavi rule. However, until the 1960s, the leading *ulama* (with certain exceptions) expressed this distrust of secular power more in terms of detachment from the political arena and its corollary of political quietism than in terms of active opposition to the existing regime.[15] The leading cleric, Ayatollah Borujerdi, who was the *marja-i-taqlid-i-motalleq* (sole source of imitation) until his death in 1961, was politically quietist and thus set the tone for the clerics' relationship with the court. This relationship underwent change with the death of Borujerdi and the rise to prominence of his former student Ayatollah Khomeini, who adopted an activist stand after his mentor's death and began to castigate Pahlavi rule as un-Islamic. Several other clerics also joined in the opposition to the shah, in part as a response to the latter's policies of economic reform (particularly land reform), which threatened to dispossess the leading *ulama* of the vast resources they controlled, thus threatening their financial autonomy.[16]

The relationship between the Shia clerics and the Iranian state changed dramatically after the Islamic revolution of 1979.[17] Politically active clerics now became state functionaries and found themselves at the center of political and economic power. Simultaneously, a variant of Islamism that combined political radicalism with social conservatism and economic etatism became the official ideology of the state and the primary instrument for regime legitimacy in postrevolution Iran. Nonetheless, several senior clerics expressed and continue to express a high degree of ambivalence toward temporal authority, even when exercised or at least supervised by the Shia *ulama*. This ambivalence, bordering on opposition, increased with the institution of the *vilayat-i faqih* (guardianship of the supreme jurist) as the cornerstone of Islamic rule in Iran. I will return to this issue later in this chapter, when discussing the Iranian model of governance.

The Divergent Trajectories of Saudi Arabia and Iran

The Saudi and Iranian cases underscore the fact that both of these states and their regimes are essentially products of modernity, especially of the processes of state building and nation formation, though in widely divergent contexts. Comparison between Saudi Arabia and Iran makes clear that Islam has played very different roles in the construction and maintenance of the Saudi and Iranian states, as has been clearly reflected in their divergent trajectories. This divergence is determined not only by the role of the religious establishment in state formation and regime consolidation but also by these two states' discrete jurisprudential traditions and specific cultural practices. Saudi Arabia's strict interpretation of Hanbali jurisprudence, popularly referred to as Wahhabism, is very distinct from the Ja'afari school of law that forms the basis of Iran's current religio-legal code. Persian/Iranian cultural practices and norms are influenced by their pre-Islamic imperial legacies as well. Similarly, tribal codes and practices of Najd, the home of the political and religious elites of Saudi Arabia, have influenced the operation of the Saudi state in no small measure, often in the guise of Islam. These two cases of state formation and centralization of state authority in self-proclaimed "Islamic" states demonstrate clearly that Islam is filtered through a number of variables that mediate and, in the process, modify Islamic norms and values.

The ruling elites of both states recognize the unique contexts and features of their two societies, even though they sometimes indulge in rhetoric that seems to imply that their regimes and states stand for universal standards and ideals and are therefore capable of being replicated around the Muslim world. Despite their occasional universalistic Islamic protestations, neither the Saudi nor the Iranian regimes have ever made any claim—even in theoretical terms—to the creation of a universal Muslim polity based on their systems of governance. Both Iran and Saudi Arabia are perfectly content to operate within a system of multiple sovereign states that, in theory, owe allegiance to no superior, a system that is itself a creation of Europe during the past four hundred years or so.[18] Consequently, it is clear that the use of the Islamic rhetoric by Riyadh and Tehran in the international arena is largely instrumental, primarily aimed at furthering their state and regime interests by portraying them as Islamic ones.

Interestingly, Saudi Arabia and Iran often reserve their Islamic rhetoric, especially that of the vituperative variety, for each other, each with the aim of demonstrating the superiority of their own system over the other. This is no coincidence; given their geographic propinquity and their clashing regional ambitions, their relationship with each other has often been adversarial or at least uneasy. Contiguous and proximate states at early stages of state making often develop conflictual relations with each other for a number of reasons, related to state and regime legitimacy and/or divergent conceptions of the regional balance of power.[19] Saudi Arabia and Iran are no exception to this rule. Their self-proclaimed "Islamic" character does not mitigate but, in fact, adds to their regional rivalry, by overlaying it with ideological rhetoric.

Comparing Political Systems

The Hereditary Monarchy of Saudi Arabia

Saudi Arabia is a hereditary monarchy whose regime draws its legitimacy from its familial and tribal connections in Najd and, above all, from its alliance with the equally hereditary Wahhabi religious establishment. As already explained, the system of rule in Saudi Arabia is basically an extension of the way Ibn Saud had governed the Kingdom of Najd. Not only the principles of governance but also the religious orthodoxy of Najd, Wahhabi Islam, was imposed on other parts of the unified kingdom, thus setting the context for all political activity in Saudi Arabia and for the close relationship—in fact, interdependence— between the political and religious establishments in the country.

All forms of constitutionalism were abhorred in Saudi Arabia until recently. Ostensibly, there seemed to be no need for a man-made constitution, since, according to the official formulation, Saudi Arabia is governed according to the Quran and the traditions of the Prophet. Only in 1992, as a consequence of heightened criticism following the Gulf War, did the king announce the Basic Law of Government and the setting up of the Consultative Council, in what amounted to nothing more than cosmetic changes to the basic monarchical character of the government. This is demonstrated by the fact that according to Article 6 of the Basic Law, "[c]itizens are to pay allegiance to the King in accordance with the Holy Koran and the tradition of the Prophet, in submission and obedience, in times of ease and difficulty, fortune and adversity." Article 7 states, "Government in Saudi Arabia derives power from the Holy Koran and the Prophet's tradition," thus making clear that the monarchy derives its legitimacy from the fundamental texts and tenets of Islam.[20]

The senior Wahhabi *ulama* continue to be the repositories of religious and legal authority in Saudi Arabia. As official interpreters of the Quran and the Prophetic traditions, they are also key enforcers of the legal principles by which Saudi Arabia is governed. Consequently, the Basic Law of 1992 does not detract from the reality that Wahhabi doctrines and their foremost interpreters continue to be indispensable to the maintenance of the Saudi system and the legitimacy of the monarchy.

This arrangement, despite its potential downside for the Saudi regime, suited the ruling elite admirably during much of the twentieth century. It meant that they could dispense with a written constitution that would require codifying a social compact with their subjects and would thus hold them accountable for their actions. It also meant that the regime, with the support of the religious establishment, could outlaw all oppositional activity by declaring it un-Islamic, since Islam brooks no *fitna* (dissension). As long as the leading Wahhabi scholars continued to justify hereditary monarchy and the position of the Saudi ruler as imam (religiously anointed leader), the monarchy and its beneficiaries could pretty much ignore liberal opposition elements as out of tune with the Islamic ethos and as troublemakers who deserved to be incarcerated, if not eliminated.

The flip side of this arrangement is that Saudi rulers have to maintain, at least in public, the image of Islamic probity and puritanical behavior enjoined by Wahhabi doctrines. Public deviation from this code of morality immediately opens them up both to religious denunciation and to political criticism couched in religious terminology. What the Saudi regime most feared and continues to fear is political opposition couched in religious terms that can be justified with recourse to puritanical Wahhabi doctrines. Such criticism has the potential to challenge the Saudi-Wahhabi elites on their own ground and to bring them into disrepute. This is what has been happening in Saudi Arabia recently; I will return to this subject later in this chapter.

Since Wahhabi doctrines, based on rigid and literal interpretations of the Quran and the Prophet's traditions, strictly circumscribe relationships with non-Muslims, they have created major problems for the Saudi regime in the context of its security dependence and close economic ties with Western powers, especially the United States. Consequently, this has traditionally been the arena of greatest vulnerability for Saudi rulers. It is no coincidence that Islamist radicals inside Saudi Arabia and outside, including Osama bin Laden, have chosen the Saudi-American nexus as the primary target of their attack aimed at the House of Saud. Bin Laden's diatribes in the 1990s against the presence of American troops in Saudi Arabia demonstrated the significance of this issue as the Achilles' heel of the Saudi regime. The criticism was very potent because it conformed to the Wahhabi worldview despite the fact that the Wahhabi religious establishment had issued a fatwa (religious edict), at the regime's behest, justifying American military deployment in the country to defend Saudi Arabia from attack. The International Crisis Group is therefore not wrong to assert, "The 1990–1991 Gulf war was the most critical event in the history of Saudi Islamism and helps explain subsequent domestic politics."[21]

The Antimonarchical Republic of Iran

Iran, in contrast to Saudi Arabia, is a fiercely antimonarchical republic that combines features of a democratic polity with elements of direct clerical rule.

Both these traits can be traced to Khomeini's own contradictory predilections, which combined democratic inclinations with authoritarian ones. It is no surprise, therefore, that both the hard-line clergy and the reformists are able to quote Khomeini in support of their respective positions.[22] But it was not only Khomeini who was responsible for the hybrid nature of the Iranian political system. He was the heir to a tradition going back to the early years of the twentieth century. The roots of Iran's current system can be traced to the Constitutional Revolution of 1905–6, when a similar debate raged among the antimonarchical forces, between those who espoused unalloyed representative government and those among the *ulama* who advocated clerical oversight of political authority.[23] The constitution adopted in 1908 included a compromise similar to the one in the current Iranian constitution. The antimonarchical coalition of 1905–8—consisting of the modern intelligentsia, the traditional merchant class, and the *ulama*—bore an uncanny resemblance, in terms of both the disparate elements that constituted it and the diversity of views expressed by them, to the coalition that brought down the shah in 1979.[24]

The fundamental laws adopted by the Iranian National Assembly following the Constitutional Revolution were essentially democratic in nature, although the representative character of the legislature was restricted by the property qualifications of the electorate. However, as Ervand Abrahamian explains, the same laws enshrined clerical supervision of the lawmaking process by constituting "a 'supreme committee' of mujtaheds . . . to scrutinize all bills introduced into parliament to ensure that no law contradicted the shari'a." Abrahamian continues, "This committee, consisting of at least five members, was to be elected by the deputies from a list of twenty submitted by the 'ulama."[25] The Council of Guardians overseeing executive and legislative functions under Iran's current constitution is a direct descendant of these provisions in the constitution adopted by the National Assembly in 1908, though the contemporary council possesses broader powers than its early twentieth-century counterpart. Today, however, both the National Assembly and the president are elected by universal suffrage, male and female, with the minimum voters' age fixed at fifteen, the lowest among countries practicing electoral democracy. Moreover, Articles 19–42 of the current Iranian constitution guarantee civic and political rights to all Iranian citizens.[26] While practice may differ from theory, the constitution does provide a benchmark that can be used to hold violators to account. In short, both the principle of clerical oversight and that of representative governance have been simultaneously strengthened in contemporary Iran, thus making reconciliation between them doubly difficult.

Although the constitutional system of 1908 was aborted due to the machinations of the Qajar court followed by the coup staged by the Cossack colonel Reza Khan, the last shah's father, its democratic and antimonarchical thrust formed an essential building block for the framers of the Iranian constitution drafted after the 1979 Islamic revolution. Since 1979, Iran's leaders have, in no uncertain terms, denounced as un-Islamic the hereditary monarchical principle. The Iranian republican system is a polar opposite of the Saudi monarchy, even if circumscribed by clerical supervision. Despite the maneuverings of the clerical establishment, electoral outcomes in Iran can produce great surprises, as in the presidential elections of 1997 and 2001, which were won with large majorities by the reformist Mohammad Khatami against the wishes of the clerical establishment and the supreme jurist. In 2005, the electorate chose a dark horse, Mahmoud Ahmadinejad, as president, on the basis of his populist appeal, thereby once again demonstrating its independent streak.[27]

Iran's Council of Guardians, composed of twelve members, half of them senior clerics and the other half elected by the National Assembly, determines the compatibility of all legislation with Islam and with the constitution. According to Article 96 of the constitution, a law's compatibility with Islam is determined by a vote of a majority of the clerics, and compatibility with the constitution is determined by a majority of the total membership of the council.[28] The council also vets candidates seeking election to the National Assembly, and in the last elections, it exercised its power arbitrarily by pruning out many reformist candidates.

Despite the oversight powers of the Council of Guardians, two successive National Assembly elections prior to the last one produced large reformist majorities. Unfortunately, their attempts at reforming the system were often stymied by the council's threat to veto legislative measures it did not approve. Even the current National Assembly, supposedly dominated by conservative elements, has acted in surprisingly independent fashion, vetoing the president's choice of ministers repeatedly. Moreover, Ayatollah Khomeini insisted, in his last years, on the creation of the Expediency Council, to mediate differences between the elected legislature and the Council of Guardians. This institution was given the power to override a veto by the Council of Guardians, a measure apparently motivated by Khomeini's desire to prevent the council from unduly interfering in legislative matters that were clearly within the purview of the parliament.[29]

The plethora of political institutions—those of the supreme jurist, the president, the Council of Guardians, the National Assembly, the Expediency Council—helps to provide checks and balances between the executive and the legislature, on the one hand, and the representative and the appointed and/or clerical bodies, on the other. Additionally, multiple crosscutting cleavages among the political classes in Iran do not conform to the simplistic division between conservatives and reformists depicted in the popular Western press. Economic progressives can be religious and political conservatives, and political and religious progressives may turn out to be economic conservatives. A major division among the conservatives is that between pragmatist conservatives and radical conservatives, who are often at odds with each other, with the pragmatists often relying on allies among the reformists.[30] Furthermore, despite the attempt by hard-liners to impose restrictions on the freedom of expression and the press, Iran is a vibrant and politically competitive society that has turned evading such restrictions into a fine art. Newspapers banned one day appear the next day under different names, with the authorities often turning a blind eye toward such transgressions. Iran is a flawed democracy but, nonetheless, a system with important democratic traits and a society and polity that is vastly different from its far more rigidly controlled counterpart in Saudi Arabia.[31]

Saudi Arabia and Iran as "Models" of Islamic Governance

While Iran and Saudi Arabia are polar opposites of each other, neither the Saudi nor the Iranian form of government can qualify as "Islamic" if one defines Islamic governance in terms of the model offered by the Prophet's rule in Medina and that of his immediate successors, the righteously guided caliphs, during the formative years of the Muslim community. It is true that the Saudi monarchical regime, based on family and clan solidarity, partially resembles a distorted version of the ideal model, just as the hereditary Umayyad caliphate did during the heyday of Arab imperial expansion. Those familiar with Islamic history will appreciate that this distortion during the earlier period was legitimized by most of the Sunni *ulama* for fear of anarchy and the disintegration of the Muslim *umma*. This has been discussed at length earlier in this book.[32] However, unlike the Umayyad and, later, the Abbasid caliphs, who traced their origins to Mecca and to the tribe of Quraysh, from which Muhammad was descended, the Saudis are of Najdi origin, from the backwaters of the Arabian Desert. They bear no kinship relation to the Prophet's tribe or clan, let alone to his family. Their background as Najdi chieftains derogates from their claim—made on the basis of heredity—to be the legitimate guardians of the holiest places of Islam, Mecca and Medina, which are located in the Hijaz, the cradle of Islam.[33]

Furthermore, the Saudi regime's oil-driven close economic relationship with the Western powers and its security dependence on the United States detract from its attempt to portray itself as the champion of Muslim causes. The more the United States is perceived by many Muslims as hostile to the interests of Muslim peoples, the more the image of the Saudi regime takes a beating because of its guilt by association.[34] Finally, despite its oil wealth, Saudi Arabia is far from being a major Muslim state. It cannot be considered on par with Turkey, Iran, Pakistan, Egypt, and Indonesia, which have large and educated populations, respectable military capabilities, and the capacity (actual or potential) to act as regional powers. Its relatively modest status among Muslim countries does not make Saudi Arabia a candidate, despite its best efforts, for leadership in the Muslim world. Its lack of military capabilities, despite huge purchases of sophisticated weaponry from the United States, was clearly demonstrated in the face of the threat from Saddam Hussein in 1990, when the United States had to come to Riyadh's rescue. Saudi Arabia's poor military record negatively affects its claim to a special role as the protector of Islam's holy places.

The Iranian model of a republican government with clerical oversight may be closer in spirit to that of the city-state of Medina, but its legislative and executive institutions, including those of the supreme jurist and the Council of Guardians, are products of the modern age and bear no resemblance to the original Islamic model. It is an irony that has gone largely unnoticed that the institution of the supreme jurist, the ultimate repository of moral and political rectitude in Iran as the stand-in for the twelfth imam during the period of occultation, is the creation of a constitution written by fallible men and women in the latter part of the twentieth century, after the 1979 Iranian revolution.[35] Furthermore, the republicanism enshrined in the Iranian constitution was pioneered by the regicidal French Revolution of 1789. There is an obvious parallel between these French and Iranian revolutions; both sought to overthrow arbitrary and unpopular monarchs and replace them with popular rule. The conjoining of the term *Republic* with *Islamic* to describe the postrevolutionary Iranian state was therefore logical. However, it was also oxymoronic. Republicanism, in the sense we know it today in Iran or elsewhere, does not have any precedent in Islamic history, despite the contrived resemblance that some may see between it and the way the early caliphs were seemingly chosen by the consensus of the elders of the community. One should not forget that it was the supporters of Ali, who later came to be known as Shia, who rejected the consensual model of the early caliphate in favor of the lineage principle that favored Ali (as the closest male relative of the Prophet) over other contenders for succession to the Prophet's temporal role. It is ironic that Shia Iran should justify its adoption of a republican model of government on the basis of the early "consensual" system that the partisans of Ali, dominant in contemporary Iran, had rejected so unequivocally.

Iran's combination of representative government with clerical supervision is also a radical departure from almost all previous models of governance adopted in the Muslim world. In fact, as stated earlier, the only precedent for such a system was the short-lived experiment in Iran in the first decade of the twentieth century, following the Constitutional Revolution. The concept of *vilayat-i faqih* (guardianship of the supreme jurist), first advocated by Ayatollah Khomeini in his seminal work *Islamic Government,* is also a fundamental deviation from Shia theological doctrines.[36] As pointed out earlier, the latter characterize all temporal rule as illegitimate until the return of the Mahdi (the twelfth imam) from occultation. This implies that, unlike the Sunni *ulama,* the Shia clerics, while acting as the moral conscience of the faithful, ought to keep a healthy distance from all temporal rulers so as not to be tainted by association, not just for political and moral reasons, but also because of religious injunction. Furthermore, the creation of the office of the supreme jurist, by equating the powers of an ordinary mortal with those of the sinless imam, can be seen as an act of blatant blasphemy. Hamid Enayat pointed out: "Khumayni's thesis . . . has certain theological implications that are not entirely free of political significance. One of them is the weakening, if not the outright rejection, of a major tenet of popular . . . Shi'ism—the anticipation of the Mahdi (*intizar*)."[37]

This background explains why the very idea of legitimizing temporal rule in the absence of the twelfth imam by creating a surrogate for the Mahdi in the form of the supreme jurist, as Khomeini did, is anathema to many of the leading Shia theologians both inside and outside Iran.[38] Moreover, the involvement of the *ulama* in running the state is seen by a number of leading Shia theologians as extremely harmful because it has the potential to bring not only the clerics but also Islam into disrepute when clerics are corrupted by their access to and exercise of temporal power.[39] As noted by Bahram Rajaee, these traditionalist theologians "represent the vast majority of the Iranian clergy that have largely remained outside government since 1979." Rajaee continues: "[T]hey are concerned with the loss of status for the clergy in Iran due to the politicization of a small number of their peers . . . [E]ven today, it is estimated that no more than three per cent of the estimated 200,000 *ulama* in Iran are such 'regime clerics.'"[40] To top it all, explains Enayat, "Khumayni's main political ideas ... obliterate some of the most important differences between the Sunnis and the Shi'is."[41] The institution of the *vilayat-i faqih*, by making the office look like a carbon copy of the ideal Sunni caliphate, epitomizes this convergence, thus making it even less acceptable to the traditionalist Shia clerics.[42]

The nature of Saudi and Iranian regimes and the systems they preside over are vastly different from each other despite attempts on the part of both to justify their rule on the basis of Islam. The radical dissimilarity between the two systems is further demonstrated by an analysis of movements and parties opposed to the Saudi and Iranian regimes. Regime opponents usually hold up a mirror to the regimes they oppose, thus helping analysts better understand the nature of regimes they seek to analyze.

The Nature of the Opposition

The nature of oppositional politics is very different between Saudi Arabia and Iran, confirming the earlier argument that the two states and their regimes are vastly different despite their attempt to proclaim themselves the true standard-bearers of Islam. Interestingly, while opposition to the Saudi regime has come most dramatically from Islamist radicals espousing a form of neo-Wahhabism that is even more puritanical and insular than the Wahhabism of the religious establishment, the main opposition to the Iranian regime has come from groups and factions that can be considered more moderate, liberal, and democratic than the clerical establishment that supervises Iran's governance. In other words, the major opposition to the regime comes from the Right in Saudi Arabia and from the Left in Iran. This is a reflection both of the greater openness of the Iranian society and polity and of the existence of a strong liberal and democratic strand in the political culture of the country, going back at least to the early years of the twentieth century. It also reflects the ingrained illiberalism of its Saudi counterpart and the relatively superficial impact of Western liberal ideas on Saudi Arabia, especially on its Najdi heartland, where the country's power resides.

Most Iranians find it difficult to contemplate an opposition that could be more reactionary than the ruling religious class, although the latter is far more open to criticism, compromise, and even change than the Saudi ruling establishment. Most Saudis find it difficult to contemplate an opposition that is liberal and democratic in nature, because the Saudi political culture—particularly the rhetoric of political debate—is intimately intertwined with its Wahhabi religious ethos and the puritanical religious idiom used by the ruling House of Saudi to justify its dominance. This does not mean that there is no liberal trend in Saudi Arabia, but liberalism there is highly elitist and without a popular base.[43] Moreover, it has been largely neutralized in the past decade or so, because the "liberals who used to stridently criticize the ruling family (and even call for their ouster) now begrudgingly acknowledge their position, in fear of the ascent of the religious right."[44]

Opposition in Saudi Arabia

The major opposition to the Saudi regime has come from religious radicals, themselves the products of Wahhabi religious education and the insular Saudi political culture. This has especially been the case since the deployment of American troops into the kingdom in 1990–91.[45] However, this challenge, although it came of age in the 1990s, was foreshadowed by the seizure of the Grand Mosque in Mecca in November 1979 by a group of religious radicals critical of the Saudi regime's corrupt lifestyle and its deviation from puritanical Wahhabi precepts. In hindsight, it is clear that the Grand Mosque incident was a harbinger of things to come. It signified the breakdown of the compact between the House of Saud and segments of the Wahhabi *ulama* that had undergirded the legitimacy of the regime since the inception of the kingdom. This social contract began to fray in the second half of the 1970s, for multiple reasons, including the demographic and educational explosion in the kingdom and the inflow of massive amounts of petrodollars following a boom in oil prices. Together, both of these factors changed lifestyles and societal expectations and created resentment among the most conservative elements.

Also important was the Saudi policy, adopted in the 1960s and determined by Riyadh's rivalry with Cairo, of giving refuge to radical members of the Muslim Brotherhood then being persecuted in Nasser's Egypt. Eric Rouleau points out: "Until the arrival of the Muslim Brotherhood, Wahhabi Islam . . . had been essentially apolitical, concerning itself mainly with puritanism in morals, the observance of proper dress, and correct religious practices per se. Under the impact of the new arrivals, however, part of the Saudi clergy progressively became politicized—and began, for the first time, to challenge the House of Saud's temporal power."[46] Several of the brotherhood's exiles were appointed to the faculty of the Islamic University of Medina. It was no coincidence that many of the leaders of the group that seized the Grand Mosque in 1979 had been or were at the time students at that institution.

Many of the exiled members of the brotherhood were disciples of Sayyid Qutb and took their cue from his radical political ideas, based on the denunciation of Muslim regimes as unbelievers (known as the practice of pronouncing *takfir*) because they were not truly Islamic but lived in a state of ignorance (*jahiliyya*) that made them legitimate targets against which holy war (*jihad*) could be waged.[47] In some ways, this was a throwback to the ideas propagated by Ibn Abd al-Wahhab in the middle of the eighteenth century but diluted in later Wahhabi teachings. What is ironic is that Qutb's teachings could be interpreted to include the House of Saud among regimes living in *jahiliyya*. However, the exiled members of the Muslim Brotherhood refrained from doing so for good political reasons. Instead, they married this radical political philosophy to the socially and culturally conservative ethos of their adopted country, thus concocting a heady brew that appealed to three critical constituencies in the kingdom—the most socially and culturally conservative, the most disillusioned and disempowered, and the most idealist—and joined them in a union potentially very destabilizing for the Saudi regime. Al-Rasheed points out, "A strong Islamic rhetoric promoting a return to Islamic authenticity attracted people who had grown frustrated with a truncated modernization, inequality, corruption of the government and close ties with the West, which began to be increasingly defined as the source of social and economic evils."[48]

The present generation of radical Islamist opponents of the Saudi regime, including those who identify themselves as members of al-Qaeda in the Arabian Peninsula (QAP), are products of this marriage between Qutbist political ideas and the innate puritanism and conservatism of the Wahhabi doctrine. Wahabism constructed from above was a pillar of the status quo. Wahhabism mobilized from below has become the mortal enemy of the same status quo. The most prominent among the contemporary religious radicals—call them neo-Wahhabi, if you will—are young *ulama* that have come to be called *al-Sahwa al-Islamiyya* (the Islamic awakening), *sahwa* for short. These are the nonestablishment *ulama* who have proven to be strident critics of the regime, several of whom were imprisoned in the 1990s for opposing the regime's decision to invite American forces into the kingdom.[49] However, after their release from prison in 1999, many of them seem to be reconciled to working with the regime and achieving their objectives through it. The regime has been receptive to such cooperation, in order to shore up its religious credentials that were being eroded because the official religious establishment had become increasingly discredited for its spineless endorsement of the regime's policies, including the decision to deploy American troops. Rachel Bronson has argued that "the regime has become entangled in a delicate and dangerous dance" with the *sahwa*. According to her, "[t]heir preachings [had] inspired bin Laden and their followers," and, "vehemently opposed to the United States," they "relentlessly criticize the traditional ulema's fawning passivity and call for greater influence over all aspects of Saudi society."[50]

Although, for the moment, the *sahwa* may be working with the regime on certain issues, such as denouncing terrorism within the kingdom, their ultimate objectives are unlikely to coincide with the regime's goals. Nonetheless, the regime seems to consider their support, however conditional, crucial in its battle against the violent militants linked to al-Qaeda who have stepped up their terrorist activities within Saudi Arabia since May 2003. One very knowledgeable analyst reports: "For now, the two camps continue to forge a strategy of co-existence if not mutual support. The clerics believe that the continued survival of the royal family is in the best interest of stability in the Kingdom as well as providing them renewed power to spread their religious message."[51] At the same time, "[w]ith the official religious establishment largely discredited, *sahwist* cooperation was considered highly valuable by rulers in desperate need of religious legitimacy."[52]

Opposition in Iran

The Iranian opposition consists of many actors who would prefer to quote Thomas Jefferson rather than Sayyid Qutb. Even those reformists who are committed to the current "Islamic" system of governance but would like to moderate it from within (e.g., former president Mohammad Khatami) speak of a "dialogue of civilizations" rather than a clash among them.[53] The *Economist*'s correspondent in Iran conceded that, despite its many flaws, the last presidential election in 2005 saw "the most pluralist election campaign in Iran's history": "[T]here was a wide range of views and a wide range of votes . . . [N]o fewer than five candidates won more than four million votes apiece."[54] Mahmoud Ahmedinejad won the runoff against the veteran pragmatist cleric and former president Akbar Hashemi Rafsanjani (who posed as a moderate on domestic and foreign issues) because of his appeal to the poor and the downtrodden. The latter also happen to be more conservative socially than the middle-class and upper-middle-class liberal constituency that supports the reformists. Ahmedinjad's election was a classic case of the masses voting against the classes.

In contrast to the Saudi situation, where the younger generation of the regime's opponents tend to be more radical in their commitment to Wahhabi Islam than the defenders of the status quo, Iranian children of the revolution, ranging from philosopher Abdolkarim Soroush to journalist Akbar Ganji, have emerged as firm opponents of clerical dominance and religious conformity and as advocates of individual freedom and political democracy.[55] One could argue that at the base of the reformist Islamic trend in Iran, which is really several trends packaged as one, lies a philosophical vision best summed up in Soroush's writings, especially his advocacy of "the possibility and the desirability of secularization of an Islamic society without a concomitant profanation of its culture."[56] Many of these reformists or modernists in Iran are "themselves former radical Islamists who have changed to be broadly reflective of the modernist Islamist impulse."[57]

In other words, Islamic reformists in Iran, following Soroush's footsteps, would prefer the separation of religion and state, but without religion being eradicated from the culture and conscience of the nation. Consequently, they are caught in the middle, under attack from both the secular purists and the religious revivalists. I do not have the space here to go into the details of this subject (which is both philosophical and political), except to point out that this framework of oppositional activity in Iran is very different from the one employed by the radical opponents of the Saudi regime. The trajectories of the main opposition movements in the two countries are therefore very distinct from each other, just as is the case with the regimes they oppose.

The relationship of the reformists to the revivalists in Iran is also unique. Its nature is more that of loyal opposition waiting for its turn in power than that of two contestants engaged in a zero-sum game. The equation between former President Khatami and Supreme Leader Khamenei symbolized this relationship, with both leaders—equally afraid of chaos and instability—trying to occupy the center of the political spectrum. The fundamentals of this relationship between reformers and radicals remain unchanged despite the recent swing of the pendulum in favor of the hard-liners. While this was engineered in part by the partisan maneuverings of the Council of Guardians during the parliamentary elections of 2004 and the presidential elections of 2005, part of the blame must also be shared by the United States. One author has pointed out, "By increasing its pressure on Iran to the point where all factions of the Iranian regime perceive an immediate national security threat, the Bush administration has facilitated the reversal of the fortunes of the modernists and the seizing of the political initiative—and Iran's foreign policy—by the very radical Islamists it seeks to sideline."[58]

Opposition and Violence

The difference in terms of the instruments used by opposition forces in Saudi Arabia and Iran is instructive. A section of Saudi radicals has of late taken increasing recourse to violence and linked up with transnational jihadi organizations, principally al-Qaeda, whose leading figure and nominal head is the Saudi-born Osama bin Laden. Known as al-Qaeda in the Arabian Peninsula (QAP), this faction—inspired by, rather than under the control of, bin Laden—has staged spectacular acts of terrorism beginning in May 2003. Although the Saudi security services seem to be gaining the upper hand in their battle against QAP, it remains a major potential threat, especially because of its capacity to recruit sympathetic Saudi jihadists returning from Iraq over the next couple of years. John Bradley notes, "[T]here is a potential for long-term blowback, just as there was when the 'Afghan Arabs' returned from Afghanistan in the 1990s."[59]

The Iranian reformist opposition has been pushed to the wall in the past few years by hard-line elements that have prevented several of its members from standing for elections and have repeatedly closed down reformist newspapers. But the reformist camp has persisted with peaceful and agitational politics and tried to get its messages across through the media and the Internet. There is little violent opposition to the Iranian regime, despite the occasional bombings attributed to the Mujahedin-i-Khalq, the exiled opposition group that had operated with relative impunity from Iraq under Saddam Hussein. Its association with Saddam Hussein (which made it suspect in most Iranians' eyes) and its evolution into a cult demanding absolute loyalty to its husband-wife leadership has detracted immensely from the movement's credibility in Iran, and it seems to have become a spent force in Iranian politics.[60]

Furthermore, the struggle between the regime and the radical Islamist opposition in Saudi Arabia, which is itself in large measure a product of the Saudi educational and religio-political system, can be very vicious and ideologically uncompromising. In Iran, the reformist opponents of the clergy-dominated regime, also products of the postrevolution Iranian system, continue to work within the system, and accommodation between the reformists and the hard-liners is not only not ruled out but keeps taking place on numerous issues all the time. As stated earlier, this is the result of multiple crosscutting political, economic, and social cleavages in Iran that promote coalition building on particular issues, even among ideological antagonists. This takes off the sharp edges of political and ideological rivalries and promotes an atmosphere conducive to accommodation rather than perpetual conflict. It also ensures that the political pendulum keeps swaying from the conservative to the reformist end of the spectrum and back, thus providing political space for almost all competing forces in Iranian society. All of these differences between the two countries reflect as much the nature of the Saudi and Iranian regimes as they do the nature of the opposition in these two countries.

Conclusion

The preceding discussion makes clear that the Saudi and Iranian political systems are vastly different from each other, are products of their unique contexts, and therefore cannot be replicated elsewhere. Both bear little resemblance to the ideal model of governance based on the times of the Prophet and his immediate successors. Both states are modern constructs and products of nineteenth- and twentieth-century circumstances, when European colonial rule had enormous impact, both direct and indirect, on Muslim societies in the political, economic, and intellectual realms. Iranian constitutionalism could not have taken root without contact with Western ideas. Saudi Arabia would not have existed within its present boundaries without British assistance to Ibn Saud at crucial points in the expansion of Saudi power from its Najdi heartland.

Despite the occasional universal pretenses in their rhetoric, both the Saudi and the Iranian leaders realize that their systems cannot be reproduced elsewhere. Moreover, the conjunction of factors that led, on the one hand, to the unification of the Arabian Peninsula by Ibn Saud in the 1920s and, on the other, to the overthrow of the Iranian monarchy in 1979 were unique to their place and time. Critical factors in the success of Ibn Saud were, on the one hand, Wahhabi ideology that provided a potent form of solidarity to the quarreling tribes of the Najd and, on the other, British interests in the Middle East that for a variety of reasons preferred the al-Saud over the Sharifian rulers of the Hijaz, despite the latter's support to the British during World War I.[61] These factors cannot be re-created elsewhere.

Similarly, the factors that led to the Iranian Islamic revolution of 1979 and the Shia clergy's role in it cannot be reconstructed in other locales and in different times. The Shia *ulama*'s financial autonomy from the state (which is unlike their Sunni counterparts in the Muslim world) and their relatively hierarchical organization were critical to the success of the Islamic revolution and the installation of a clerical-led government in the country. Despite some cross-fertilization of ideas among Sunni and Shia radicals in the second half of the twentieth century (especially the influences of Qutb and Mawdudi on Khomeini), the political and religious universes of the Sunni countries, which form the vast majority in the Muslim world, are vastly different from those of Shia Iran. This precludes the type of mullah-led mobilization that became the hallmark of the Iranian revolution. In short, both the Saudi and Iranian cases are sui generis developments that defy replication.

CHAPTER 4

Between Ideology and Pragmatism

Egypt and Pakistan provide examples par excellence of the quest for ideological purity on the part of Islamist thinkers as well as of the Islamist movements' ability to adapt to changing political circumstances. The two cases also highlight the importance of regime policies in determining Islamist trajectories. Cumulatively, these factors clearly demonstrate the validity of the proposition that expressions of political Islam in discrete countries are grounded in social and political realities specific to their contexts and that Islamist movements undergo metamorphosis in response to changing situations and regime policies.

This chapter compares the leading Islamist movements in Egypt and Pakistan—the Muslim Brotherhood (MB) and the Jamaat-i-Islami (JI), respectively—to analyze, among other things, how far their strategies have been shaped in response to regime policies and restraints imposed on them. However, given the fact that the JI's and MB's strategies cannot be fully comprehended in the absence of an understanding of the seminal ideas propounded by their founders/ideologues, a comparison of their three major figures—Hassan al-Banna, Abul Ala Mawdudi, and Sayyid Qutb—is deemed essential for the purpose of this chapter.

Pakistan and Egypt: The Background

The division of British India on the basis of Muslim and Hindu majority areas created Pakistan. Islam is therefore the primary cementing bond among its diverse ethnic groups, a fact that was clearly understood by its irreligious founders, who perceived religion principally in instrumental terms. The potency of political Islam therefore presented a major challenge for the modernist Pakistani elites, because they could not deny outright the political and legal role of Islam in a country created in its name. The Islamist parties in Pakistan, especially the JI, were able to exploit this situation to promote what they characterized as an Islam-based agenda. This consisted principally of the infusion of selected provisions of sharia law into the legal code and the vetting of legislation to determine that it was compatible with Islamic law.[1] The Islamists' political agenda has been a constant cause of tension between Pakistan's modernist regimes and the Islamists, who have considered Pakistan's rulers as promoters of Anglo-Saxon law and thus as against the sharia.

Egypt, by comparison, took its Islamic character for granted, with a Muslim majority of around 90 percent going back centuries. However, during the first half of the twentieth century, its quasi-liberal, modernizing elite and its royal court failed to end the de facto British occupation of the country that had begun in the 1880s, making them easy targets of popular anger. The venality of Egypt's semifeudal ruling elite added to popular discontent. The situation became more acute at the end of World War II, with Egypt "facing critical internal and external problems and ruled by men without a semblance of popular support."[2] It was in this context that Islamist political ideology took root in Egypt, with the MB, the principal Islamist movement, projecting itself as the defender both of Egyptian national interests and of Muslim dignity against the foreign occupiers and their domestic collaborators.

A comparison of these two movements, the JI and the MB, which have led the charge for Islamization of their respective societies and polities, demonstrates how different the Islamist movements have been in the two countries, despite the similarities in their idioms and concepts that continue to be couched in Islamic terms. Admittedly, there has been a certain degree of cross-fertilization of ideas; the influence of JI founder Abul Ala Mawdudi's writings on the ideas put forward by Sayyid Qutb, the MB's chief ideologue during the1950s and 1960s, is clear. However, it is also evident that the two scholars-cum-activists were reacting to distinct challenges that required unique responses. Similarity in the concepts and idioms used by Mawdudi and Qutb and in their respective movements often concealed the different stimuli that led the two Islamist thinkers to expound their fundamental ideas and develop their theories in the first place.

Mawdudi, the chief theoretician of the JI, which he founded in 1941, was initially reacting to the challenge of preserving an Islamic identity under British rule in religiously plural India, where Muslims formed less than one-third of the total population. Then, in the run up to the partition of India in the 1940s and after the creation of Pakistan in 1947, he was responding to the challenge of establishing an Islamic state in Pakistan, whose foundational ideology of (Indian) Muslim nationalism he had opposed. He had done so on the basis that nationalism was incompatible with Islam and that the secular nationalist leaders of the Muslim League were bound to create a "Kemalist" state in the name of Islam while surrendering the rest of India to unadulterated Hindu domination. In Mawdudi's view, if Pakistan was to be created in the name of Islam, it had to be an "Islamic" state, not one that was predominantly Muslim merely in a demographic sense. Once Pakistan had been established, his program "was no longer to save Islam in India but to have it conquer Pakistan," and the JI "was therefore opposed not to Pakistan but [to] the [un-Islamic] Muslim League."[3] It is this latter struggle of Islamizing Pakistan that JI has been engaged in for the past six decades.

Hasan al-Banna, who founded the MB in 1928, was reacting to the British political and military presence in Egypt and to the Egyptian elite's collaboration with their de facto colonial masters. He did not have to wrestle with the problems of Muslim/Islamic identity in a plural society the way Mawdudi did. He took the existence of the Egyptian nation-state for granted and found no incompatibility between Egyptian nationalism and Islam: "Within appropriate bounds, nationalism, al-Banna held, was consistent with Islam . . . The Muslim Brethren was a religious movement that embraced but transcended nationalism."[4] He went even further to argue that "Egypt's role is unique [in the Muslim world], for just as Egyptian reform begins with Islam, so the regeneration of Islam must begin in Egypt, for the rebirth of 'international Islam,' in both its ideal and historical sense, requires first a strong 'Muslim state.'"[5]

While the two movements shared ideological similarities and used vocabulary drawn from Islamic sources, there were differences that went beyond merely nuance and were in many cases of a substantive character reflecting the differences in the contexts in which the JI and the MB were founded. At the same time, the leading theoreticians of both organizations demonstrated a high degree of innovation in their interpretation of Islamic terminology. Their conceptions of Islamic polities included characteristics that were distinctly modern and had no precedents either in Islamic jurisprudence or in the traits exhibited by the idealized Islamic state of the time of the Prophet and the first generation of Muslims.

Ideological Foundations: Mawdudi, al-Banna, and Sayyid Qutb

Mawdudi was the most seminal thinker of all the ideologues of the Islamist movement. His approach to Islam was quintessentially political. Two characteristics distinguished Mawdudi—and therefore his party—from the *ulama* and their organizations in both India and Pakistan. The first was his denial of free volition as a consequence of the true Muslim's total surrender to God's command, a position that brought forth ripostes from leading theologians in the subcontinent. More relevant to our discussion is the fact that Mawdudi "accepted only politics as a legitimate vehicle for the manifestation of the Islamic revelation and as the sole means for the expression of Islamic spirituality, a position that correlated piety with political activity, the cleansing of the soul with political liberation, and salvation with utopia."[6] Consequently, to him, Islam was, above all, a political ideology that required its adherents to bend all their energies toward realizing the Islamist utopia of setting up an "Islamic" state.

The concept of the Islamic state, as propounded by Mawdudi and increasingly accepted by Islamists of various hues, was itself novel and a product of modernity, although its advocates made it look like a hoary Islamic institution. As stated earlier in this book, the modern sovereign nation-state bears little resemblance to the classical Islamic polities, whether of the time of the Prophet or that of the early Arab empires. Despite the lip service paid by Mawdudi to the concept of the universal *umma,* his practical aim was to make Pakistan Islamic by capturing political power and enforcing the sharia within the boundaries of the state. It was clear that Mawdudi's "Islamic state" sacrificed universality at the twin altars of particularism and pragmatism.

Mawdudi's idea of the Islamic state was based on the concept of God's sovereignty (*hakimiyya*). Accepting God's sovereignty implies that such a state would be governed according to the path laid out by God for Muslims to follow (the sharia). At the same time, he emphasized human agency in the implementation of God's will by stating that "the Quran vests vicegerency in the entire Muslim citizenry of the Islamic state," thus "[t]he right to rule belongs to the whole community of believers."[7] This vicegerency, according to Mawdudi, is implemented, above all, through the institution of a strong and pious executive, selected by the community from among its most upright members and committed to the implementation of the sharia with the help of advice from a consultative council made up of equally pious and wise Muslim males. However, Mawdudi emphasized that human agents, whether the executive, the elected representatives, or the judiciary, could only interpret, execute, and adjudicate God's law; they could not create new, man-made laws (except in exceptional circumstances), for that would by definition contravene Islamic teachings.

In theory, therefore, Mawdudi abrogated the independent legislative function of the state, limiting it almost entirely to the interpretation of God's law, the sharia, with the exception of those cases where the Quran and the sunna were silent. In such cases, the consultative council, the legislative wing of government, could exercise *ijtihad* (independent reasoning) and formulate laws as long as they were not in violation of the sharia. Where God's commands and the Prophet's practices were not self-evident, the legislature could presumably plug in the holes, but it would have no right to change the basic legal architecture as laid out in the Quran and the sunna. Its role would be to supplement the sharia, not to replace it. However, since the Quran and the sunna are silent on a large number of issues that the modern state has to tackle, this meant a great amount of latitude in the exercise of power for the legislative as well as the judicial and executive organs of Mawdudi's Islamic state, giving these institutions far greater power in practice than his theory seemed to allow.

Furthermore, Mawdudi averred that Muslim citizens of the Islamic state would have "limited popular sovereignty": "In effect, Mawdudi was claiming that both the will of God and the will of the people were effective loci of sovereignty since the latter would necessarily conform to the former."[8] This is why Mawdudi called his preferred system "theo-democracy," where the Muslim citizenry acts as the agent of God's will. One can see the impact his ideas may have had on Khomeini's conception of the Islamic republic in Iran, whose constitution also assumed that both the will of God and the will of the people should be reflected in the governance of the country and that they would not run contrary to each other.[9]

It was clear that Mawdudi was not bent on re-creating the system of the city-state of Medina under the Prophet, despite the limitations he imposed on the state's legislative functions. He was taking his cue from Western representative institutions while adapting them to his concept of Islamic governance. That Mawdudi was fully cognizant of the requirements of twentieth-century polities and their organizational structures was reflected in his tripartite division of governmental functions among the principal organs of the Islamic state. The formal structure of the state, which included the separation of powers, was built on the model of representative governments found in Western democracies: "In his proposals and discussions, Mawdudi seldom made comparisons with the ethical teachings of other religions, but he did with various Western theories and systems of political organization and government, from communism to democracy."[10] Mawdudi's constant obsession with adapting Western forms of government while attempting to remain true to his conception of the Islamic state resulted in his institution of the "democratic caliphate," an executive elected by the people and responsible for ruling on the basis of God's law, with the legislature and the judiciary performing adjunct functions.

As mentioned earlier, Mawdudi laid great emphasis on the Islamic state's function of interpreting and implementing God's law. At the same time, Mawdudi set the stage for contemporary Islamist thinkers to repudiate the importance of the accumulated wisdom of earlier interpretations and legal precedents. He argued that the function of interpretation could not be restricted by the existence of earlier *tafsir* (interpretative commentaries) and/or precedents in *fiqh* (jurisprudence). Answers to legal, political, economic, and social questions were to be traced to the Quran and the hadith and to the practices of the first generation of Muslims, before they became corrupted by *bida* (innovations): "In Mawdudi's view . . . the history of Islam stopped with the rightly guided caliphs, for the social and political institutions that followed were incapable of reflecting the ideals of Islam in any fashion . . . The Islamic state therefore had to stand outside the cumulative tradition of history of Muslim societies. . . . In effect, the history of Islam would resume, after a fourteen-century interlude, with the Islamic state."[11]

This device of going back to the fundamental sources of law could be both constraining and liberating. It could be constraining in the sense that it limited options that had been provided especially by the more liberal schools of Sunni jurisprudence, such as the Hanafi school that was predominant in India and Pakistan. It was liberating because it did not insist on *taqlid*, or strict adherence to earlier theological and jurisprudential opinions, thus opening the way for innovative interpretations as long as they could be justified by analogy with decisions taken during the Prophet's time or that of his immediate successors. It could therefore act as an avenue for the introduction of novel concepts and ideas that were not available in the existing jurisprudential literature.

Mawdudi's approach to the construction of an Islamic polity was basically a top-down one. Vali Nasr points out: "Mawdudi believed in incremental change rather than radical ruptures, disparaged violence as a political tool, did not subscribe to class war, and assumed that Islamic revolution will be heralded not by the masses but by the society's leaders." Consequently, Nasr continues, "[t]he Jama'at's efforts have always aimed at winning over society's leaders, conquering the state, and Islamizing the government."[12] The JI's collaboration with General Zia-ul-Haq's military dictatorship in the 1980s conformed to a large extent to its founder's philosophy of capturing the state by Islamizing the ruling elite and implementing Islamic law in order to then Islamize society.

Despite his rhetoric that constantly referred to Islam as a revolutionary force, Mawdudi's idea of revolutionizing society and polity was very evolutionary, and he aimed at achieving his objective of creating an Islamic state in piecemeal fashion: "[W]hat Mawdudi meant by the term revolution was a process of changing the ethical basis of society, which should begin at the top and permeate into the lower strata."[13]

Mawdudi's ideas about jihad were also far more moderate than the ideas of many of his contemporaries, especially Sayyid Qutb and those influenced by Qutb's thinking. Mawdudi made clear in 1948, in the context of the first India-Pakistan war over Kashmir, not only that Pakistan was bound by a cease-fire agreement it had reached with India but that only a properly constituted state authority could declare jihad over Kashmir or any other issue. Individuals and groups could not declare jihad on their own, for this, according to Mawdudi, would be in contravention of Islamic principles.[14] Moreover, according to Mawdudi, jihad "was not war, but a struggle—a struggle not in the name of God but along the path set by God"; he made clear in 1954 that jihad could only be undertaken against an external enemy (not an internal one), only if the country was "actually, and not potentially at war," and then "only if the war was with *daru'l-harb* (abode of non-Muslims)."[15]

Unlike Mawdudi, al-Banna was, above all, an organizer and activist, rather than a political philosopher or even an ideologue. His primary legacy in Egypt is the tightly knit organizational character of the MB, fashioned to some extent on Sufi brotherhoods and owing unconditional allegiance and absolute obedience to a supreme guide. Al-Banna's conception of social order was embodied in the organization he founded, which had to be a total system covering all aspects of a Muslim's life: "He envisaged an Islamic utopia with no political parties, no class antagonism, and no legitimate differences of personal or group interests: the Islamist equivalent of the utopian Marxist classless society. In the case of the brotherhood, however, the utopia to be achieved in the future was based on restoring the utopia deemed to have existed in the past, at the time of the Prophet Muhammad and the rightly guided caliphs."[16] One can see the combined influences of the modern totalizing ideologies in the ideological and organizational framework espoused by al-Banna.

The MB under al-Banna, unlike the JI, was committed to a bottom-up strategy of first Islamizing society before making an attempt to capture power. This did not prevent al-Banna and the MB from participating in political maneuverings during the 1940s and from extending limited support to one or the other of the contending parties. But, overall, "Banna and the Society [MB] had a traditional platform that the Society should exercise power only when the nation had been truly 'Islamized,' and thereby prepared to accept the principles for which the Brothers stood."[17]

For al-Banna, "[t]he *sharia*—its implementation or non-implementation—was the determinant in the definition of a true Islamic order." However, for al-Banna and for his successor as supreme guide of the MB, Hasan al-Hudaybi, the implementation of an Islamic order did not mean a return to the form of government that existed in the time of the Prophet and his immediate successors. For them, "the existing constitutional parliamentary framework in Egypt, if reformed, would satisfy the political requirements of Islam for a 'Muslim state.'"[18] Here, one finds considerable similarities between al-Banna's views and those of Mawdudi, whose conception of the Islamic state, as analyzed earlier, is remarkably like that of a quasi-democratic, representative system, in that it featured a strong executive, a consultative council with restricted legislative functions, and an independent judiciary, with the people staffing the various organs of government, acting as human agents of God's will.

The model of the Islamic state as adumbrated by its leading exponents was usually limited to an enunciation of general principles without dictating a particular form of government. The latter could be left to the exigencies of time and place. Al-Banna was no exception in this regard. The MB in Egypt under al-Banna and his successors stipulated only three principles essential to the Islamic state: "(1) the Quran is the fundamental constitution; (2) government operates on the concept of consultation (*shura*); (3) the executive ruler is bound by the teachings of Islam and the will of the people." Moreover, "Banna described the relationship of ruler and ruled as a 'social contract' . . . in which the ruler is defined as 'trustee' . . . and 'agent' . . . Since the ruler is the 'agent contracted for' by the nation, he is 'elected' by it. The Quran designated no specific ways of holding elections."[19] As these general principles denote, representative government, whether parliamentary or presidential, would qualify as "Islamic" as long as laws promulgated by such a government did not contravene the sharia, defined as God's commands embodied in the Quran and the Prophet's practices, as attested to by the sunna based on hadith that are considered robust by authorities trained in the art of hadith verification. Such a definition, one could argue, not only is minimalist in character but has enough flexibility built into it for it to accommodate itself to contemporary political and social circumstances, whether in Egypt or Pakistan or elsewhere in the Muslim world.

The separation of the concept of the sharia from jurisprudential traditions forms the hallmark of modern Islamist thinking, especially in the writings of Qutb and Mawdudi: "Qutb, for example, notes the confusion between the sharia and 'the historical origins of Islamic jurisprudence.' The rulings of the legists of the Islamic tradition are obviously inadequate, he says, for the needs of society through time."[20] The return to the original sources of religion, the Quran and the sunna, and the rejection of the intervening traditions (spanning centuries of praxis and interpretation) could be progressive, in the sense of being responsive to contemporary societal demands, or could signify a return to a romanticized and ahistorical past, divorced from context. It could also lead to a combination of these two apparently contradictory tendencies, thus producing a hybrid that was both retrogressive and progressive at the same time. It is this hybrid that Islamism has turned out to be in general and especially in Egypt and Pakistan.

The strategy of downplaying—if not totally ignoring—the rich traditions of Islamic jurisprudence allowed the Islamists, especially Mawdudi and Qutb, much greater license in terms of envisioning their ideal polity than would have been the case had their imaginations been circumscribed by clearly defined jurisprudential rules. Without the jurisprudential baggage encumbering their imaginations, they could construct the past de novo while not being oblivious to the requirements of the contemporary era. As mentioned earlier, this process of imagining the golden age of the past while being sensitive to the realities of the present was demonstrated best in their conceptions of the "Islamic state." It is clear that the existence of sovereign states within clearly defined boundaries limits the geographic scope of the Islamists' imagination. While they pay lip service to the concept of the universal *umma*, their prescriptions for the ills of their society have limited relevance beyond their nation-state and are in fact designed to apply within existing political boundaries. This is also the case with the model that they advocate as the alternative to existing political systems, a model that is commonly known as the "Islamic state." This model takes the existence of sovereign states as given and does not attempt to replace them by a universal polity. All it does is advocate replacing existing political systems based on the "laws of men" with a system based, in theory, on the "laws of God."

It is instructive to note that Mawdudi, al-Banna, and Qutb were not primarily theologians by training. Although Mawdudi did receive a certificate that qualified him to become an *alim* (religious scholar), he abandoned a religious vocation for a secular one, began his career as a journalist, and then became a scholar-reformer and political organizer. In fact, Mawdudi was very critical of the *ulama*, who he considered largely responsible for producing a fossilized form of Islam that was not relevant to the modern world.[21] While several of the founding members of the JI in the 1940s were religious scholars, Mawdudi's disdain for the *ulama*, his authoritarian tendencies that gradually stifled debate within the party, and his dismissal of the wisdom of much of accumulated tradition strained his relations with the *ulama* within the JI fold and forced most of them to leave the party. However, Mawdudi's disapproval of the *ulama* did not prevent him and the JI from cooperating with *ulama*-based parties to further the Islamist agenda in the Pakistani parliament and outside.

Al-Banna and Qutb both came out of the secular educational system in Egypt and were self-taught in theological matters. Both worked for the Egyptian ministry of education as schoolteachers. Qutb, in fact, began his writing career as a literary critic and spent two years in the United States on a government scholarship. The lay background of these leading Islamist figures is one of their foremost distinguishing characteristics. Among other things, it explains their contempt for the *ulama*, documented earlier in this book.[22] As Richard Mitchell explains, Al-Banna's "revulsion at the sense of futility in the Azhar in the face of the currents battering away at Islam can be said to mark his disenchantment with it as a citadel of defence for the faith," and his movement "was a direct challenge to Azhar authority and a demonstration of its impotence."[23]

Sayyid Qutb and the Radicalization of Political Islam

Sayyid Qutb, the foremost ideologue of the MB in the 1950s and 1960s, provided the major ideological thrust to the MB during the last fifteen years of his life and made a very distinctive contribution to the structure of Islamist thought. While he built on some of Mawdudi's ideas, such as *hakimiyya* (sovereignty of God) and *jahiliyya* (age of ignorance), he went much further than Mawdudi had done in giving these concepts radical content. Carl Brown observes: "Qutb built on Mawdudi's ingenious interpretation of a venerable Muslim term—*jahiliyya* or the time of 'ignorance' before God's message to Muhammad—to make it describe not a historical period but a condition that can exist at any time. In the Mawdudi/Qutb formulation, even professed Muslims who do not live up to God's comprehensive plan for human life in this world and the world to come are living in a state of jahiliyya."[24] Brown further points out: "Qutb's mature political theory . . . may be seen as a rigorously logical and consistent working out of the implications of his three concepts: jahiliyya, hakimiyya, and jihad. In simplest terms it comes down to this: God's sovereignty (hakimiyya) is exclusive. Men are to obey God alone. Men are to obey only rulers who obey God . . . [whose] mandate is clear and comprehensive. It is available for mankind's guidance in the Shari'ah. To set aside the clear and comprehensible divine mandate is to lapse into jahiliyya. Rulers who so act are to be resisted. Resistance under these circumstances is a legitimate act of jihad. The ruler's claim to being a Muslim ruling a Muslim state is null and void."[25]

While Mawdudi had also made a distinction between true and nominal Muslims, he had never given up on the latter and never declared them beyond the pale, the way Qutb did: "He tried to appeal to their religious, intellectual, and, ultimately, their political sensibilities. His concern lay with politics; hence, he needed to extend the reach of his message and persuade greater numbers to his cause."[26] Moreover, given Mawdudi's top-down strategy of Islamization, it was inconceivable that he and the JI would excommunicate members of the ruling elite, thus changing their relationship with successive Pakistani regimes into zero-sum games. Such a strategy would be totally counterproductive in their scheme of things and fatal to the cause they espoused.

Qutb was responding to a very different situation from those faced by Mawdudi and al-Banna. He was reacting against an authoritarian and repressive Arab nationalist regime in Egypt, which had cracked down severely on Islamist political formations, particularly the MB. He considered Nasser's regime, which had initially flirted with the MB and then turned against it, a product of *jahiliyya* (ignorance of God's commands, akin to the ignorance of the pre-Islamic pagans of Arabia) and, therefore, the equivalent of rule by infidels. Qutb's pronouncement of *takfir* (excommunication) against the Egyptian rulers and the political system they presided over has no parallel in the doctrine and rhetoric of Mawdudi.[27] This demonstrates, among other things, that while the hostility between the state and the Islamists had become a zero-sum game in Egypt in the 1950s and 1960s, it never reached a situation of irreversible antagonism in Pakistan. In the 1970s and 1980s, some of Qutb's more militant followers took his ideas to their extreme conclusion by declaring the whole Egyptian society—not just its regime—to be in a state of *jahiliyya* and, therefore, a legitimate target for jihad. This set off a chain reaction of violence and counterviolence, including the assassination of President Sadat in 1981, major terrorist attacks in the first half of the 1990s, and subsequent brutal repression by the Egyptian state.

Political Pragmatism

The preceding analysis makes clear that while there may be considerable correspondence in the idioms used by the JI and the MB and significant similarities
in ideas espoused by the principal theoreticians of Islamism in Pakistan and
Egypt, one should not conclude that the JI and the MB are cut from the same
cloth. They were and continue to be very different sorts of organizations in
terms of their strategies, with their respective characters determined largely by
the milieus in which they have had to operate over several decades. Regime
policies have formed a significant—in fact, dominant—component of their
respective milieus, determining to a substantial extent the character of both
Islamist movements, which have seen themselves as opponents of the existing
normative and political order even when they have at times collaborated
closely with regimes presiding over such an order.

Lisa Anderson has captured this reality very well: "Opposition . . . has the
unusual characteristic of being defined partly by what it opposes; it develops
within and in opposition to an ideological and institutional framework and, as
such, reveals a great deal not only about its own adherents but also about the
individuals, policies, regimes, and states in authority."[28] The action-reaction
pattern between the state and Islamist formations is often determined by the
former, with the latter largely reacting to regime policies. In the case of Egypt,
as Maye Kassem has pointed out, the state's policy of "adopting 'cooperative'
and 'coercive' tactics constituted a cycle that was not simply maintained and
enhanced in the post-1952 republic, but significantly contributed toward determining the disposition of Islamist opponents in the contemporary era."
Kassem continues: "On one level, [the Nasserite regime] crushed the Muslim
Brotherhood movement in a manner unprecedented to date. On another level,
the brutality involved in the regime's approach to the Brotherhood produced a
reactionary Islamic ideology that not only was extremist in its interpretation,
but was also the foundation of the more radical Islamist groups that emerged
in the late 1960s."[29]

Pakistan has always been a more open polity than Egypt, even when under
military rule. Given the political culture of the Indian subcontinent and the tradition of parliamentary politics inculcated from times of British rule, Pakistan's military rulers have usually felt compelled to use democratic forms to
bolster their legitimacy. Pakistan has therefore remained a "semidemocracy"
most of its life. This has provided the JI and other Islamist parties considerable
political space to test their strength among the general public. In the process, it

has also strengthened their commitment to democratic functioning, however imperfect. They perceive the democratic system as the primary bastion preventing them from being crushed by military regimes that, with the exception of Zia's rule, have tended to be relatively secular and modernist and, therefore, not well disposed toward Islamist groups. This is why the JI, despite its Islamist activism, became committed to a constitutional political process from the 1950s despite the fact that it considered the political system in Pakistan to be un-Islamic. According to Nasr, "[t]he alliance between secularism and martial rule reinforced the party's commitment to Islamic constitutionalism, which could be the means for restoring the Jama'at's political fortunes."[30]

Despite ups and downs in its relations with the Pakistan government, the JI (unlike the MB in Egypt) has continued to operate as a legal political party during much of Pakistan's independent existence. The initial inroads that the Islamist forces were able to make during the constitution-writing process between 1949 and 1956 were neutralized to a substantial extent by the military coup of 1958. Relations with the government remained tense during the secularly inclined rule of General Ayub Khan between 1958 and 1969, when the JI opposed his policies as insufficiently Islamic and his regime as undemocratic. However, its relations with the army improved during the civil war of 1971, when its members in East Pakistan collaborated with the military in violently repressing supporters of Bengali independence from Pakistani rule.

The JI's relations with the Pakistan regime improved dramatically in the 1980s, for a couple of very important reasons. First, General Zia-ul-Haq, who seized power in 1977 and ruled until 1988, made Islam a principal component of his regime's legitimacy formula. He did so in order to fend off demands for a return to democracy. Second, the JI and other Islamist formations became major beneficiaries of the 1980s Afghan insurgency launched, with massive assistance from the United States and Saudi Arabia, against Soviet occupation. The JI and other Islamist groupings and their offshoots became major partners with the Pakistan military in acting as conduits for financial and ideological support as well as for weapons supplies to various Islamist groups fighting the Soviet-supported regime in Afghanistan.

Even during the 1990s, when the Afghan war came to an end and Pakistan returned to civilian rule, the JI and other Islamist parties continued to have close relations with the Pakistani military, the real power behind the throne even when the country was under civilian rule. The Pakistani military's policy of supporting the Taliban in Afghanistan coincided with the objectives of the Islamist parties. Although this relationship has frayed somewhat since General

Musharraf's volte-face on the Taliban issue following 9/11, the JI and other Islamist parties continue to selectively collaborate with the military regime in order to keep the relatively secular parties—the Pakistan People's Party (PPP), led by Benazir Bhutto, and the Muslim League, led by Nawaz Sharif—out of power. The collaboration with Pakistan's military elite has been consistent with the JI's top-down strategy of Islamizing Pakistani society by first Islamizing the ruling elite. One wonders, however, who has been using whom in this relationship between the military-dominated regime and the JI.

The MB, despite its periodic flirtations with Egyptian regimes (first with Nasser in 1952–54 and then especially with Sadat during the 1970s), has never come as close to using the levers of power for its own ends as the JI did during Zia's rule in Pakistan. Even when Sadat encouraged the Islamists in the early 1970s to participate in the public life of the country in order to neutralize socialist and Nasserite elements opposed to him, his government closely circumscribed the MB's activities in order to prevent it from becoming too powerful and acting beyond the state's control. Although it was allowed to operate as a semilegal network and even publish its own newspapers and magazines, the MB was not permitted to function as a legal political party and to participate in elections under its own banner. Furthermore, the honeymoon ended in 1977 with Sadat's visit to Israel, and extremist members of an Islamist grouping, the Islamic Jihad, assassinated Sadat in October 1981.

While Sadat had cracked down on the MB following its opposition to his visit to Israel, his successor, Hosni Mubarak, once again attempted to provide limited public space to the MB, in order to co-opt it into the system and use it against his secular and socialist opponents. However, violence by extremist Islamist groups during the first half of the 1990s, the MB's impressive performance in elections to professional bodies (many of which it came to control), and its expanding network of social services (which came to fill the void that the state could not) convinced Mubarak that it was more of a threat to his rule than a potential ally.[31] He changed course in the mid-1990s and once again suppressed MB activities with a heavy hand. The MB, by now accustomed to adapting itself deftly to bad times, lowered its political profile and waited for the next round of political liberalization to begin. At the same time, it meticulously distanced itself from extremist Islamist elements that had perpetrated violence in Egypt during the 1990s, thus preserving its moderate image among the Egyptian populace.

The Mubarak regime once again began to somewhat liberalize its authoritarian rule in the early part of this decade, in great part due to American pressure on Middle Eastern governments to democratize. But it stopped short of granting the MB legal party status. Part of a breakaway and more moderate faction of the MB, which called itself al-Wasat (the Center), also attempted to gain the status of a legal political party and failed. However, the regime did permit the still technically illegal MB to campaign more openly than before in the parliamentary elections of November and December 2005. This tactic was adopted primarily to convince the Western publics and their governments of two things: first, that the regime intended to genuinely open up the political system; second, that given the MB's popularity, the only alternative to the present order was a takeover of Egypt by Islamists who are likely to gravely threaten Western interests. That this was primarily a tactical, not a strategic, move on the part of the Mubarak regime became very clear when the regime, worried about the MB's electoral performance going beyond what it found comfortable, ordered the security forces forcefully to stop MB supporters going to the polls in the last phase of the elections, leading to a dozen or more deaths.[32] This incident exposed both the potential strength of the MB and the limits within which the regime expected it to operate.

Metamorphosis

As has been stated earlier in this chapter, what makes Egypt and Pakistan very important examples of Islamist political activity is the fact that the Islamist formations in the two countries, principally the MB and the JI, have developed the most elaborate and sophisticated rationale advocating the establishment of political orders in the modern world based on Islamic principles. Even more remarkable is that Islamists in both countries were and remain convinced that this God-given order could only be implemented through the medium of a very modern instrument, the political party, which has no precedent in Islamic political traditions. In fact, one could argue that political parties, since they divide the *umma* on partisan bases, would be considered a source of *fitna* (dissension) according to traditionalist interpretations of Islamic teachings. Nonetheless, these twentieth-century political instruments for the implementation of God's will, the JI and the MB, were conceived as vanguard parties imbibing the values of discipline, hierarchy, and unquestioning loyalty to its leaders. In other words, they were and continue to be well-organized cadre parties in the Leninist tradition. This makes clear that the ideologues and leaders of the MB and the JI were fully cognizant of the requirements of twentieth-century politics and that their organizational structures reflected these requirements. They were thus very much products of modern circumstances, rather than throwbacks to the early period of Islam.

Moreover, the JI (from the 1950s) and the MB (at least from the 1980s) have developed a vested interest in the democratic functioning of their respective polities. The JI's restrained approach toward political activity was reflected in Mawdudi's antipathy toward violent change. Nasr notes that even after the first military coup in Pakistan that attempted to move the country toward a more secular direction, the JI "did not radicalize, a development which stands in clear contrast to revivalist movements in Pahlavi Iran and Nasser's Egypt." Nasr continues, "Mawdudi wanted above all to avoid the fate of Egypt's Muslim Brotherhood under Nasser and to that end steered the Jama'at clear of radical solutions to the challenges posed by the Ayub regime."[33]

Although the JI entered into a de facto alliance with General Zia's authoritarian regime in the late 1970s and into the 1980s, it became increasingly disenchanted with the regime as time wore on. Nasr notes that Zia's authoritarian tendencies became particularly galling to the JI "as it became apparent that the martial-law regime had in good measure dissipated Islam's political appeal and diminished the ability of religion to legitimate political action and authority." As Nasr observes, "Zia's triumph had proved to be a Pyrrhic victory for Islam."[34] However, the alliance with the regime provided the JI with opportunities that compensated to some extent for its guilt by association with an increasingly unpopular government. Nasr explains that it did so by opening the "government to the Jama'at's influence to an unprecedented extent," as the JI "now began to infiltrate into the armed forces, the bureaucracy, and important national research and educational institutions."[35]

Although the JI began as an elitist, vanguard organization consisting of ideologically committed members, its involvement in the day-to-day politics of Pakistan created the need to build coalitions with other groups and parties and to achieve accommodation with authoritarian and semiauthoritarian regimes. This soon turned the JI into a pragmatic political party that de-emphasized ideology while increasing its commitment to the democratic political process, which it saw as the best guarantee against arbitrary suppression by unrepresentative governments. As a consequence, the JI's revivalist agenda not only moderated but took on a distinctly democratic hue.

A similar story has been repeated in the case of the MB in Egypt. The MB's posture today is a far cry from the ideologically charged and uncompromising stance its leaders had adopted during the period between 1954 and 1966. The latter position, most eloquently expressed in Sayyid Qutb's writings, was in fact repudiated by the MB's supreme guide Hasan al-Hudaybi as early as 1969, in an attack ostensibly aimed at Mawdudi's ideas. However, Hudaybi's views could be construed as unequivocally repudiating Qutb's radical ideas, since the latter's key concepts were borrowed from Mawdudi and often taken to conclusions that Mawdudi had never contemplated: "According to Hudaybi, the task of the Brethren was to preach Islam in the society in which they lived. He did not characterize the society as *jahiliyya,* but merely noted that many Muslims remained in a state of *juhl* . . . [T]he latter means no more than ignorance of the sort that can be remedied by mere preaching . . . There are Muslim sinners, of course, but one hardly excommunicates a Muslim merely because he has sinned."[36] The year 1969 was too early for the MB leadership to directly criticize the "martyr" Qutb. This stage was reached in 1982, when Hudaybi's successor, Umar al-Talmasani, wrote that "Sayyid Qutb represented himself alone and not the Muslim Brethren," thus distancing the MB conclusively from Qutb's radical views.[37]

The MB had long rejected Qutb's political line, by accommodating itself to the realities of political life under Sadat from the early 1970s and even cooperating with the regime on certain fronts (without openly admitting it was doing so). Now it had finally emerged ideologically from under the shadows of Qutb's extremist interpretation. Certain Islamist groups, some disenchanted offshoots of the MB, continued to uphold the purity of Qutb's ideas and even take them to further extremes, but they were roundly condemned by leaders of the MB. The MB's criticism of Sadat's trip to Jerusalem in 1977 and the Israeli-Egyptian Peace Treaty of 1979 had soured its relationship with the regime, and Sadat had incarcerated a number of MB activists in prison during the last year of his life, but the MB did not advocate any form of violent resistance to the regime's repressive policies.

Mubarak's decision cautiously to open up the polity during the early years of his regime provided the MB with some political space that it used to good measure. Although, as stated earlier, Mubarak cracked down on the MB during the latter half of the 1990s, its political base held remarkably well, due in part to its social welfare and educational activities and in part to its image as the only organized political force capable of standing up to authoritarian rule and advocating the protection of human rights. The MB's moderation from the 1970s onward has been largely linear, despite the ups and downs in regime policies that have tended alternately to permit a controlled expansion of its activities or to restrict them further. The MB's trajectory has demonstrated the validity of Carrie Rosefsky Wickham's argument that "political openings [even short of democratization] can encourage Islamist opposition leaders to moderate their tactics."[38] The difference between today's MB and that of yesteryear can be explained largely in terms of regime policies. Mubarak's harshest treatment of the MB comes nowhere close to what the party and its leadership suffered at the hands of the Nasserite regime in the 1950s and 1960s, and this has made it feasible for the MB to find a niche within the system that it can exploit to its advantage.

The attempt by a breakaway faction of the MB to create a Center Party, Hizb al-Wasat, in cooperation with certain non-MB intellectuals and political activists, including some Christians, demonstrates even more strongly the increasing moderation among a section of the MB, especially its middle-generation leadership. This moderation is the result both of a cost-benefit analysis and of a process of political learning that this generation has gone through while working within the political space provided to it by a regime alternating between repression and partial liberalization. The latter not only has attuned them to taking advantage of the limited opportunities available under Mubarak's rule but also has inculcated in them a habit of cooperation with Egypt's non-Islamist opposition in an attempt to preserve and broaden democratic space. What may have started as a tactical maneuver seems to be well on the way to transmuting into a commitment to democratic values, based on the understanding that only the implementation of these values can protect Islamists and non-Islamists alike from the regime's arbitrary acts of repression.[39] While the veracity of this proposition remains to be fully tested (especially in the Arab world), there are strong signs that this may indeed be happening in Egypt and elsewhere. Augustus Richard Norton has argued that the emergence of al-Wasat is not an isolated phenomenon in the Muslim world but could well be the forerunner of an increasingly popular trend: "Al-Wasat was not a shot out of the blue, but a culmination of tajdidi [reformist] trends that have been developing dramatically since the 1980s . . . It is a modern manifestation of liberal Islam, but its commitment to interpret *shariah* flexibly flows also naturally from the modernism of Muhammad 'Abduh, almost a century ago . . . It is an instructive sample of modern political parties that will appear with increasing regularity throughout the Muslim world."[40]

Such moderation is not limited to the al-Wasat faction, which has broken away from the MB and been denounced by the latter for departing from its Islamic roots.[41] The MB itself has undergone a similar metamorphosis, demonstrated by its near-open participation in the parliamentary elections of 2005, often in cooperation with other political forces. This has brought it considerable returns. Despite the attempt by the regime to restrict the number of seats it could capture, the MB won eighty-eight seats, making it the second largest political force in the country after the ruling National Democratic Party (NDP), which is less a party than a patronage network-cum-governmental agency. It is very clear that had the regime not prevented many MB supporters from voting in the last phase of the elections, nearly all of its 130 candidates would have won parliamentary seats.[42] Simultaneous with its participation in the elections, there has been a concerted attempt by the MB to demonstrate its democratic and pluralist credentials. Writing in a leading British daily newspaper under the title "No Need to Be Afraid of Us" while the votes were still being cast, the MB's vice president stated in no uncertain terms: "Our aim in seeking to win a limited number of seats in parliament is to create an effective parliamentary bloc that, in conjunction with others, can energize an inclusive debate about the priorities of reform and development. Not a single political, religious, social or cultural group should be excluded from Egypt's political life. The objective must be to end the monopoly of government by a single party and boost popular engagement in political activity . . . The success of the Muslim Brotherhood should not frighten anybody: we respect the rights of all religious and political groups."[43]

The attempt by the MB to project its image as a party committed to democracy and pluralism is not merely a veneer. Its travails over the past several decades have led its leadership to conclude, just as the JI leadership did much earlier, that a constitutional democracy is the best guarantee for the party's protection from arbitrary repression. This has led one commentator to conclude: "The Muslim Brotherhood's success at the ballot box does not merely reflect the growing popularity of the Islamist group. It also marks a fundamental change in the Brotherhood's strategy; the group is now working toward active political participation, rather than merely seeking to survive."[44] Participation in democratic activity, even if undertaken in very restrictive circumstances, such as those currently prevailing in Egypt, has a way of transforming participants whose initial orientation may have been nondemocratic, if not antidemocratic.

On the whole, the current situation in Egypt is well summed up in an International Crisis Group briefing that asserts that despite the government's refusal to allow the MB to function as a legal political party, its "social presence dwarfs that of all potential political rivals, including the ruling NDP." The briefing explains: "[I]f legalized, there is a real possibility of it overwhelming the political scene . . . But this situation is partly of the government's own making: by hampering legal opposition parties and refusing to legalize new ones, it has facilitated [the MB's] . . . virtual monopoly in this sphere."[45] Much will depend, however, on whether the regime sees the MB's credible performance in the last elections as a prelude to its co-optation into a genuinely liberalized system or as a means to demonstrate to the United States and its Western allies that political liberalization in Egypt will open the floodgates of Islamism, which is innately hostile to the West. If the regime follows the latter strategy in an attempt to garner international support for a crackdown on the MB, it would mean a return to the days of unalloyed authoritarianism. This may end up pushing the MB toward greater radicalism and confrontation, thus turning the regime's rhetoric into a self-fulfilling prophecy. It will also impede the trend toward moderation and compromise now clearly visible among Egyptian Islamists.

Islamist Ulama *and Lay Islamists: Changing Equations*

As stated earlier, the JI has been more fortunate in its relations with governments in Pakistan than the MB has been in Egypt. However, its electoral performance had been meager until the last parliamentary elections in 2002, when it joined *ulama*-based parties, the leading among them the neo-Deobandi Jamiat-ul-Ulama-i-Islam (JUI), to form a united "Islamic" bloc known as the Muttaheda Majlis-i-Amal (MMA), the United Action Front. The two parties could not be more dissimilar: the JI is an elitist urban-based party that until recently had strong support among the urban, educated community of *muhajir* (refugees from India) concentrated in the port city of Karachi and the middle and lower middle classes in urban Punjab. The JUI, led by puritanical Deobandi *ulama,* is populist in character, with a strong base among the Pashtuns, rural and urban, living in the North-West Frontier Province (NWFP) and Baluchistan. While the JI's *muhajir* base has been eroded over the past two decades by the emergence of an ethnic *muhajir* party, JUI's Pashtun base has been augmented during the same period by the Afghan jihad and the consequent convergence of Islam and Pashtun nationalism in the areas bordering Afghanistan.

After the overthrow of the Taliban by U.S.-led forces in early 2002, the JUI embarked on a two-pronged strategy: supporting Musharraf against the moderate secular parties, the PPP and the Muslim League, and acting as the mouthpiece of Islamic radicalism combined with Pashtun identity/nationalism that made it highly critical of Musharraf's policy toward Afghanistan.[46] The MMA's electoral performance in 2002 cannot be understood in isolation from the JUI's two-pronged strategy. The MMA fared rather well in elections to the National Assembly, garnering 11 percent of the popular vote, which translated into a disproportionate number of seats, 59 out of 342.[47] It performed much better in the provincial elections in the NWFP and Baluchistan; it came to power on its own in the former and in partnership with Musharraf's party in the latter. Interestingly, however, its strongest performance came in areas that are considered bastions of the JUI, the NWFP and Baluchistan. The MMA performed much worse in those areas where the JI was expected to have popular support, urban Sindh and urban Punjab. This makes clear that the JUI is very much the senior partner in this alliance and that the combination of Pashtun nationalism and traditionalist Islam (rather than the lay Islamism of the JI variety) has the greatest political appeal in Pakistan.

These results signaled a major shift in the Islamist center of gravity in Pakistan, from the JI to the JUI and related groups, a process that began in the 1980s but reached its culmination in the 1990s and was demonstrated clearly in the elections of October 2002. The real agent of change in this case was the external variable of the Afghan jihad, the importance of the Pashtun groups in this jihad, Pakistan's support to Islamist fighters during the war, and the Pakistani military's role in bringing the overwhelmingly Pashtun Taliban to power in Afghanistan. The Afghan venture allowed the Pashtun-based JUI to become the lead player among Islamist groupings. Its populist agenda and mass base gave it great advantage over the JI, with its elitist image and a middle-class urban base.

The JUI is an *ulama*-based party that appeals to the more puritanical among the traditionalists. The JUI *ulama* and madrassas linked to them provided the foot soldiers for the party during the 2002 elections. The proliferation of madrassas in the 1980s and 1990s helped the *ulama*-based parties, particularly the JUI, to reverse their equation with the JI in terms of their capacity to mobilize public opinion. Furthermore, the Pashtun anger at Musharraf's reversal of course and his decision to join the United States in its war against the Taliban worked to the advantage of the Islamist parties, particularly the JUI, which was already entrenched in the Pashtun areas.

The cooperation in Pakistan between the JI and the JUI—until recently ideologically poles apart—demonstrates a convergence between lay Islamists and sections of the *ulama* that is a consequence in part of the radicalization of a segment of religious scholars and their renunciation of their traditionally politically quietist and, by implication, pro-establishment stance. This is a phenomenon also witnessed in recent years in Egypt, where a segment of the *ulama,* including elements from within al-Azhar, the institution of the Islamic establishment par excellence, have adopted postures that are very critical of the government's domestic and foreign policies. As the lay Islamists mellow in both Pakistan and Egypt and as a segment of the *ulama* are radicalized as a result of domestic repression and/or external stimuli, it may lead to not merely a convergence of the two streams but their hybridization. This could result in the emergence of a form of Islamism that is much more respectful of traditional religious practices and the corpus of jurisprudential knowledge than has been the case so far.

In fact, it can be argued that the religious establishment with al-Azhar at its apex has been more successful since the 1970s than the lay Islamists, including the MB, in making Egyptian society more Islamic and making legal norms conform increasingly to the sharia. It has been able to do so as a consequence of an unwritten compact with the regime by which the religious establishment has been allowed free rein as far as cultural and religious matters are concerned in return for its acquiescence into the state's near total control of the political and economic spheres. Political sterility has been bought by the regime at the cost of cultural and social conservatism and de facto censorship of views that run counter to those of the religious establishment. Al-Azhar and associated institutions, despite occasional divisions within and among them, have constantly pushed the limits of their influence, and the state has usually given in on secondary issues, such as culture and societal norms, as long as the religious establishment has refrained from directly criticizing its political, security, and economic policies. This increasing Islamization of society has also created fertile ground for the propagation of Islamist political views. While the MB and al-Azhar may ostensibly be at loggerheads in Egypt, there seems to have developed a division of labor between the two as far as furthering the Islamist agenda is concerned.[48]

Extremist Violence

As the mainstream Islamist movements have moderated and committed themselves to play by the rules of the political game, a number of breakaway, extremist factions have appeared that have taken recourse to violent, terrorist actions. While such organizations do not have the support of significant segments of the populations either in Egypt or in Pakistan, their dramatic acts of terror have often grabbed headlines both domestically and internationally. It is therefore imperative that we analyze this phenomenon of Islamist extremism as well, in order to round off our discussion of political Islam in the two countries.

The drift toward violence and extremism in Islamist politics in Egypt was induced by governmental repression that radicalized the ideology and then the strategy and tactics of Islamist factions. Maye Kassem has pointed out: "[W]hile Nasser's ruthless crackdown on the Brotherhood gave birth to radical militant Islamism, Sadat's crackdown enhanced radical militant tendencies. The reinforcement of such tactics by the state under Mubarak not only reinforced this predicament, but consequently elevated it to the international level as well."[49] The emergence of al-Jama'a and the Egyptian Islamic Jihad and their increasingly violent attacks on foreign tourists as well as Egyptians can be directly traced to state repression that set off a chain of violence and counterviolence that reached its apogee in the mid-1990s.

Consequently, in the second half of the 1990s, the leaders of the Islamist movements, al-Jama'a in particular, "came to realize," as Kassem observes, "that the state's blatant use of aggression in its efforts to control and contain them had inadvertently baited them into retaliation, and that they had started an armed struggle that they could not win." Kassem continues, "Equally important, in the process they saw themselves being marginalized from the sphere of political activity and being pushed into the category of terrorists."[50] The decision of the internal leadership of al-Jama'a to abjure violence in jail in 1997 was endorsed by most of the external leaders in March 1999. However, some extremist leaders and groups, especially the faction of the Egyptian Islamic Jihad led by Ayman al-Zawahiri working in exile from Afghanistan, denounced what they saw as the "capitulation" of the internal leadership. Many of them joined Osama bin Laden in launching a jihad against the "far enemy," the United States, because they had not succeeded in overthrowing the "near enemy," the Egyptian regime.[51] The violence that had been undertaken by extremist Egyptian factions has been now largely transferred to the global level, providing the Egyptian regime some respite.

In Pakistan, the drift toward violence and extremism was largely the result of the nexus that developed between the military, particularly the Inter-Services Intelligence, and certain Islamist factions in the context of the Afghan jihad and the subsequent decision by the Pakistani military to unleash Islamist terror in Indian-administered Kashmir.[52] This nexus was in many ways the intensification of an ongoing (although uneasy) relationship between the Islamist parties and the military to curtail the moderate and secular parties' room for maneuver. However, not just the military has used the Islamists for its own purposes. Aqil Shah has pointed out: "Since independence in 1947, the Pakistani elite generally—not just the military—has sought to accommodate and manipulate Islamists. Yet, just who has been using whom has not always been clear."[53]

The proliferation in Pakistan of terrorist outfits, such as Lashkar-e-Taiba and Jaish-e-Muhammad, in the 1990s is a direct result of the support they have received from segments within the military and political elites. The latter have perceived such groups as useful instruments of Pakistani policy that would help destabilize Indian-administered Kashmir in the context of the insurgency in the region against Indian control and the popular support that the insurgency has received in the Kashmir Valley. However, some of these groups have developed an ambivalent relationship with the Pakistani regime since 2001, when, under American pressure, President Musharraf tried to curb their activities because they were funneling men and material into Afghanistan in support of the Taliban, then under attack by the United States and its allies. Nonetheless, the Pakistan government has failed to put the genie back in the bottle, partly because there is continuing support for jihadist groups among elements within the military, based on the strong belief that the Pakistan army can use them in the future for its own ends just as it had done in the past.[54]

Pakistan's military rulers also face a conundrum on the broader issue of the relationship between the military and the mainstream Islamist parties, especially those grouped within the MMA. Some analysts have argued that the equation between the military and the mainstream Islamists in Pakistan is now moving in favor of the latter. Nasr reports: "As pressures mount, the military . . . will not likely remain politically active without fuelling Islamism. The notion of secularizing the military has become a contradiction in terms. As the military faces stiff resistance to its authority, it is likely that it will give in to the MMA [the Islamist political alliance], returning to the framework of relations that governed military-Islamist relations the 1980s. However, this time . . . the balances of ideology and power are very different . . . This may well present Islamists with the first serious opportunity to emerge as viable mainstream political actors."[55]

In both Egypt and Pakistan, Islamist parties appear to be gaining ground because of regime policies, even if the two governments have adopted different strategies in their attempt to confront and/or co-opt major Islamist parties. In Egypt, the MB is clearly the most credible alternative to the current regime and is likely to replace it if free and fair elections are held. In Pakistan, the situation is much more mixed, with the Islamist groupings and the military joined together in an uneasy relationship to prevent the more secular parties from coming to power through democratic means. However, the Islamist-military marriage of convenience is replete with contradictions that may surface at any time. One should not be surprised if the Islamist parties move away from their alliance with the military in the near future and team up with the left-of-center PPP and/or the right-of-center Muslim League (Nawaz) to demand a return to full democracy. After all, as the JI experience demonstrates, constitutional limits on the government's executive powers have played a major role in protecting the party from arbitrary acts of governmental repression. The JUI, it should not be forgotten, was an ally of the PPP in the NWFP not so long ago.

Conclusion

This chapter demonstrates not only that the Islamist phenomenon in Pakistan and Egypt is distinct from expressions of political Islam elsewhere but also that the two Islamisms are different from each other despite their use of similar vocabulary. It also demonstrates that both these expressions of political Islam are prisoners of their respective contexts. Furthermore, it reveals that mainstream Islamism in both countries has mellowed considerably and turned pragmatic, as a result partly of regime policies and partly of self-evaluation of their interests as extremist strategies have failed and as moderation has brought them closer to the centers of power. Both cases demonstrate that if there is a discernible long-term trend in Islamist politics, it points toward moderation and constitutionalism, not violence and extremism.

These conclusions are especially striking given the fact that Pakistan and Egypt were home to the most prominent Islamist thinkers—Mawdudi and Qutb, in particular. These thinkers expressed total philosophies that combined sophisticated and systematic analyses of the world around them with remarkable degrees of innovative thinking, laying out "Islamic" solutions to the predicaments faced by their societies. Pakistan and Egypt are also home to the two best-organized Islamist parties, the JI and the MB, which boast of dedicated cadres and the "purity" of their Islamist creed. None of these factors that could be expected to militate against pragmatism and compromise have prevented the mainstream Islamist formations in the two countries from moderating and becoming normal players of the political game according to the rules set by their countries' regimes, which have usually been unsympathetic to the Islamist cause.

The ability of Islamist parties in Egypt and Pakistan to adapt to their respective situations and work within the constraints imposed on them demonstrates how much context matters in Islamist politics when conducted under authoritarian and/or semidemocratic regimes. Chapter 5 will test the same proposition—the importance of context in the formulation and execution of Islamist agendas—in democratic and democratizing settings, by analyzing and comparing Islamist political formations, their agendas, and their political maneuverings in Turkey and Indonesia.

CHAPTER 5

Muslim Democracies

Democratic forms of governance, imported from the West as part of the colonial experience, are new to Muslim countries, as they are to all postcolonial and non-Western states. As pointed out in chapter 1, the classical tradition of governance in the Muslim world emphasized order for fear of anarchy and the division of the *umma*. Even those scholars and political actors who stressed the notion of *adl* (justice) as an important characteristic of rulership did not equate just government with popular rule. They were concerned primarily with the character of rule, rather than with how the rulers were chosen. Popular sovereignty, the precursor of democracy, was a concept alien not only to the classical age of Islam but also to Europe until the French Revolution of 1789. It did not put down intellectual roots in Europe until well into the nineteenth century. Even then, its practice was heavily circumscribed by property, gender, racial, and educational qualifications.

Some Muslim thinkers had achieved familiarity with the terminology of liberal thought and democratic governance in the nineteenth century, as these ideas spread from Europe.[1] But only in the second half of the twentieth century did a considerable number of Muslim countries begin to experiment with representative institutions. Many such experiments were aborted soon thereafter, for reasons having to do more with colonial legacies, social structures, regime characteristics, and regional security environments than with Islam.[2] By examining the cases of Indonesia and Turkey, this chapter aims to show that there is no inherent and irreconcilable contradiction between Islam and democracy. Circumstantial variables and contextual factors have constrained the growth of democracy in large parts of the Muslim world.

Religion, State Making, and Democracy in the West

Liberal democracies, as we know them today, have had a very brief history in the West itself. One can argue quite convincingly that liberal democracies in Europe and North America were established no earlier than the twentieth century and are products of a long process of gestation that began several centuries ago. Moreover, liberal democracies in the West have usually had very violent pasts. These have included domestic and interstate wars of religion and wars of colonial expansion in the case of Europe and the near total extermination of the native population, the practice of slavery and the inhuman treatment of African slaves, and a very bloody civil war in the United States. Such violence, as Charles Tilly points out in the case of Western Europe, has been crucial to the process of state making and nation formation in these regions.[3] Modern nation-states, which currently draw their legitimacy from the identification of the ruled with the rulers, have been constructed largely through policies of blood and iron.[4] Nonetheless, the establishment of such nation-states has been an essential prerequisite for the development of democratic forms of governance based on social contracts that bind both the governors and the governed.

Contrary to popular belief that modern nation-states are products of the triumph of the secular over the sacred, religion has played a very crucial role in their formation in the Western world. Talal Asad has argued very convincingly: "Religion has been central to the formation of many European identities: Poland, Ireland, Greece, England, and others. In the New World, Protestantism played a vital part in the construction of the new American nation, and religion continues to be important despite the constitutional separation of church and state . . . The established church, which was an integral part of the state, made the coherence and continuity of the English national community possible. We should not say that the English nation was shaped or influenced by religion: the established church (called 'Anglican' only in the nineteenth century) was its necessary condition."[5] In many cases, shared religious beliefs acted as the bedrock on which political loyalties were constructed and national identities established. The best way for the rulers to cultivate the loyalties of the ruled was to demonize the religious "other." Anthony Marx points out: "The absolutist French state was . . . built with the crutch of religious exclusion . . . By the time of the French Revolution, expulsion had produced relative religious homogeneity allowing for a liberal rhetoric of more inclusive nationalism." Marx continues: "The exclusion of Catholics to unify Protestants became the bedrock for English nation-building, reinforced later by foreign wars in which the French were seen as religiously linked to the internal 'other.'"[6]

Only after nation-states were firmly established and their ruling elites securely entrenched was the exclusionary model of nation formation gradually transformed into an inclusive and civic model of nationalism. However, this is still an incomplete process in Europe, as recent instances of Islamophobia demonstrate very clearly. It is instructive to remember that modern liberal nationalism has been built essentially on illiberalism, a lineage that most current advocates of liberal democracy try their best to ignore.

Religion, State Making, and Democracy in the Muslim World

Perceived from a linear perspective in which religious intolerance performed the role of midwife for the birth of modern nation-states in Europe and in which the latter acted as the essential prerequisites for the establishment of social contracts that produced democratic governments, the experience of the non-Western world, including its Muslim component, is unlikely to appear unique or even exceptional. Religion has acted as the identity marker helping the process of nation formation in Europe. That it plays a similar role in defining national identities and political preferences in the Muslim world today should come as no great shock to students of state formation and nationalism. The same record that was played in Europe until not too long ago is currently being replayed in the postcolonial world, including its Muslim component.

However, what is unique is that most postcolonial states, including Muslim ones, have had neither the luxury of centuries of time (as was the case in Western Europe) to build modern nation-states nor the autonomy to fashion their own political boundaries through war and diplomacy (as the Europeans did). Their mostly artificially constructed boundaries drawn by European colonial powers largely for reasons of imperial convenience—the Indonesia-Malaysia, Pakistan-Afghanistan, Syria-Lebanon, and Iraq-Syria borders immediately come to mind—have immensely complicated the twin processes of nation formation and democratic governance in many postcolonial, including Muslim, countries.[7] This is reflected in great measure in the interaction between religion and politics in Muslim countries, including the deliberate use of Islam in defining nationhood within artificially constructed states in the absence of other forms of solidarity. It is also reflected in the authoritarian nature of many regimes in Muslim countries and in the authoritarian tendencies among rulers even within Muslim democracies. Incomplete processes of state making and nation formation lie at the root of all of these phenomena.

As they have done in the case of postcolonial states in general, colonially crafted boundaries and lack of adequate time to complete the twin processes of state making and nation building have complicated the move toward democracy on the part of Muslim countries. This has led to the assertion by some analysts that Islam is inherently incompatible with democracy. The truth is that Islam has little to say on the question of democracy, since it does not prescribe a single model of governance that is applicable to all societies across time and space. According to one scholar, the "Qur'an . . . knows no such concept of an 'Islamic' state, least of all one with the coercive powers of a modern leviathan."[8] The comparison in chapter 3 between the models presented by the two leading self-proclaimed Islamic states, Saudi Arabia and Iran, forcefully drives home the point that there are serious divergences of opinion as to what an ideal Islamic polity ought to be. The bottom line is that there is nothing in Islam that militates against Muslim polities adopting democratic forms of rule, just as there is nothing in Islam that prevents autocratic rule in Muslim countries.

As stated earlier, the answer to the Muslim world's poor democratic record lies elsewhere. It lies in the Muslim countries' current stage of state making and nation building. It lies in the particular contexts within which predominantly Muslim polities have developed and in the specific issues they have had to countenance in their processes of state and nation formation. It lies in the composition and nature of ruling elites and in their commitment or lack of it to the establishment of representative institutions. It lies in the regional security environment and how conducive it has or has not been for the development of representative institutions and democratic politics. Finally, it lies in the policies of external great powers that, in several cases, have intruded in significant ways into the domestic politics of strategically important Muslim countries and therefore into their state-building and nation-making processes. Quite often, great powers have supported authoritarian regimes since the latter have served these powers' strategic and economic interests more willingly and efficiently than their democratic counterparts. Such policies, during both the cold war and post–cold war periods, have been very deleterious from the perspective of democratic development in the Muslim world.

Despite all the negative factors, the Muslim world's democratic record is not as bad as it is made out to be. Important Muslim countries, such as Malaysia, Bangladesh, Turkey, and Indonesia, have made substantial strides toward democratic governance during the past few decades. It is in the Arab world that Muslim countries have remained exceptionally authoritarian. But even here, as the examples of Lebanon, Kuwait, and even Morocco and Jordan demonstrate, there has been movement toward greater political openness than was the case in the past.

In recent years, Islamist parties and movements in both Arab and non-Arab countries have, in several cases, contributed substantially to the development of democratic ethos in predominantly Muslim states and to the legitimization of representative institutions among their populations. They have done so by enthusiastically welcoming political liberalization and participating in the political process wherever there have been opportunities, however limited, that permit such participation. Their embrace of political democracy, even in small doses, is the result of the fact that they have realized that democratic polities provide the best assurance for the free expression of their political views and the best guarantee against regime suppression of political tendencies that rulers find unpalatable. The Islamists' attraction to democratic governance may have been undertaken initially for tactical reasons. However, their participation in competitive politics and the realization that their interests are best served by an open, democratic polity strongly suggest that they have moved beyond the tactical stage to a more genuine appreciation of the democratic system. This augurs well both for the future of democracy in the Muslim world and for the further socialization of Islamist parties into the democratic ethos.

Comparing Turkey and Indonesia

Turkey and Indonesia provide good examples of both democratic transition and the subsequent consolidation of democratic forms of governance. They also provide strong evidence of the Islamists parties' contribution to and incorporation into the democratic system. Furthermore, the two cases demonstrate clearly that democratic settings promote multiple expressions of political Islam in Muslim countries, thus debunking the myth that Islamism is a monolithic phenomenon.

I have also chosen Indonesia and Turkey for detailed analysis of the prospects for "Muslim democracy" because of their demographic and strategic importance, respectively, within the Muslim world. Indonesia is the largest Muslim country in terms of population and has undergone a recent successful transition to democracy that has been quite painful and at times chaotic. Turkey, strategically located at the point where Asia and Europe meet, is a long-standing member of the North Atlantic Treaty Organization (NATO) and an aspirant for membership in the European Union (EU). Most important, despite all the imperfections of its political system, Turkey has had the longest engagement with representative institutions and democratic politics in the Muslim world, going back at least six decades. It also has a history of Islamist parties participating openly in the political arena at least from the early 1970s.

Both cases also demonstrate the validity of Vali Nasr's argument that "Muslim Democracy rests not on abstract, carefully thought out theological and ideological accommodation between Islam and democracy, but rather on a practical synthesis that is emerging in much of the Muslim world in response to the opportunities and demands created by the ballot box." Nasr concludes: "The depth of commitment to liberal and secular values that democratic consolidation requires is a condition for Muslim democracy's final success, not for its first emergence . . . [I]t is the imperative of competition inherent in democracy that will transform the unsecular tendencies of Muslim Democracy into long-term commitment to democratic values."[9] This conclusion is corroborated by the earlier experiences of European countries where liberal values have triumphed after a long and often violent and exclusionary process. As earlier comments in this chapter indicate, Europe would have stagnated in a highly authoritarian condition had liberal values been considered not as end products of their successful operation but as essential prerequisites for the introduction of representative institutions.

State and Religion in Turkey and Indonesia

Unlike in most other Muslim countries, where political Islam has either been suppressed or co-opted by regimes, Turkey and Indonesia demonstrate a much more complex relationship between religion and state. During the first two decades of its existence, the Turkish Republic functioned as an authoritarian one-party state that suppressed all expressions of Islam in the public sphere. However, for the last six decades, as the system has gradually liberalized, political Islam and the secular state have had an uneasy relationship that has oscillated between the state's successive attempts to close down Islamist parties and its toleration of Islamist political activity when these parties have resurfaced under different names. At times, as in the 1980s, the secular state has in fact attempted to form a working relationship with Islamist factions, under the guise of what has been euphemistically called "the Turkish-Islamic synthesis," to counter leftist tendencies in the country when the latter have been strong. This vacillation on the part of the state between hostility and tolerance has had dual effects. On the one hand, it has restrained Islamist political activity to some degree. On the other, it has provided enough space for Turkish Islamism to operate in the political arena and has prevented it from being driven underground and morphing into a clandestine and violent movement.

Following the military's "soft coup" of 1997 that ousted the Islamist Refah (Welfare) Party from power, most Turkish Islamists have learned how far they can realistically push constitutional restraints imposed by the militantly secular state without fear of backlash.[10] Capitalizing on their experience, they have repackaged themselves in such a fashion as to remain impeccably within constitutional bounds. They have also built a broad coalition that cuts across class and rural-urban cleavages and goes well beyond their original Islamist constituency. Consequently, the Adalet ve Kalkinma (Justice and Development) Party (AKP), which has firm Islamist roots, succeeded in winning the parliamentary elections in November 2002 with a massive mandate and remains in power without significant opposition, until recently, from the secular military that had forced its Islamist predecessor from office. The recent tension between the AKP and the military erupted over the AKP's decision in the spring of 2007 to nominate foreign minister Abdullah Gul as its presidential candidate. Gul was expected to easily win the presidency given the AKP's majority in parliament, which elects the president. Secularists saw Gul's Islamist background and the fact that his wife wears a headscarf as threatening to Turkey's secular foundations. The military, considered to be the guardian of Kemalist secularism, threatened indirectly that it might intervene if the AKP went ahead with Gul's election. The constitutional court declared the first round of elections invalid on a technicality and the AKP decided to call fresh parliamentary elections on July 22, 2007. The party is expected to win these elections thus clearing the way for the election of its preferred candidate by the Parliament.[11]

The AKP, confident of its support base, has also proposed a constitutional amendment that would change the current procedure of electing the president by parliament and instead have him or her elected directly by the people. While the current president has vetoed this amendment, it is likely to become an issue again after the next elections. However, it appears that the prospects of a confrontation between the military and the AKP are exaggerated. There are now too many stakeholders—both domestic and foreign—in Turkey's democracy for the military to attempt to overthrow an elected government as it had done in earlier times.

In the case of Indonesia, the relationship between Islam and the state was debated vigorously during the first decade of independence. Despite the state's secular bias, adequate political space was provided for Islamist parties to remain in the public eye and to participate in public debates, even if in rather muted ways. This remained the case during the parliamentary era (1948–58), during Soekarno's "guided democracy" (1958–65), and during Soeharto's "New Order" regime (1966–98). The transition to democracy in 1998 opened up this political space greatly, initially leading to a cacophony of Islamist voices that both surprised and alarmed Islamist intellectuals in Indonesia.[12] Since then, Islamist parties have robustly engaged in the public propagation of their ideas while simultaneously attempting to build coalitions with parties representing different—and often contrary—political perspectives.

Turkish democracy has undergone remarkable consolidation since the late 1990s, especially following the parliamentary elections of November 2002 that brought the Justice and Development Party to power. Indonesia stands out as a remarkable case of successful transition from authoritarian rule to democratic governance, despite the problems that accompanied such a transition. Turkey provides a fine example of democratic consolidation that encompasses increasing concern for human rights and a substantial decrease in the political clout of the military. Currently, both Turkey and Indonesia have democratically elected governments. As stated earlier, a party with Islamist roots, the AKP, heads the government in Turkey. It was not so long ago that the leader of the largest Islamic movement in Indonesia, the Nahdlatul Ulama (NU), occupied the post of president of that country. At least two major Islamist parties form part of the coalition that governs Indonesia today. Most significantly, Indonesia and Turkey point the way to what could lie ahead for much of the Muslim world in the not-so-distant future in terms of the incorporation of religiously inspired political formations into broadly secular political systems.

Both countries also provide good examples of the multiple expressions of political Islam through a variety of political parties and organizations, thus negating the thesis that political Islam is a monolith, even within specific countries. In Indonesia, the split between the modernist Muhammadiya and the traditionalist NU has been a fixture of political life since before the birth of the republic and has spawned a number of political parties and tendencies that have often competed with each other for the Islamist political base. While the intra-Islamist competition was muted to a large extent during Soeharto's authoritarian regime (1965–98), it has resurfaced since the fall of the dictatorship and the reemergence of democratic politics. Moreover, Greg Barton points out: "[T]he moderate nature of Indonesia's two mass-based organizations, the 40-million-strong Nahdlatul Ulama (NU) and the 30-million-strong Muhammadiyah is widely seen as underwriting the essentially quiescent and tolerant nature of Indonesian Islam. Together the two organizations represent a major portion of all Indonesian Muslims, and the great majority of all *santri* Muslims, the observant Muslims who pray and fast regularly and observe orthodox practices."[13]

In Turkey, where representative institutions have functioned—even if imperfectly and with periodic interruptions—for the past fifty years or more, the moderate and modernist Islamists split from the more hard-line and conservative ones to form the Justice and Development Party, which won the 2002 elections with 35 percent of the votes and two-thirds of the parliamentary seats. Its less accommodating rival, the Saadet (Felicity) Party, won only 2.5 percent of the votes and is not currently represented by any parliamentary seats.[14] But even before the split, the Islamist party, in its various incarnations in Turkey, had basically worked within the framework of Turkey's constitution, despite the fact that the constitutional cards were stacked against it because of the sacrosanct position attached to the official ideology of Kemalism, which is uncompromisingly secular and subordinates religion to the secular state.[15]

The cases of Turkey and Indonesia drive home the point that even with all the shortcomings on display in these two countries, political democracy creates political space for Islamist parties while simultaneously neutralizing the more extreme and rigid manifestations of Islamism that often thrive under autocratic rule. At the same time, democracy's competitive nature helps to split the Islamist base, cutting individual Islamist political formations down to size and drastically reducing the possibility that a monolithic Islamist bloc will take and hold power. Furthermore, political democracy provides the opportunity for non-Islamist political formations of different hues, suppressed under authoritarian rule, to compete in the political arena, thus presenting the electorate with a diverse range of options to choose from. As Daniel Brumberg points out, this has been a major factor that has moderated the Islamist agendas in the two countries under discussion: "[I]n Indonesia and Turkey secularists and traditional non-Islamic [read 'non-Islamist'] Muslim parties have retained organized political support in society, a situation that has compelled Islamists to shelve religious agendas, such as the imposition of Islamic law or, more ambitiously, the quest to establish an Islamic state, in favor of the politics of accommodation."[16]

Encounters with Secularism

In some ways, the Turkish and Indonesian democracies share remarkably similar backgrounds despite their geographic location at two ends of the Muslim world and their very diverse historical experiences, including their widely differing encounters with Western powers. The first major similarity they share is the fact that secularism, although interpreted somewhat differently in the two contexts, formed a foundational basis of the two republics when they came into existence. In Turkey's case, the triumph of secularism over religion, a function of the disintegration of the Ottoman Empire, was very clear and enshrined in the republican constitution. This did not mean the strict separation of state and religion but the dominance of the religious sphere by the secular—indeed, antireligious—state.

Since its inception, the Turkish state's control over the religious sphere has been carried out by the Directorate of Religious Affairs, which appoints all religious functionaries (down to the prayer leaders in mosques) in all towns and villages. As a result, the directorate has become the second largest public employer in the country, next to the Ministry of Defense, which controls the armed forces. One perceptive observer of the Turkish scene notes: "The state thus aimed to supervise religious observance, its content, and the limits within which it could be practiced . . . Thus secularism, in its inception, was intimately linked to state authority . . . An authoritarian, single-party regime had initiated and instituted the secularizing reforms at the cost of democratization . . . The process of democratization in the country, in turn, was intimately linked to relaxing state control over religious life."[17] In other words, the implicit authoritarianism of the secular Kemalist state provided political Islam the opportunity to don the mantle of democracy and turned symbolic Islamic issues, such as the wearing of head scarves by women in universities and public offices, into major human rights issues.

Unlike in Turkey, the relationship between Islam and the state in the case of Indonesia remained ambiguous from the time the state was founded in 1948. Islamist political forces had contributed in no mean measure to the Indonesian struggle for independence from Dutch colonial rule, and there were important "Muslim"—if not "Islamist"—strands within the Indonesian nationalist movement.[18] In fact, one of the earliest of the modern anticolonial movements in the Dutch East Indies, now Indonesia, was Sarekat Islam, which Clifford Geertz referred to as the first mass nationalist organization in Indonesia and "an expression as much of the impulse to religious self-purification as to political self-assertion."[19] Nonetheless, the constellation of political forces in Indonesia, which included the nationalists, the Communists, the military, and Islamist organizations, kept Islamism in check while providing it sufficient avenues for political expression. The furious debate over the role of Islam and over the place of the sharia in the Indonesian constitution during the first decade of independence attests to the importance of Islamist opinion in the early Indonesian polity. The failure of the Islamists to include references to the sharia in the constitution in turn demonstrates the countervailing power of secular-nationalist forces during the formative years of the Indonesian Republic.[20]

In both Indonesia and Turkey, constitutional constraints on the expression of political Islam have had a moderating influence on Islamist political forces. According to Ziya Onis, "the progressively more moderate course that the Islamists have been adopting in Turkey in recent years reflects, in part, the impact of the Kemalist modernization project, with its strong emphasis on the principle of secularism."[21] This does not mean that there is a simple causal linkage between secular authoritarianism and moderate Islamism or that the latter would have taken a more radical course if the former constraint were not present. Turkey's moderate Islamism owes its origins to a number of factors, of which secular authoritarianism is but one. In fact, one could argue on the basis of events of the past decade that as the Turkish system has retreated from its authoritarian tendencies, the Islamist party in the country has moderated further, thus establishing a linkage between democratization and Islamist moderation. There might indeed be a circular relationship among secular authoritarianism, Islamist moderation, and democratic consolidation, with the latter two reinforcing each other in order to preclude the Kemalist military and civilian elites from reimposing authoritarian rule.

Furthermore, it is clear that there has been a greater salience of Islam in Turkish social and political life in recent years despite the increasing moderation of the Islamist party. This is related not so much to the clash of ideologies between Islamism and secularism in an increasingly democratic context as to the changing nature of the equation between the center and the periphery in Turkey. This is represented by, among other things, the demographic invasion by the rural periphery of the urban center (in search of economic opportunities) and the increasing importance of the provincial bourgeoisie, largely religiously observant, in Turkish economic and political life.[22] Omer Taspinar explains: "What has periodically been perceived as the 'revival of Islamic fundamentalism' is rather part of a sociopolitical process whereby the traditional culture of the Anatolian periphery is carried to the political center. In other words, instead of an alarming situation signaling the imminence of an Islamic revolution, the rising visibility of Islam in Turkish society and politics is essentially related to the democratization of state-society relations within the framework of a healthy departure from aggressive laicism."[23]

The Indonesian Islamist formations have undergone dissimilar experiences from those in Turkey, and their trajectory has therefore been different from that of their Turkish counterparts. But the fact that they have had to find accommodation with secular forces is equally clear. It is instructive to note that the leading figure in the Indonesian nationalist movement during the anticolonial struggle and the first president of the republic after independence, Soekarno, was greatly influenced by the Turkish experience of separating state from religion: "Separating Islam from state, Soekarno argued, would liberate Islam from the tutelage of corrupt rulers and unleash its progressive potentialities."[24] Moreover, for the revolutionary Soekarno, as for Kemal Ataturk, "there was no 'return'" to Islam; rather, "Islam had to catch up its thousand years of backwardness."[25]

However, unlike in Turkey, where Islam was initially banished from public life by fiat, an uneasy accommodation between Islam and secularism was achieved in Indonesia, after an acrimonious public debate—centered on what came to be known as the Jakarta Charter—during the first decade of independence.[26] This accommodation was enshrined in a composite state ideology termed Pancasila (meaning "five principles"), which included belief in one God, nationalism, humanism, democracy, and social justice but did not directly refer to Islam. The concession to Muslim sentiments took the form of reference to "one God" rather than "God" as originally proposed by the nationalists. Furthermore, the Indonesian government, like its Turkish counterpart, set up its Ministry of Religious Affairs, both to placate Muslim opinion and to control the propagation of religion, especially Islam, in the country.

The Pancasila formula was further modified after Soekarno proclaimed Indonesia to be a "guided democracy" in 1958 and curtailed political and civil rights. He proclaimed "NASAKOM" to be the ideology of the state. The acronym was composed of the first letters of the Indonesian words standing for nationalism, religion, and communism. It was an attempt by Soekarno to balance the major political forces at work in Indonesia and thus to find an equilibrium that would stabilize and legitimize his rule by catering to the demands of all the important political tendencies operating in the country at that time. While Soekarno banned the modernist Muslim party, Masyumi (the political arm of the Muhammadiyah movement), because it opposed his idea of "guided democracy," his regime attempted to incorporate the traditionalist, *pesantren* (madrassa)-based NU into the power structure, although in limited ways.

The Soeharto regime came to power in 1965, after the failed leftist coup that upset the equilibrium that Soekarno had tried to establish, especially between the army and the Communist Party of Indonesia (PKI). The regime at first collaborated with the NU Islamists in visiting vengeance on Communist supporters, leading to the massacre by the army and vigilante death squads of about five hundred thousand people, large numbers of them in Java. However, it soon reversed course and, to the disappointment of the Islamists, "adopted a mixed regimen that combined severe controls on political Islam with guarded support for Islamic spirituality."[27] The NU, which had expected to receive major benefits because it had supported Soeharto's rise to power, was quickly sidelined, losing its sole representative in the cabinet in 1971.

At the same time, the regime shunned the modernist Muslims represented by Masyumi and its later incarnation Parmusi and tried its best to debilitate modernist Muslim organizations whom it perceived to be the greater threat because of their open opposition to the regime's antidemocratic tendencies. By the mid-1970s, the traditionalist NU had also become a strong critic of the regime. The latter in turn set up an official Muslim party, the United Development Party (known by its Indonesian acronym PPP), as one of the three official parties allowed to operate publicly in the hope that it would act as the public face of Islam acceptable to the authorities and also draw support away from groups opposed to the regime. At the same time, by bringing together both modernist and traditionalist elements into the newly formed party, the regime ensured that it would remain in a perpetual state of internal friction and deadlock and would not pose a challenge to the established order.

Autonomous political activity by the Islamists was anathema to the Soeharto regime. However, the regime was not averse to the spread of Islamic social mores, in the hope that it would help maintain law and order and also convey the message that the regime was not against Islam but merely against its uncontrolled political expression, because it had the potential to upset the political equilibrium. Robert Hefner notes the paradox of the regime's stance: "[T]his peculiar tactic of suppressing Muslim politics while encouraging Muslim piety offered more room for Muslims than other society-based organizations . . . Eventually the resurgence [of Islam] forced Soeharto to rethink his policies on Islam."[28] Hefner concludes: "By the late 1980s, the [Islamic] revival had decisively altered the rules of the political game. From now on the struggle to capture Muslim allegiances was to be a key feature of national politics."[29]

This latter trend culminated in the 1990s in Soeharto's attempt to woo the most conservative elements among the Muslim political and religious classes. It was a deliberate and desperate attempt by the Soeharto regime to use its newly acquired "Islamic" credentials to neutralize the pro-democracy movement that was gathering force. The strategy failed, thanks in part to the Asian financial crisis of 1997, which had devastating effects on the Indonesian economy and created great disillusionment with the regime. Nonetheless, the attempt left hard-line Islamists with a legacy—in terms of financial and material support—from of the remnants of the Soeharto regime that contributed to intercommunal violence in the wake of Soeharto's fall.

Although most Islamist groupings joined the opposition that eventually brought down the Soeharto regime in 1998, this did not mean the triumph of Islamism in Indonesia. Islamist political forces not only had to contend with secular and nationalist elements but also had to come to terms with the fact that they were bitterly divided among themselves. The end of the Soeharto era and the transition to democracy spawned several "Muslim" parties, often in contention with each other and constantly in search of coalition partners among secular political formations. Despite the fragmentation of Islamist forces, mainstream Islamist parties have found their niche in the democratic political system and have simultaneously come to accept the rules of the political game in Indonesia that rule out the creation of an Islamic state or the introduction of sharia law.

As in Turkey, Islamist forces in Indonesia, while reconciled to the reality of the secular state, attempt to influence the course of state policy toward "Muslim," if not "Islamic," directions. In both cases, Islamist formations have moved toward post-Islamism, exchanging their Islamist agendas for those based on what Jenny White has called "Muslimhood."[30] In other words, they have replaced their preoccupation with the implementation of sharia law with the attempt to infuse Islam's socio-moral teachings into the public arena. In the process, they have reconciled themselves genuinely to the rationalist ideas of modernity, embracing a considerable degree of Westernization.[31]

This transformation has been aided by the fact that, unlike in most Arab states, globalization has affected Turkey and Indonesia to a much larger extent because of their export-oriented economies and their consequent greater integration into the international economy. This is particularly clear in the case of Turkey, where substantial segments of the religiously inclined provincial bourgeoisie, traditional supporters of Islamist parties, have benefited economically from access to global markets and technology following economic liberalization beginning in the 1980s under Turgut Ozal, as prime minister and, later, president. It is instructive to note that they have done so at the expense of the established bourgeoisie at the center of power in Istanbul and Ankara, who had been the principal beneficiaries of the secular Turkish state's etatist economic policies.[32]

Consequently, the traditional supporters of the Islamist party in Turkey have developed a vested interest in greater economic interaction with the outside world, especially the industrialized democracies of Europe, and have further internalized the values of political democracy. This has led, among other things, to a transformation of Islamic political identity in Turkey, away from rigid literalism and anti-Westernism and toward a more liberal definition of the faith resulting in moderation and accommodation with Europe.[33] It is no surprise that the AKP is firmly committed to economically liberal policies, in part because of Turkey's dependence on the International Monetary Fund and in part because it suits the interests of its traditional supporters in Anatolia. While the causal linkage between economics and politics is not as clear in the case of Indonesia, economic incentives related to globalization seem to have played a similar role in that country, strengthening the liberal tendency among Indonesian Islamists of different hues. This has augmented their commitment to democracy and their acceptance of secularism as the dominant state ideology.

Political Islam and the Authoritarian State

In both Indonesia and Turkey, political Islam has had to contend not only with the secular state but with the authoritarian state as well. In both cases, the state's authoritarianism has rested on the role and power of the military in domestic affairs. Furthermore, the military in both Turkey and Indonesia has been generally antagonistic toward political expressions of Islam. The dialectic between authoritarianism and democracy in Turkey and Indonesia has thus become intertwined with the encounter between political Islam and secularism in both countries.

The Turkish state's authoritarian tendencies are a legacy of the strategy of forced modernization adopted by Kemal Ataturk and his colleagues during the initial decades of the republic's existence. The first-generation republican elite considered Turkey's ills to lie in the backwardness of the Ottoman Empire (which drew its legitimacy in part from Islam) and in its refusal to fall in step with "civilization" as epitomized by Europe. Modernity, including changes in the alphabet and in dress codes as well as a militant form of laicism, was therefore forced down Turkish throats whether the people wanted it or not. The Turkish military, with its high prestige as the founder and protector of the republic, was charged with safeguarding the revolutionary legacy, a role enshrined in the constitution.

The military had and continues to have dual functions in Turkey: to protect the country from external attack and to safeguard the Kemalist order from internal subversion, whether through secessionism or Islamic revivalism. The primary instrument for the military's involvement in politics is the National Security Council (NSC), which includes the top military brass and important cabinet ministers and is chaired by the president of the republic. The NSC acts as a supercabinet. Established by Article 118 of the 1982 constitution, which was adopted after the military coup of 1980, the NSC provides the military high command the opportunity to influence, pressure, and often dictate to the government in matters of national security. Since "security" has been traditionally defined in Turkey to embrace internal as well as external issues that the secular elite finds "threatening," the military has traditionally exercised virtual veto power on issues relating to political Islam and Kurdish ethnonationalism that the Kemalists perceive as threats to national security.[34] Although the role of the military brass within the NSC has been reduced in recent years in response to the pressure exercised by the EU, the institution continues to be a major avenue through which the military commanders can influence civilian decision making on "security" related issues, including the state's response to Islamist political activity.

There is a striking similarity between the Turkish military's role as the guarantor of political order and the role of the military in Indonesia. In the initial years of the republic, the Indonesian military, formed during the armed struggle against Dutch colonial rule in the 1940s, possessed similar prestige to its Turkish counterpart for being the primary instrument responsible for the creation of the republic and the defense of its borders. It was a major political actor during Soekarno's rule, especially in its role as a counterweight to the Communist Party of Indonesia (PKI), which had a very strong presence in Java. Simultaneously, it kept Islamist forces in check, although it was not averse to cooperating with the latter against the Communists.

The military's political role was formalized under Soeharto's New Order regime, which publicly proclaimed the doctrine of *dwifungsi* (literally meaning "two functions") to describe the armed forces' dominant position in the Indonesian polity. According to the doctrine of *dwifungsi*, the Indonesian military had two roles: it served as armed defender of the republic from external threats and as the sociopolitical force responsible for maintaining internal order and security.[35] Given the fact that the military was Soeharto's primary support base, the top brass of the armed forces carried great weight in the formulation and implementation of the regime's policy. Soeharto's New Order regime therefore came to be seen as a military dictatorship with a thin civilian veneer.

In both cases, the military remained wary of Islamist political forces, seeing them as potentially popular—and therefore credible—challengers to the established order. The predominant role of the military in the politics of both countries and the military's penchant in both cases for imposing variants of what has been termed "authoritarian secularism" no doubt curbed Islamist political tendencies to a significant extent.[36] At the same time, however, this has had the unintended consequence of allowing Islamist formations to project themselves as defenders of human rights and democracy in both Turkey and Indonesia. This is a pattern seen in other parts of the Muslim world as well (e.g., in Egypt and Algeria). However, it has achieved greater salience in Turkey and Indonesia because these two countries have undergone genuine democratic transitions that have allowed Islamist parties to translate their image as defenders of civic and political rights into electoral gains.

Both countries have also shared the experience of having their militaries and regimes use Islam for instrumental purposes in the political arena, including making opportunistic alliances with Islamist extremists against leftist forces and, in the case of Indonesia, against both Muslim and secular democrats. Taspinar points out, "Even the staunchly secularist Turkish military did not hesitate to use Islam after the 1980 military take-over in order to eradicate the leftist tendencies in Turkish society."[37] The state-Islam nexus was formed as a result of the ideological polarization between the Left and the Right in the 1970s that culminated in the 1980 military coup aimed at eradicating leftist forces from Turkey's political life. Taspinar explains: "[T]he secularist leadership of the 1980 coup did not adopt a strict version of Kemalist secularism; instead, they supported an ideology that came to be known as the 'Turkish-Islamic' synthesis. In other words, by encouraging the fusion of Sunni Islam and national solidarity, the military government tried to de-politicize and homogenize Turkish society. It was hoped that the Turkish-Islamic synthesis would generate a united national front against the ideological influence of the left and put an end to the ethnic, sectarian and political differences that had polarized the country during the 1960s and the 1970s."[38]

This nexus between the Turkish military and Islamist elements came to an end in the early 1990s. With the leftist forces crushed and the Kurdish insurgency under control, the military became increasingly wary of the rise of Islamist political forces—some of whom it had abetted—in the country's political life. The Turkish military's opportunistic use of Islamist groups against leftists and Kurdish separatists is very reminiscent of the Indonesian military's use of the Islamist NU and affiliated organizations to eliminate PKI cadres in 1965, a campaign that left a half-million people dead, most of them in Java, the stronghold of the PKI. It also has a parallel with the attempt by the Soeharto regime in its waning years to encourage conservative Islam, flaunt the president's newly acquired devotion to Islamic practices, and use extremist Islamist elements to confront and neutralize both secular and Muslim democrats engaged in challenging the authoritarian system. The latter episode spawned intercommunal strife that led to considerable loss of life and property but did not prevent the fall of the Soeharto government.

There have also been reports that in the 1980s, at the height of the Kurdish insurgency in southeastern Turkey, elements of the Turkish security apparatus—the "deep state," as it is known in Turkey—used Kurdish Islamist extremists to fight a "dirty war" against Kurdish separatists led by the Kurdish Workers Party, known by its Turkish acronym PKK. It has been alleged that Islamist vigilante squads armed by the military were responsible for killing leading Kurdish intellectuals as well as PKK cadres and for spreading a considerable amount of mayhem in the Kurdish areas. This collaboration seems to have come to an end in the late 1990s, when the "Kurdish Hizbullah" was perceived as no longer useful by the Turkish security services. The breakdown of this relationship may have contributed in part to the decision by armed remnants of the extremist faction to demonstrate their continuing capacity to employ acts of dramatic terror by engaging in suicide bombings that killed dozens of people in Istanbul in November 2003.[39]

In both Indonesia and Turkey, the military has had to beat a retreat from the political arena. In the case of Indonesia, the military-backed regime was overthrown and replaced by a democratic one. The process was facilitated by the fact that the Indonesian regime was highly personalistic: Soeharto's fall meant the collapse of the entire regime. The lack of ideological and political homogeneity among the top brass of the Indonesian military during Soeharto's waning years further reduced the capacity of the military to resist democratic change. Several of the top generals were, in fact, co-opted into the emerging democratic system. This process of co-optation reached its culmination in the election of a former general to the presidency in Indonesia's last election, which was by all accounts free and fair. General Yudhoyono was supported for the presidency by a couple of Islamist parties, especially the Partai Keadilan Sejahtera (PKS). The Islamist PPP, which had belonged to the opposing alliance, switched sides after the elections and also threw its support behind the newly elected President Yudhoyono. Islamist groupings are now represented in the government and form a significant base of support for the new president.[40]

In the case of Turkey, the role of the military in politics has been significantly reduced, despite the fact that it operates as a cohesive institution rather than as an instrument of personal power. This reduction in the military's political influence is partially the result of pressure from the EU, which deems civilian supremacy essential for Turkey's entry into the EU. However, it is also a result of important domestic developments. The latter include not only the moderation of the Islamist party and the winding down of the Kurdish insurgency but also the emergence of new and strengthened socioeconomic forces (especially the religiously oriented provincial bourgeoisie) that form an important source of support for the AKP and have a major interest in the consolidation of democracy in the country. These new social forces, which have been major beneficiaries of Turkey's economic liberalization and its increasing integration into the global economy, also have a vested interest in the country gaining admission to the EU. One analyst explains, "In Turkey, the success of the AKP's Muslim Democratic platform is less a triumph of religious piety over Kemalist secularism than of an independent bourgeoisie over a centralizing state."[41] It appears that a powerful domestic-external nexus that has developed in Turkey has forced the military on the defensive and increasingly into the barracks.[42] While it is unlikely to relinquish its political role at one stroke, the linear trend points toward the military's continuing political marginalization in Turkey.

Democratic Transition, Democratic Consolidation, and Political Islam

As stated earlier, both Turkey and Indonesia now have functioning democratic governments. Indonesia has undergone a recent transition to democracy, but there are enough indications—including two rounds of parliamentary and presidential elections—to suggest that the process is, for all intents and purposes, irreversible. Turkey, despite periodic hiccups, has gone beyond the transitional phase and is headed toward democratic consolidation. Again, as stated earlier, Islamist parties have been an integral part of the processes of democratic transition in Indonesia and democratic consolidation in Turkey.

Not only has Islamism mellowed in the process of democratization, but Islamist parties have themselves entered what may be called their "post-Islamist phase." This may not mean a complete abandonment of Islamism but certainly signifies a major transformation in terms of both the substance and the style of Islamist politics. The AKP in Turkey is a clear example of this phenomenon, so much so that it has led a keen observer of the Turkish scene to declare: "In the case of Turkey, we see . . . the process of post-Islamism or the shift from the politics of identity to the politics of service . . . based on compromise and cooperation. A new social and political contract, as a result, is evolving in the case of Turkey on the basis of neoliberal economic and political values . . . The JDP [AKP], being a product of these transformations, is not a party of identity but rather a party that strives to provide better services . . . [and] acts as an agent of the country's integration into liberal political and economic spaces."[43]

However, another scholar of Turkey, Jenny White, has argued that the reality is more complex and that the AKP's transformation does not amount to it abjuring the politics of identity. According to White, the transformation that has occurred is from Islamism to Muslimhood, which "limits Islam in politics to ethical and moral inspiration of individual behavior and individual choice." White argues, "The party supports democracy because it guarantees freedom of individual belief and expression and thus religious expression and its own survival."[44] White's depiction of the AKP's model of Muslimhood has close parallels with what has been happening in Indonesia. In fact, the major Islamist organizations in Indonesia, above all the NU, had led the way toward this transformation to post-Islamism by giving up, several decades ago, the idea of including references in the constitution to the sharia as a basis for law and by accepting the secular foundations of the Indonesian political system.

The Indonesian Islamists' commitment to a secular state while maintaining an Islamic ethical approach to public life has been characterized as "secular-inclusive." This perspective stands in direct contrast to "secular-exclusive" views represented by the Kemalist elite in Turkey and the secular-nationalist parties and elements within the military in Indonesia, which attempt to exclude Islam almost totally from the public sphere. According to one scholar of Indonesia, the secular-inclusive camp argues that "'Muslims' should pursue not the establishment of an Islamic state but the development of Islamic society"; thus, while de-linking Islam from the state, the secular-inclusive camp claims "that it is natural and legitimate for 'Muslims' to expect the government to reflect the moral values of Islam while maintaining its non-religious-based state." The same Indonesian scholar concludes, "The focus is no longer on how to bring Islam into the foundation of the state, but how to bring Islamic coloration into state policies."[45]

In the last parliamentary elections in Indonesia, parties supported by the two largest Muslim organizations, the NU and the Muhammadiyah, adopted secular-inclusive agendas. Even the PKS, the party considered to be the most Islamist and sharia-oriented in its approach, "shrewdly chose to downplay its Islamist ideology and focus instead on issues of wide appeal to Islamist-leaning and non-Islamist voters alike."[46] It won over 7 percent of the vote in the last elections. Currently, the Islamist PKS is part of the ruling coalition and is represented in the cabinet, headed by a president who cannot be considered an Islamist by any stretch of imagination. The secular-inclusive Muslim parties were able to garner 32.8 percent of the votes in the Indonesian parliamentary elections held in 2004.[47] This is very similar to the 35 percent won by the AKP in the November 2002 elections in Turkey. Both countries, therefore, have significant support bases for post-Islamist or secular-inclusive policies and agendas. Such secular-inclusivism, unlike advocacy for the implementation of sharia law, is not antithetical to the commitment to pluralism that is necessary for the successful functioning of democratic government.

Democracy demands compromise and the building and maintaining of coalitions. Ideological inflexibility can therefore be a distinct disadvantage in such a political system. It is no wonder that wherever democracy has begun to flourish in the Muslim world, it has forced Islamist parties to moderate their stand in order to survive politically. After a while, demonstrating ideological flexibility in order to build coalitions becomes an ingrained habit and a part of the organizational and political culture of such parties. Once this occurs, post-Islamism takes over. This is exactly what has been happening in Indonesia and Turkey over the past several years.

Islamist Extremism in Democratic Contexts

Democracy does not automatically solve the problem of Islamist extremism, which may continue to persist as a fringe phenomenon even after mainstream Islamist parties have embraced post-Islamist agendas and stances. This has been true in both Turkey and Indonesia. The latter has been home to several dramatic acts of terror carried out by Islamist extremists, with support from their transnational peers. The bombings in Bali and elsewhere attributed to Jemaah Islamiyah, which has tentacles spread around much of Southeast Asia, rank among the worst acts of terrorism carried out by extremist organizations.[48]

However, it would be wrong to confuse such acts of terrorism with mainstream Islamist and post-Islamist political activity in Indonesia. The terrorist groups obviously have some support in society, but this is minuscule compared with the social bases that can be boasted of by mainstream Muslim organizations, such as the NU and the Muhammadiyah. Also, the extremists' violent agenda is marginal, if not irrelevant, to the main issues that face the Indonesian society and polity and that the mainstream groups attempt to address. Like al-Qaeda, which will be analyzed in chapter 7, Jemaah Islamiyah and related groups may commit headline-grabbing acts, but their impact is ephemeral in character. The same goes for the occasional acts of terror attributed to extremist Islamist organizations in Turkey, such as the Turkish/Kurdish Hizbullah.

The fate of Turkish and Indonesian democracies and the place of Islamist formations within them will be decided not by these fringe elements but by mainstream Islamist organizations, such as the AKP and the NU. Here, the picture is much more optimistic not only for the individual countries concerned but as examples for the rest of the Muslim world as well. However, this does not mean that there will be no bumps on the road toward democracy and Islamist moderation, as recent tensions between the military and the AKP in Turkey over presidential elections has demonstrated. In fact, the Turkish and Indonesian cases demonstrate the hurdles that had to be overcome to attain democratic transformation and to achieve accommodation between Islamism/Muslimhood, on the one hand, and the secular state, on the other. The two cases also demonstrate that such transformation and accommodation is not beyond the realm of the possible. This is the lesson that the rest of the Muslim world needs to learn from Turkey and Indonesia.

CHAPTER 6

Islamist National Resistance

There are a few important cases where Islamist political groupings with territorially circumscribed objectives—including those of liberation from foreign occupation, secession, or irredentism—clearly straddle the violent and nonviolent worlds. In many such cases, Islamism blends with nationalism, particularly in the context of resistance against non-Muslim foreign domination and/or occupation. Islam thus becomes an instrument for the mobilization of Muslim populations against control or domination by predominantly non-Muslim political authorities or foreign occupiers, thus giving the resistance its religious color. Such instances arise mainly in those cases where ethnicity and Islam coincide to a substantial extent; therefore, the latter can be used as a marker to define ethnic identity in opposition to the ethnoreligious identity of the dominating or occupying non-Muslim ethnic groups. This phenomenon is evident in such diverse locales as Russian-controlled Chechnya, Indian-administered Kashmir, and Israeli-occupied Palestine.

Movements of national and/or ethnic resistance that aim at liberation, secession, or irredentism usually turn to Islam as their principal instrument for mobilization when secular parties and groups fail to achieve their nationalist goals, be they ending foreign occupation or gaining autonomy/independence from existing parent states. This is clearly demonstrated in the Palestinian and Kashmiri cases, where popular support shifted to Islamist movements and organizations following the failure of more secular groups to achieve nationalist objectives. In the process, ethnonational movements also become ethnoreligious ones. When such movements take up arms under the banner of a hybridized ideology that combines nationalism and religion, major powers apprehensive of Islamist radicalism brand them "terrorist" organizations. Both Hamas in Israeli-occupied Palestine and Hizbullah in Lebanon have suffered this fate.

However, the label "terrorist" lumps such movements together with those engaged in transnational violence, such as al-Qaeda. This blurs a very important distinction between the two sets of groups—namely, that the formers' objectives as well as their base of operations are territorially circumscribed, while the latter choose their targets around the globe and carry out activities transnational in character. The first group works within the parameters of the state system, aiming at liberation or secession, while the second operates in defiance of such parameters, in near total disregard of national boundaries.

Hizbullah and Hamas

The foremost examples of Islamist national resistance movements are Hizbullah in Lebanon and Hamas in Israeli-occupied Palestine. This is the reason they have been chosen for detailed study in this chapter. The violence in which they engage in pursuit of their nationalist objectives has often been lumped together, in Western analyses and policy proclamations, with the transnational violence perpetrated by al-Qaeda under the blanket term *terrorism*. In 2002, Richard Armitage, then U.S. deputy secretary of state, went to the extent of describing Hizbullah as the "A-team of terrorists," suggesting that al-Qaeda may well be the "B-team."[1] However, on closer scrutiny, it becomes clear that there is an enormous difference between Hizbullah and Hamas, on the one hand, and al-Qaeda, on the other—in terms of both objectives and strategies. Unlike al-Qaeda, the violence that Hizbullah and Hamas have engaged in has been the product of struggles that are context specific, nationally and territorially bounded, and principally determined by the fact of foreign occupation.[2]

The use by Hizbullah and Hamas of Islamic rhetoric and imagery to resist foreign occupation is reminiscent of nineteenth- and early twentieth-century movements in Muslim countries resisting the imposition of colonial rule or attempting to overthrow it. Hizbullah and Hamas are in the tradition of these earlier movements that used the concept of jihad to justify resistance against foreign domination, thereby popularizing the modern interpretation of jihad as primarily defensive war against foreign occupation, aimed at driving out the occupier.[3] While both organizations have been careful to control and direct the exercise of violence by their members, the obligation of jihad to resist foreign occupation has been couched by them in terms of the individual duty of every Muslim under such occupation.[4]

This interpretation has been used as a mobilizing tool to recruit members to engage in resistance activity against very heavy odds. At the same time, it has been responsible for attacks on civilian targets carried out by individual members of these organizations, including suicide bombings. One must note, however, that Hizbullah and Hamas are not the only organizations to undertake suicide bombings, which were initially made popular by the predominantly Hindu Tamil Tigers fighting for independence from the Buddhist Sinhalese-dominated Sri Lankan state. Even in the discrete Palestinian and Lebanese contexts, other nationalist and resistance organizations have participated as frequently in suicide attacks as the members of the two Islamist movements. According to Robert Pape, who has done extensive research on what motivates suicide bombers to do what they do, only eight of thirty-eight Lebanese suicide bombers who attacked Israeli targets were members of Hizbullah; the large majority belonged to leftist groups and included three Christians. Pape contends: "What these suicide attackers—and their heirs today—shared was not a religious or political ideology but simply a commitment to resisting a foreign occupation. Nearly two decades of Israeli military presence did not root out Hizbollah. The only thing that has proven to end suicide attacks, in Lebanon and elsewhere, is withdrawal by the occupying force."[5]

Hizbullah and Hamas are part of a larger trend that has come to combine nationalism with Islam in the Arab world since the 1970s. Such a tendency is partly a reaction to the failure of the secular Arab nationalist ideology and of parties and movements that represented that ideology, such as the Baath and the Nasserite groups, to deliver power, wealth, or dignity to Arab peoples. The failure of Arab nationalism as a potent force was demonstrated, above all, in the humiliating defeat of Egypt and Syria by Israel in 1967. That event spawned two different tendencies as successors to Arab nationalism. The first was the particularistic nationalisms within individual Arab countries, exemplified in the case of the Palestinians by the Fatah's takeover of the Palestinian Liberation Organization, which until then had been an instrument used by Arab rulers, especially Nasser of Egypt, to further their own objectives. The second tendency was the return of political Islam to the center stage of Arab politics in dramatic fashion. In several cases, Islamist formations became the foremost spokespersons for popular national grievances, and Islamist vocabulary came to be routinely used to promote nationalist agendas.

Political Islam thus became a surrogate for nationalist ideologies, seamlessly combining nationalist and religious rhetoric in a single whole. Francois Burgat observes, "Much more than a hypothetical 'resurgence of the religious,' it should be reiterated that Islamism is effectively the reincarnation of an older Arab nationalism, clothed in imagery considered more indigenous."[6] Hizbullah and Hamas are unambiguous examples of the successful combination of nationalism and Islam in the Lebanese and Palestinian contexts, respectively.

Ideological Antecedents

Shia Activism and Hizbullah

Despite their similarities, Hizbullah and Hamas have their roots in very different Islamic religio-political traditions. Hizbullah is a product of Shia activism in Lebanon, going back to the 1960s and initially inspired and led by Ayatollah Musa al-Sadr, until his mysterious disappearance in 1978 while on a trip to Libya.[7] In the 1960s, Musa al-Sadr broke from the politically quietist mold of the Shia clergy in Lebanon at about the same time that Khomeini did so in Iran, and it is clear that he received inspiration from the latter's ideas and activities.

Shia activism in Lebanon gained further momentum as a result of the Iranian Islamic revolution of 1979 and of the increased political consciousness among the Lebanese Shia in the 1970s following economic changes and the outbreak of civil war in 1975. Given the traditionally close links between the Shia clergy in Iran and Lebanon, Ayatollah Khomeini's revolutionary interpretation of Islam, including his doctrine of *vilayat-i faqih*, had major impact on the Lebanese Shia clergy and lay activists. Coming as it did in the midst of the civil war in Lebanon and the first Israeli invasion of Lebanon in 1978, which primarily affected the Shia south, this revolutionary religious impulse became an important instrument of radicalization among the Lebanese Shia. When it was formed in 1985, Hizbullah openly acknowledged Khomeini as its supreme guide in religious matters, and it continues, after his death, to acknowledge his successor, Khamenei, in the same role.[8]

However, accepting Khomeini and his successor as supreme guides did not mean that Hizbullah became subject to the dictates of the Iranian regime or committed to the promotion of Iranian state interests that did not coincide with its own. Hizbullah justified its autonomy of action by arguing that while it was subject to the supreme jurist's orders in terms of the "undisputable implementation of the doctrinal Shari'a principles," Khomeini himself had sanctioned its autonomy by recognizing "the objective and specific conditions of every group or country." The Hizbullah leadership, therefore, has "substantial independence at the practical level not necessitating direct and daily supervision by the Jurist-Theologian."[9]

Despite the fact that the bombing of the American embassy and U.S.

marine barracks in Beirut in 1983 have been attributed to groups linked to Hizbullah, the movement did not formally come into existence in its present form until 1985. Moreover, since its formal proclamation, Hizbullah has demonstrated over the past two decades that it is not interested in waging a global war against the "far enemy," the United States in particular. This was true even during the period when it was waging an armed struggle to end the Israeli occupation of south Lebanon. It also held true during the fighting between Israel and Hizbullah in July and August 2006, despite the fact that the United States rushed sophisticated weapons to Israel to help it attack Hizbullah and other Lebanese targets. A leading scholar, writing before the Israeli withdrawal from Lebanon in May 2000, pointed out: "In the ideology of Hizballah, Israel is anathema. In contrast, while the United States is considered an adversary and is disliked for its support of Israel, Hizballah's secretary general has claimed that the United States is not a target of attack."[10] This stance draws a sharp distinction between Hizbullah and al-Qaeda, which is fixated on attacking American targets around the world.

The Muslim Brotherhood and Hamas

The ideological roots of Hamas are very different from those of the Shia Hizbullah. Hamas is the political arm of the Palestinian Muslim Brotherhood, itself an offshoot of the Muslim Brotherhood (MB) established in Egypt in 1928 by Hasan al-Banna. Like its parent organization, Hamas is a product of the Salafi tendency in Sunni Islam, which is doctrinally opposed to un-Islamic accretions and seeks to return to a pure and pristine Islam of the imagined golden age during the time of the Prophet and the first generation of Muslims. While the philosophical epicenter of Salafism may have moved away from the enlightened Salafi ideas propagated by Muhammad Abduh in nineteenth-century Egypt to those of his Syrian disciple Rashid Rida and the literalist and scripturalist interpretation of Islam favored by the Wahhabis, Salafi thinking is far from being monolithic. Salafism is diverse enough to accommodate both the highly political—and therefore ideologically malleable—Muslim Brotherhood and the more literalist, rigid, and less overtly political tendencies evidenced in the Gulf and Saudi Arabia. Hamas is an offshoot of the Muslim Brotherhood and, like its parent body, falls toward the pragmatic end of the Salafi spectrum. Furthermore, Hamas's political ideology has been shaped by the interrelated Palestinian experiences of loss, expulsion, and occupation. It thus marries the relatively strict code of Salafi Islam to the current Palestinian situation of dispossession and occupation, seeking in Islam answers to and remedies for the Palestinian predicament and advocating in theory the creation of an Islamic Palestinian polity as the panacea for the sorry plight of the Palestinian people.

Hamas therefore acts as a religiously inspired Palestinian political force that poses as an alternative to the secular nationalist Fatah, which dominates the Palestine Liberation Organization (PLO) and until recently controlled the Palestinian Authority as well.[11] While inspired by the MB ideology first propagated in Egypt, Hamas fashions its political strategies not according to the dictates of the Egyptian MB but in response to Palestinian realities, particularly the Israeli occupation of Palestinian lands. Its political relationship with its Egyptian counterpart is, if anything, even weaker than Hizbullah's relations with the Iranian clerical establishment. In the final analysis, both Hizbullah and Hamas are autonomous organizations that respond to local situations and the needs of their constituencies as they see them. They are not part of international Shia or Sunni organizations—there is no "Comintern" of Shia or Sunni Islam—and they do not follow dictates from abroad on political issues.

As is the case with other Islamist formations, Hamas considers itself "an integral part of the world Islamic movement, affecting it and affected by it, both positively and negatively."[12] At the same time, it is a flexible organization, as Andrea Nusse observes: "Hamas is a modern political movement involved in a struggle for power, whose oppositional discourse is based on religious references. It is a national organization that is surprisingly pragmatic and clearsighted in its analysis of international politics. Despite the repetitive use of supposedly fixed concepts, it demonstrates an impressive ideological flexibility."[13] Hamas's ideological flexibility is borne out, above all, by the assertion in the Hamas Charter that the territory of Palestine is sacred to Islam and, therefore, that its liberation is an Islamic duty. According to Hamas, commitment to Palestinian nationalism is therefore perfectly compatible with the commitment to the idea of the universal *umma*. The charter states unequivocally that "Fatherland (*watan*) and nationalism (*wataniyya*) are . . . part of the Islamic creed."[14] These assertions make it clear that Hamas, despite its commitment to an Islamist ideology, "views itself as a natural extension of the Palestinian resistance . . . to the Zionist invasion."[15]

Hamas shares the worldview of most Palestinians—and, indeed, of most Arabs and Muslims—that Zionism and later Israel were and are part of the larger Western design to keep the Arab/Muslim world in submission and to prevent any challenge against Western hegemony from emerging from the

Arab/Muslim world. Israel is seen as a willing instrument of this design because it reaps huge benefits from acting as the West's vanguard in the strategically placed and resource-rich Middle East.[16] However, unlike transnational Islamist movements (e.g., al-Qaeda) that deem almost all Western targets legitimate, "Hamas considers its battle to be with Israel and Zionism and has declared its policy of not picking fights with regional and international powers."[17]

Hamas has continued to hold fast to this position despite the fact that the United States and its allies have declared it a terrorist organization, have refused to have any contact with the Palestinian Authority since Hamas's election to office in January 2006, and have imposed rigorous sanctions on the Palestinian territories in order to punish the Palestinian people for daring to elect Hamas to power in the most recent elections to the Palestinian National Council. This makes it clear that Hamas, like Hizbullah, does not share ideological or political kinship with al-Qaeda and other transnational Islamist organizations that have no compunction in attacking American and other Western targets, from North America to Southeast Asia. Like Hizbullah, Hamas adheres to objectives that are territorially confined, despite its occasional rhetorical recourse to Islamic universalism.

Political Origins

Lebanese Occupation and Hizbullah

Hizbullah emerged as the major Shia resistance movement against the Israeli invasion of Lebanon in 1982 and Israel's subsequent occupation of the Shia-dominated southern part of the country. While it was born in the midst of the civil war in Lebanon, which pitted several confessional groups against each other, it was not a direct product of that war and was only tangentially connected to it. The initial protagonists in the civil war were mainly Maronite, Druze, and Sunni factions, the latter supported by the PLO. The main Shia participant in the civil conflict was Amal, the Shia political grouping that emerged out of the "Movement of the Deprived" founded by Ayatollah Musa al-Sadr. Amal gradually moved in a secular direction and away from its Islamic roots as it became a participant in the civil war as well as a patronage network for its constituency. Hizbullah emerged out of a split within Amal between the more religious and the more secular factions. The religiously oriented factions, inspired by the Iranian revolution of 1979 and with the blessings of Ayatollah Khomeini, coalesced to form their own organization and called it the Party of God, or Hizbullah, formally announced in 1985.[18]

Not until after the second Israeli invasion of Lebanon in 1982 and particularly its continued occupation of southern Lebanon did Hizbullah emerge as a resistance organization becoming a formidable force, gaining considerable support from the Shia population of southern Lebanon, the Bekaa Valley, and the poor Shiite-populated suburbs on the southern outskirts of Beirut. It soon overshadowed Amal and flourished during the two-decade-long Israeli occupation of predominantly Shia south Lebanon, where it launched a disciplined and effective guerrilla campaign against the occupation forces and the South Lebanese Army, a Christian-led militia allied with Israel. Paradoxically, there may have been no Hizbullah today had Israel not invaded Lebanon in 1982 and not occupied the predominantly Shia south for eighteen years: "Without the raison d'etre of opposing the occupation, Hizballah would not have been able to build a broad Shi'i constituency."[19]

The party's leadership does not contest the fact that Hizbullah was aided militarily and politically by Iran and Syria in its resistance to Israeli occupation. However, such assistance should not be confused with the factors that led to Hizbullah's creation and to the credibility it attained as the leading defender of the community's interests among the Shia of Lebanon and as the primary resistance force against the Israeli occupation. Its appeal was based on the fact that it was responsive to the socioeconomic plight of the Lebanese Shia, their perceived political impotence within the Lebanese system, and, above all, their resentment against the prolonged Israeli occupation of predominantly Shia south Lebanon. Hizbullah's actions continue to be determined largely by Lebanese considerations, even if they are on occasion coordinated with policies followed by Syria and Iran and may have beneficial outcomes for one or both of its supporters: "While Hizballah's operations in the south [against Israel] were coordinated with Syria . . . and substantial Iranian and Syrian support facilitated its development . . . there is no doubt that Hizballah is very much an indigenous organization."[20]

Palestinian Occupation and Hamas

The combination of political Islam and national liberation that distinguishes Hamas from other major Palestinian factions did not take place suddenly. The MB, of which Hamas is a progeny, had been active in Palestine since the 1930s and had taken part in the Great Palestinian Rebellion of 1936–39 and in the first war over Palestine against the Zionists in 1948. The creation of Israel divided the Palestinian MB, with the West Bank movement submerging itself into the Jordanian MB and with the Gaza movement maintaining its strong links with the Egyptian MB. Although the MB in Gaza continued to be the more radical of these two movements, a conscious decision was made by its leadership to keep a low political and military profile and to concentrate on educational and *dawa* (missionary) activities. This course was adopted to create a successor generation steeped in the Islamic ethos and at the same time capable of fighting the Zionist enemy successfully.

The Gaza MB's reluctance to participate in the Palestinian resistance movement against Israel during the 1950s and 1960s led to the emergence of Fatah from the wombs of the brotherhood itself. Several leading members of the MB in Gaza, including Salah Khalaf (Abu Iyad) and Khalil al-Wazir (Abu Jihad), broke away from the brotherhood to found the national liberation organization that came to be known, by its acronym, as Fatah. Although the situation changed drastically with the Israeli occupation of Gaza and the West Bank in 1967, the Palestinian MB, especially in its stronghold in Gaza, continued to refrain from organized resistance to the Israeli occupation, concentrating instead on educational and social welfare activities again aimed at inculcating the Islamic ethos in the generation that would finally overthrow Israeli rule.

The initial split on issues of strategy between the Fatah-led PLO and the MB, later Hamas, has continued to this day despite the decision by the Palestine MB in the mid-1980s to become actively involved—both politically and militarily—in the resistance against Israeli occupation. Hamas was born as a result of this decision, as the political wing of the MB. It was publicly established in December 1987, just as the first Palestinian intifada was taking shape. However, the Palestinian MB had decided, probably as early as 1984, to change course, having made the assessment that its relatively apolitical stance had lost it a great deal of support among the Palestinian population. Additionally, observes Nusse, "the defeat of . . . the PLO in Lebanon in 1982 led to a situation of confusion and reorganization that propelled political Islam to the forefront."[21] In an interesting reversal of roles, from 1993 onward, following the signing of the Oslo Accords, Hamas has come to represent the more militant face of Palestinian resistance to Israeli occupation. The Fatah-dominated PLO, which signed the Oslo Accords and was, as a result, transformed into the Palestinian Authority, has now come to be seen as the moderate face of Palestinian nationalism.

Even from this very brief account, it is clear that the strategies of Hamas and its parent organization, the Palestinian MB, have been shaped primarily by factors related, first, to fighting the Zionist project in Palestine that succeeded in establishing Israel and, since 1967, to resisting the Israeli occupation of Gaza and the West Bank. They have also been shaped by Hamas's political competition with Fatah and the PLO within the occupied territories. Despite its occasional universalistic Islamist rhetoric, Hamas remains as much a Palestinian phenomenon as Hizbullah is a Lebanese phenomenon.

Combining Resistance and Politics

Hizbullah: From Clandestine Militia to Mainstream Political Party

Both Hizbullah and Hamas cut their teeth in the field of resistance to Israeli occupation. However, both have gradually but surely moved into the arena of competitive politics and become near normal players of the political game without giving up their right to resisting occupation with or without arms. The end of the Lebanese civil war in 1990 led to Hizbullah's transformation from a radical, clandestine militia to a mainstream political party with an armed resistance wing committed to driving Israel out of all Lebanese territory. The continued Israeli occupation of southern Lebanon gave Hizbullah's claim to act in both capacities great credibility, even among those Lebanese not sympathetic to its ideology. Thanks also to its vast network of social services that caters to the needs of the most underprivileged and vulnerable sections of Lebanese society, including segments of the non-Shia population in the country, it has become an important player in Lebanon's political game.[22]

Hizbullah has participated in elections since 1992 and has performed quite well, even though the seats allocated under Lebanon's confessional system to the Shia have had to be shared almost equally between Hizbullah and Amal, the weaker of the two main Shia political formations in Lebanon. Hizbullah has had to share seats largely to placate the Syrian regime, which saw Amal as its surrogate in Lebanon and was wary that Hizbullah's acquisition of too much popularity and power could lead it to defy Syria's wishes and hurt Syrian interests. This was an acknowledgment on the part of Damascus that it could not control Hizbullah and therefore wanted its parliamentary presence curtailed. That Hizbullah had at heart the interests of its Lebanese constituency, rather than those of Syria, became clear during the events following the assassination of former Lebanese prime minister Rafiq al-Hariri and the subsequent withdrawal of Syrian forces from Lebanon. Hizbullah held a massive demonstration, with Lebanese flags flying, to thank the departing Syrians for their service to Lebanon, not to demand the retention of Syrian forces.

Syria's withdrawal from Lebanon freed Hizbullah from the shackles of residual Syrian influence, thus allowing it to demonstrate clearly that it was the senior partner in the Hizbullah-Amal Shia alliance. In the 2005 elections,

Hizbullah continued its pattern of sharing seats with Amal, largely because the Hizbullah leadership did not want the Shia vote to fracture at a crucial stage in Lebanon's political development. But it is clear that Hizbullah has become the dominant force among the Shia and a major participant not only in the political process but also, until November 2006, in the government of Lebanon. Hizbullah and its allies, including Amal and a Christian faction, left the government partly on the issue of an international tribunal established to investigate Rafiq Hariri's assassination and partly because the major Sunni, Maronite, and Druze factions in the government were unwilling to give Hizbullah and its allies greater representation in the cabinet.

Hizbullah has been very eclectic in building coalitions with other parties and factions, including some of the most hard-line Maronite elements that would normally be considered its natural antagonists. Its principal non-Shia ally following the elections of 2005 is the parliamentary group headed by the Maronite leader Michel Aoun, the former general who had been a strident opponent of Syria's presence in Lebanon and had spent years in exile until the Syrian withdrawal from Lebanon. In another interesting twist, in 2005, Bahiyya al-Hariri, the sister of the assassinated Sunni former prime minister, was elected unopposed to a parliament seat from Sidon in south Lebanon, as a candidate of a list dominated by Hizbullah and its ally Amal.[23]

The withdrawal of Israeli troops from south Lebanon in May 2000 augmented Hizbullah's prestige as the only Arab force capable of compelling Israel to cede conquered Arab territory. One author claims: "It now commands respect among nearly all Lebanese, and its popularity among Shi'ites is immense. Having been never involved in intra-Lebanese infighting, it elicits trust even though its military wing refuses to disarm, citing continued Israeli presence on a sliver of disputed borderland known as the Sheba'a Farms."[24] Paradoxically, the Israeli withdrawal also appeared to make Hizbullah largely redundant as a military force and compelled it to emphasize its political role as a participant in the Lebanese polity committed to defending Lebanese sovereignty and Lebanese national interest. Consequently, its dual role as a resistance movement and a political party has resulted in "Hizbullah's oscillation between militancy and political pragmatism in the pursuit of its goals," which "has left most scholars and policy makers perplexed."[25]

This oscillation is best explained by the fact that Hizbullah's political reputation rests in considerable measure on its role as a resistance movement. The United States and its allies have put pressure on Syria and Lebanon—through UN Security Council Resolution 1559 and by other means, directly and indirectly—to force Hizbullah to disarm. This has led the organization to reemphasize its resistance role in order to preserve its military capacity, which is closely tied, in its perception, to its political credibility. The crisis of 2006 resulting in full-scale conflict between Hizbullah and Israel technically began with the kidnapping of two Israeli soldiers by Hizbullah in July of that year. However, this action was not unrelated to the fact that Israel had bombed Hizbullah positions in May in response to rocket attacks on Israel by a Palestinian splinter group. Furthermore, regardless of the immediate provocations, it is clear that Hizbullah's decision in July 2006 to take on the much stronger Israeli army was the result, in large measure, of international pressures to disarm, which were forcing Hizbullah into a corner. Hizbullah's decision to escalate tensions with Israel seemed to reflect the considered view of its leadership that resumption of this conflict was essential for Hizbullah to retain its resistance role and the military capacity so essential to its political image.[26]

Hizbullah's actions in 2006 demonstrate its unwillingness to undergo a total transformation into a normal political party abjuring the use of arms. Such unwillingness can be understood in light of the fact that there is enormous imbalance between Israeli and Lebanese power, with Lebanon's armed forces incapable of defending the country's borders against Israel. Hizbullah therefore considers itself the defender of Lebanese sovereignty against incursions by Israel on the pattern of the 1982 invasion, a claim that strikes a sympathetic chord among the large majority of Lebanese, in many sectors of Lebanese society: "Before the war [between Hizbullah and Israel in 2006], just over half the Lebanese said they supported Hizbullah's role as an armed resistance group that deterred Israeli attacks. Two weeks after the fighting started, more than 85 percent of Lebanese in one poll said they supported Hizbullah's military attacks against Israel."[27] Regardless of the military outcome and the diplomatic intricacies of a settlement worked out within or outside the United Nations, Hizbullah is likely to emerge from the battles of 2006 with its political strength augmented rather than diminished: "The war has . . . seriously damaged Lebanese confidence in the United States. The 'March 14' anti-Syrian coalition of Christian, Sunni and Druze parties expected U.S. support to transform Lebanon into a truly democratic, sovereign and prosperous country. Instead, Washington's unqualified backing of Israel has pushed more Lebanese toward Hizbullah."[28]

Where there has been a distinct change in Hizbullah's stance as a result of its transformation into a Lebanese political party is on the question of turning Lebanon into an Islamic state, which was the organization's avowed objective during the early years of its existence. The compromises it has had to make to participate in the Lebanese political process has diluted Hizbullah's original vision of turning Lebanon into an Islamic polity à la Iran. Now, Hizbullah leaders openly accept the reality of Lebanon as a multiconfessional polity, while stressing their special role as an Islamic pressure group within that polity and their commitment to parliamentary politics.[29]

Hizbullah's leaders have tried to explain away their retreat from the party's original stand by claiming that an Islamic order cannot be imposed by force; it can only be introduced if it is the willing choice of the people of Lebanon. Sheikh Naim Qassem, deputy secretary general of Hizbullah, asserts: "Where the freedom of choosing a governing system is attributed to our people in Lebanon, they will not find a better alternative to Islam. Hence, we call for the implementation of the Islamic system based on a direct and free choice of the people, and not through forceful imposition as may be assumed by some."[30] Given the multiconfessional nature of Lebanon's population, the introduction of an Islamic system based on Shia law through democratic means remains a fantasy. It is evident that in this case, Hizbullah's socialization into democratic politics has led it to jettison, for all practical purposes, its goal of turning Lebanon into a Shia Islamic state. It is reconciled to working within a multiconfessional democracy as a full participant in the system, but on the condition that its role as a resistance movement is respected until it decides to give up that role voluntarily, possibly following the augmentation of the Lebanese state's capacity to protect Lebanon's security vis-à-vis Israel.

Hamas: From Resistance to Interrupted Moderation

Hamas, like Hizbullah, was born as a resistance movement and has gradually turned into a political party. However, functioning under Israeli occupation limits its capacity to act as a normal party even more than is the case with Hizbullah. Ironically, Israel may have had more to do with Hamas's emergence than most Israelis and Westerners are willing to acknowledge. It appears that the Palestinian MB's ostensible apolitical stance between 1967 and 1984 led the Israeli leadership to assume that it could be used as an effective antidote to counter the PLO's increasing stature and popularity among the occupied Palestinian population as the sole voice of national resistance and, consequently, the sole representative of the Palestinian people, both within the occupied territories and outside.

Israel's tacit, if not explicit, encouragement of the Palestinian MB has led some to argue that Israel was responsible in part for building up the MB in occupied Palestine in the 1970s and 1980s, in order to divide Palestinians who overwhelmingly supported the secular, Fatah-dominated PLO. Some argue that Israel did so by providing space for the MB's front organization, the Islamic Association, to build mosques and set up charitable institutions in the occupied territories without let or hindrance. This conclusion is borne out by remarks made by Daniel Kurtzer, then U.S. ambassador to Israel, at a seminar in Jerusalem in December 2001. Kurtzer argued that the growth of Islamist movements in the occupied territories, principally Hamas, was achieved "with the tacit support of Israel" because "Israel perceived it to be better to have people turning toward religion rather than toward a nationalistic cause."[31]

However, Israeli calculations went awry when the Palestinian MB decided to abjure political quietism and become explicitly involved with the Palestinian resistance to Israeli occupation. The first Palestinian intifada, which began in late 1987, acted as the crucial catalyst for the overt politicization and the subsequent militarization of the Palestinian MB. Largely because of the intifada, "[t]he Islamists reinvented themselves, making the transition from being a social-educational-proselytizing movement . . . to a political, armed resistance organization."[32]

While Hamas was able to build a popular following during the first intifada, the Madrid peace conference of 1991 and the ensuing Oslo Accords of 1993 led to it being largely overshadowed by the PLO, which now took charge of the Palestinian Authority (PA). But as the PLO failed to liberate Palestinian lands according to the timetable envisaged under the Oslo Accords, Palestinian opinion began to turn against the Oslo process. In great part, this was the result of Israeli policies of continued Jewish settlement and interminable delays regarding turning over territory to Palestinian control. The sight of PA "president" Yasser Arafat held in his headquarters in Ramallah as a prisoner of the Israeli occupation further showed up the fact that Palestinian autonomy was nothing more than a charade. Consequently, Hamas gained greater popularity, since it had declared its unequivocal opposition to the Oslo process and predicted that it was not going to lead to the liberation of occupied territories. Hamas, successfully combining nationalism and Islam, thus became "the Palestinian incarnation of politicized Islam in the Middle East."[33]

Hamas's popularity was also related in substantial part to the PLO's conversion into the PA, whose corruption and inefficiency stood in stark contrast to Hamas's moral probity and its record of social service, thus adding to the latter's appeal. Furthermore, with Israel's policies becoming more oppressive and strangulating the Palestinian economy and with the PA unable to deliver social services, Hamas's network of charitable organizations moved in to fill the void.

This was particularly true in terms of providing help and succor to the most disadvantaged segments of Palestinian society, especially in the overcrowded refugee camps and shantytowns of Gaza.

At the same time, Hamas developed a military wing, especially in Gaza, which carried out attacks against Jewish settlers, the occupying Israeli military, and civilians within Israel. It is clear that for Hamas, since the mid-1990s, "the notion of liberating Palestine has assumed greater importance than the general Islamic aspect."[34] While the concept of liberating Palestine is often left deliberately vague, so that it could refer either to the entire Palestine mandate from the Jordan River to the Mediterranean Sea or to the territories occupied in 1967, the Hamas leadership has increasingly begun to emphasize the importance of Israeli withdrawal to the 1967 borders as the precondition for a long-term truce (*hudna*). Hamas's leaders have also accepted the idea that the future of Palestine ought to be determined either on the basis of a popular referendum or by freely elected representatives of the Palestinian people and that Hamas will abide by such a decision. Such statements have often implied that the long-term truce as conceived by Hamas leaves open the possibilities of mutual recognition by Palestine and Israel and of a settlement based on the borders of 1967, if the Palestinian people accept it of their own volition.[35]

Hamas's decision to participate in the 2006 elections to the Palestine National Council after having boycotted the 1996 elections because they were held within the Oslo framework is probably the best indication that it has decided to work within the two-state framework, without explicitly admitting that fact. Several considerations went into the Hamas decision to participate in the elections held in January 2006, among them the unpopularity of the PLO and the increasing Palestinian disenchantment with the Oslo process. Nonetheless, its participation was an implicit recognition of the fact that the two-state solution was the only feasible option available to the Palestinians and that the job of the elected PA was to get the best deal within the constraints imposed by that framework.

Statements made repeatedly by leading Hamas figures in the aftermath of the party's surprise victory in the parliamentary elections of January 2006 signaled the possibility of their eventual acceptance of the two-state solution, although under certain specific conditions. Mutual recognition and a two-state solution were clearly outlined by Mousa Abu Marzook, the deputy chief of the Hamas Political Bureau, in an article in the *Washington Post* soon after election results were announced: "We will exert good-faith efforts to remove the bitterness that Israel's occupation has succeeded in creating, alienating a generation of Palestinians . . . There must come a day when we will live together, side by side once again."[36] It was apparent that Hamas was following in the footsteps of the PLO in terms of moderating its stance and accepting the fact that Israel cannot be wished away. The PLO gave up its maximalist goals when presented with the opportunity to attain power in the occupied territories, and there is little reason to believe that Hamas would act otherwise. Moreover, Hamas's base is primarily in the occupied territories and not in the refugee camps outside Palestine that continue to be largely loyal to the Fatah-dominated PLO. This further constrains Hamas's options and is likely to force it toward moderation, since there is clear indication that most Palestinians within the occupied territories support a two-state solution that delivers a viable and secure Palestinian state to them.[37] Maximalist rhetoric may be essential to keep the Palestinian resistance alive in the face of Israeli intransigence. However, maximalist policies will quickly lose credibility with Hamas's constituency in the occupied territories once prospects for the end to Israeli occupation become significantly bright.

Where Hamas genuinely differs from the PLO is in its stand that Palestinian recognition of Israel must be tied to complete Israeli withdrawal from the occupied territories, including East Jerusalem, and must be part of a package of mutual recognition by the two states. Unlike the PLO, Hamas is unwilling to fritter away its most valuable card without attaining full Israeli recognition of a Palestinian state within the borders of 1967. This has been stated repeatedly by both internal and external leaders of Hamas since its election victory in January 2006.[38] While Hamas has moved increasingly toward accepting a two-state solution, its leadership is not willing to accept Israel's legitimacy as a state unless and until it is certain of what Israel has to offer in return. When asked whether Hamas is willing to accept Israel's right to exist, Hamas leader Mahmoud Al-Zahar responded, "If Israel is ready to tell the people what is the official border, after this we are going to answer this question."[39] Khaled Meshal, the top Hamas leader living in exile, stated in Cairo in late November 2006 that "the Palestinians would launch a new uprising unless there was clear progress toward a Palestinian state along the 1967 borders."[40] One can read this statement as a strong signal by Hamas that it would be willing to accept a Palestinian state within the 1967 borders.

It is unfortunate that the United States, Israel, and the European powers were and are unwilling to give Hamas the benefit of the doubt and engage with it as the elected government of the PA. Instead, they boycotted it by branding it a "terrorist" organization; imposed economic sanctions on the PA following the election of Hamas; and imposed on it conditions, such as the immediate recognition of Israel, that Hamas was bound to reject. The counterproductive nature of the American, European, and Israeli policy of boycotting Hamas and imposing economic sanctions on an already financially bankrupt PA is self-evident.

External pressures have hardened Hamas's position while simultaneously discrediting its internal political leadership (which decided to join the PA government) in the eyes of its military wing. The latter seems to be acting more and more in collaboration with other militant factions (including the Al-Aqsa Martyr's Brigade, which owes allegiance to Fatah) and not taking its directions from Hamas's political leadership.[41] The kidnapping of an Israeli soldier in June 2006 by the Qassam Brigades (Hamas's military arm) without consultation with the political leadership is clear evidence that this is the case. Current pressures, both external and internal, are likely to push Hamas back almost totally into a resistance mode, escalating conflict between Palestinian factions as well as between Israel and Palestine and eventually leading to the collapse of the PA and the demise of the two-state solution.

This is the scenario that appears to be currently unfolding in the occupied territories, especially in Gaza. Continuing Israeli incursions from the ground and attacks from the air a year after Israel's unilateral withdrawal from Gaza and following Hamas's election to office have led Hamas to declare its cease-fire null and void and to return to its earlier position of armed resistance, including suicide bombings. This has, in turn, led to a full-fledged Israeli attack on Gaza, thus ending the prospects for Hamas's continuing moderation. All this has prompted one analyst to remark, "The offensive against Gaza is designed to destroy Hamas for daring to win an election."[42] What is even worse is that internecine warfare erupted in Gaza between Hamas and Fatah with the latter, supported by the United States and Israel, refusing to permit Hamas control of the PA's security apparatus despite Hamas's electoral victory. Attempts by the Saudi king in the form of the Mecca accord to form a unity government also failed due to machinations by outside powers—including the United States supplying arms to Fatah-linked militia to fight Hamas—and the refusal of the entrenched Fatah functionaries to give up their power and privilege. Although Hamas has won a military victory in Gaza by rooting out Fatah from the strip, Fatah continues to wield power in the West Bank where the Hamas military presence is much weaker. Egged on by the United States and Israel, Palestinian president Mahmoud Abbas has removed the elected Hamas prime minister, dissolved the "unity" government established under the Mecca accord, and set up his own government that totally excludes Hamas. This has led to the de facto division of the Palestinian territories, with Hamas in control of Gaza and Fatah of the West Bank. The PA has in effect collapsed while Hamas and Fatah fight over its carcass. All this may well have been avoided had Hamas been allowed to take power smoothly after the January 2006 elections without hindrance from within and without and socialized into accepting democratic outcomes.

It is interesting to note that both Israel and the United States opened up their coffers in support of the Abbas government immediately after the split between Hamas and Fatah and between Gaza and the West Bank. This gives the distinct impression that the division of the West Bank and Gaza suits their purposes, especially since it will allow Israel to impose its own version of a two-state solution by unilateral disengagement and to incorporate large chunks of Palestinian territory into Israel. However, in the long term, such an outcome will not be conducive to the amelioration of the Israel-Palestine conflict and is likely to make the dispute even more intractable than it is today. A major casualty of such a result will be the democratic process in Palestine and the consequent reversal of Hamas's movement toward becoming a normal political party willing to work within a democratic system and, therefore, to be subject to popular opinion on issues relating to a solution of the Israel-Palestine conflict. Such an outcome will fuel both intra-Palestinian conflict and conflict between Israel and the Palestinians.

Conclusion

It is clear from the preceding discussion that Hizbullah and Hamas are more similar to the Irish Republican Army than to the al-Qaeda network. They are national resistance movements whose primary aim has been to end foreign occupation of their lands. Simultaneously, they are political parties that participate in national politics with the aim of influencing their countries' domestic and foreign policies and shaping their future. In the process, they have engaged in broadening their political base, building coalitions, and turning increasingly pragmatic. As the democratic process began to take hold in Lebanon and in occupied Palestine, it seemed, until recently, that they had increasingly come to accept the rules by which the political game is being played. Their leadership and rank and file were becoming increasingly socialized into the culture of democratic politics, leading one to believe that they were well on their way to becoming "normal" parties.

However, the events of 2006 and 2007 have put in grave doubt the future of both political formations as normal political parties. Both the Lebanese and Palestinian political systems—the former as a result of the innate weakness of the Lebanese state and the latter by the fact of continuing Israeli occupation—are extremely penetrable and hostage to the behavior and interests of outside actors. This is particularly true of occupied Palestine, but it also captures the reality of the Lebanese system to a great extent. The escalating hostilities between Hizbullah and Israel in 2006 and the pressure on the former to disarm seem to be forcing Hizbullah back into its original resistance mold. The Israeli "reoccupation" of Gaza and its incarceration of dozens of Hamas legislators, including ministers, and the factional war between Fatah and Hamas have aborted the democratic process in the occupied territories, thus turning Hamas once again exclusively into a religio-nationalist resistance movement. It appears that it is only a matter of time before the next intifada is launched in occupied Palestine. The bottom line is that abnormal situations of occupation and state debility—along with the corollary of external intrusion—do not produce normal political actors or normal political processes. It is clear, however, that it is not their Islamist ideologies that prevent Hizbullah and Hamas from transforming themselves into political parties; the unusual situations in which they find themselves—much of which are not of their own making—make such a transition impossible.

Nonetheless, events of the past decade provide a ray of hope that, if the situations in Palestine and Lebanon normalize, both Hamas and Hizbullah have the potential to refashion themselves as normal political parties and that it is not too far-fetched to envisage the transformation of these Islamist resistance movements into normal players of the political game within democratic settings. But for this to happen, the occupation of Palestine must end and the Lebanese state must build its strength to a level where it can insulate itself from unwanted external intrusion. There is little to suggest that either will happen quickly or painlessly.

CHAPTER 7

Transnational Islam

The last several chapters have attempted to demonstrate, on the basis of case studies drawn from some of the most important Muslim countries, that mainstream and nationally bounded Islamist political formations, whether in opposition or in power, represent the vast majority of Islamist groups in terms of numbers, membership, and their impact on politics and society within the Muslim world. A major reason for the preeminence of national formations is the fact that political Islam cannot be relocated from one place to another easily. This is the case because transplanted forms of Islamism will not be adequately sensitive to context, which, as earlier chapters have demonstrated, matters a great deal in determining the success or failure of Islamist movements.

Transnational Islam loses both relevance and authenticity in the process of transplantation. Peter Mandaville explains: "Teachers in conservative Deobandi madrasas in Pakistan, while they may share certain of his views, do not disseminate the fatwas of Omar Bakri Muhammad from London. Student reading groups at universities in Indonesia, while they may share Tariq Ramadan's emphasis on the democratic, multicultural possibilities of Islam, have never read his books . . . [I]t is important not to overstate the case when it comes to transnational Islam. While we may identify tendencies and general varieties of discourse, it becomes much more difficult to establish direct causal linkages."[1] This conclusion is corroborated by Fawaz Gerges's authoritative study of al-Qaeda. It clearly makes the point that militant transnational jihadis form a very small minority not only among Islamist political formations as a whole but also among militant jihadis themselves. However, as Gerges points out in his book, the transnational jihadis form "a tiny—but critical minority" among Islamist groupings.[2] They are "critical" particularly for the international image of political Islam, because they engage in the most violent acts in the name of Islam across the globe. Consequently, they have the most dramatic impact outside the Muslim world, helping to shape the image of political Islam globally as a violent and extremist ideology.

Paradigmatic Change

The transnational jihadi groups, which are increasingly denoted by the catchall term *al-Qaeda,* go beyond the local regimes to target the "far enemy," the West in general and the United States in particular. The latter are perceived by these groups as crucial supporters and sustainers of the "near enemy," the authoritarian and repressive regimes that stand in the way of turning the Muslim world into a true and borderless *dar al-Islam* based on the militants' conception of the ideal Islamic model.[3] The transnational jihadis have therefore turned the largely "defensive" mode in which mainstream Islamists operate both domestically and globally into an "offensive" one, by attacking the source of the problem—as they see it—that is located outside the Muslim world.

For transnational jihadis, offense on a global scale is the best defense locally. They believe that the only way to stop the West's unwanted interference in *dar al-Islam* is to inflict damage on Western interests where it hurts most, thereby weakening the resolve of Western powers, especially the United States, to intervene in matters affecting the Muslim world. Their stated objective, reiterated time and again, is to eject Western powers, principally the United States, from the Muslim world, not only militarily, but also in terms of their capacity—politically, economically, and culturally—to influence developments in Muslim countries. In this sense, they not only represent the other side of the coin in terms of Huntington's clash of civilizations but also pose a paradigmatic challenge to the current Western-dominated international order. While offensive in tactical conception, al-Qaeda is able to portray this strategy as a part of the Muslim world's ongoing resistance to Western domination, in large part due to American policies in the Middle East that are perceived by large segments of Muslim populations as deliberately hostile to Muslim interests, especially Washington's unqualified support to Israel's occupation of Palestine and, more recently, the invasion and occupation of Iraq. Al-Qaeda's strategy of offense as the best defense was conceptualized in the statement "Jihad against Jews and Crusaders" issued by the World Islamic Front (led by Osama bin Laden) on February 23, 1998. This statement pronounced the following ruling: "To kill the Americans and their allies—civilians and military—is an individual duty incumbent upon every Muslim in all countries, in order to liberate the al-Aqsa Mosque [in Jerusalem] and the holy mosque [in Mecca] from their grip, so that their armies leave all the territory of Islam, defeated, broken, and unable to threaten any Muslim."[4]

This is a very major change in paradigm in Islamist strategies, because it moves the focus of activity from the national to the global level and makes indiscriminate violence, rather than agitation and mobilization, the primary instrument of political action. It is therefore important for us to examine the ideology and activities of these transnational extremist networks, such as al-Qaeda, and to assess the impact of their words and deeds on Western perceptions and the global image of political Islam as well as on the philosophy and activities of mainstream Islamist groups. The latter also take the transnational jihadist challenge very seriously, because it has the capacity to undermine their credibility among their own support base by demonstrating that, unlike the transnational militants, the mainstream Islamist parties have been contained, if not co-opted, by local regimes and, by extension, the United States and its allies.

Transnational Islamism: Background and Context

Before analyzing the contemporary transnational extremist and violent groups (above all, al-Qaeda), we need to be clear about two facts. First, transnational Islamism in its modern sense—that is, as embedded in a system first of colonial empires that divided the Muslim world into several colonially crafted political entities and then of multiple sovereign states—is not a recent phenomenon. It has a hoary tradition going back at least to the second half of the nineteenth century. Then, it was termed pan-Islam, and Jamal al-Din al-Afghani, an Iranian-born scholar and activist, was its leading advocate.

Al-Afghani was remarkably catholic in his approach. Born a Shia in Iran, al-Afghani portrayed himself as a Sunni activist in order to gain credibility among Muslims worldwide. He frequented the court of the Ottoman sultan-caliph, the titular head of the Sunni Muslim world, to enlist his support for a pan-Islamic movement that he envisioned as the best way to force European colonial powers out of Muslim lands. The Ottoman sultan, who had devised his own pan-Islamic strategy to save his decaying empire by bolstering his role as the caliph of Islam, was more than willing to use al-Afghani for his own ends. But he was unwilling to support al-Afghani's formulation of the pan-Islamic agenda, which the sultan considered to be too radical and potentially deleterious to his state and regime interests and to the Ottoman Empire's relationship with major European powers.

Al-Afghani was himself a bundle of contradictions. An exponent of pan-

Islam and Muslim unity across national boundaries as the panacea for Muslims' weakness when faced with the European colonial onslaught, al-Afghani was at the same time a supporter of nationalist movements that aimed at overthrowing colonial rule. He was, in particular, an admirer of the Indian national movement led by the Indian National Congress. He advised Indian Muslims to make common cause with their Hindu compatriots to drive the British from the subcontinent. He severely criticized the great Indian Muslim reformer and educationist Sir Sayyid Ahmed because of the latter's pro-British stance that, according to al-Afghani, isolated Indian Muslims both from Muslims around the world and from their Hindu countrymen.[5] Al-Afghani considered nationalism and pan-Islam two sides of the same anticolonial coin; for him, adopting one or the other was a matter of tactics, to be determined largely by the different contexts in which anticolonial movements operated.[6]

According to the eminent historian Albert Hourani, for al-Afghani, pan-Islam meant that "the Muslim rulers should cooperate in the service of Islam": "There is no sign that he had in mind to create a single Islamic State or to revive the united caliphate of early times. When he talked of the caliphate he meant by it some sort of spiritual authority or else simply a primacy of honour."[7] Al-Afghani was perfectly willing to work within the system of multiple and sovereign states as long as he could advance the cause of Muslims and Islam against the forces of Western colonial domination. His pan-Islam was therefore not as transnational in character as many people assume. He was very sensitive to context and fashioned his strategies based on local circumstances.

The second fact worth clarifying before proceeding with contemporary analysis is that most contemporary transnational Islamist activities do not fall within the "jihadist" description. In fact, the transnational jihadi groups form a small minority among transnational Islamist actors, just as they do among jihadi groups themselves, most of whom operate within national boundaries and have local, rather than global, objectives. Gerges terms these formations, including Egyptian and Algerian groups that were the largest and most violent among the jihadis, "religious nationalists," to distinguish them from the transnational jihadi networks, such as al-Qaeda.[8]

It is important, therefore, that before moving on to discuss the transnational jihadist movements, principally al-Qaeda, we consider two other forms of transnational Islamist activity that are salient in the Muslim world today. The first is transnational missionary activity, referred to as the *dawa* (literally, "call"), aimed at making existing Muslim populations better Muslims in terms of following Islamic ritual practices and codes of moral behavior. The other is an explicitly political trend of transnational Islam that seeks to re-create an Islamic caliphate based on the model of the "righteous caliphs" of early Islam, without openly advocating violent activity. While doctrinally motivated by the Salafi conception of the age of the righteous caliphs, this latter trend takes its polemical bearings from the dismemberment of the Ottoman Empire in 1918 and the abolition of the caliphate in 1924, both of which it attributes to the machinations of Western powers and their agents in the Muslim world. The missionary trend is represented above all by the Tablighi Jamaat, and the revival of the caliphate tendency is represented by Hizb ut-Tahrir. These two organizations will be studied here in some detail, to distinguish them from transnational militant groups as well as to demonstrate where their agendas overlap.

The Tablighi Jamaat and Transnational Missionary Activity

The principal aim of the Tablighi Jammaat (TJ), founded in India in the 1920s, is faith renewal—that is, to make nominal Muslims good practicing Muslims by helping them to get rid of un-Islamic accretions and observe Islamic rituals faithfully.[9] The TJ works across national boundaries through groups of volunteers who crisscross the globe at their own expense to spread the message of faith renewal to Muslim communities, including those living in the West.[10] The TJ is not explicitly political and makes it a point to emphasize that it is interested in moral regeneration, not political transformation (let alone political unification of the *umma*). The TJ also does not delve into matters of *fiqh* (jurisprudence), thus eschewing controversy that would accompany its endorsement and privileging of one jurisprudential school over the others.

In this sense, the TJ is nonsectarian, although it is deeply imbued with the reformist and puritanical ethos that permeates the Deobandi subschool of Hanafi jurisprudence, which developed in colonial India in the second half of the nineteenth century.[11] The founder of the TJ, Maulana Muhammad Ilyas (1885–1944), was a product of the Deoband theological seminary himself and imported the Sufi-tinged revivalist ethos of the seminary into the TJ. The roots of both the Deobandi and the Tablighi movements go back to the same source of reformist and revivalist Islam in the Indian subcontinent that traces its origins to the teachings and writings of the eighteenth-century theologian Shah Wali Allah. This reformist trend sought to purge non-Islamic practices accrued by Indian Muslims from the Hindu ethos surrounding them, as the first step toward the community's regeneration.[12]

Despite the TJ's attempt to portray itself as nonsectarian, the Wahhabi religious establishment of Saudi Arabia looks at the movement with great suspicion. Leading Wahhabi *ulama* have denounced it for being "deviant" and "un-Islamic" because it does not follow their strict Hanbali code. Shaykh Abdul-Azeez ibn Baaz, the powerful head of the Saudi religious establishment until his death a few years ago, went "so far as to announce that the Tablighis are destined to perdition in Hell . . . and . . . , for all purposes, are not Muslims at all."[13] Consequently, one can surmise that TJ ideology would be anathema to the Wahhabi-inspired jihadi groups, such as al-Qaeda.

Although avowedly apolitical in its orientation, the TJ does not engage in a pluralist discourse, is very introverted, and is not particularly interested in dialogue with non-Muslims. In countries with Muslim minorities (e.g., India, Britain, and the United States), the TJ encourages Muslims to insulate themselves against the contaminating influences of majority cultures by remaining within their own circles of true believers, considered islands of belief within countries largely populated by unbelievers.[14] However, as Yoginder Sikand has argued cogently, the TJ's strategies change depending on context. In Muslim minority countries or in those predominantly Muslim countries in which Islamist political activity is harshly suppressed, the TJ follows a strictly apolitical line. In fact, Muslim regimes who are fighting Islamist opponents often see the TJ as a viable antidote to politically active Islamist groups and thus as an ally in helping to maintain the status quo. Such regimes perceive the TJ as an important vehicle for depoliticizing Muslim masses and preventing them from succumbing to antiregime Islamist propaganda. Pakistani regimes, when opposed by the Islamist Jamaat-i-Islami (JI), have often taken recourse to extending patronage to the TJ, in an effort to pit it against the JI and reduce the latter's appeal among the masses.

In circumstances more congenial for Islamist political activities, some TJ members, including some of its leading lights, play active political roles, normally in and through Islamist parties. Although the TJ officially does not take political stands and sticks to an apolitical line, one can deduce that, given the compatibility between its long-term aims and those of Islamist political formations, it has the potential to act in a supporting role to the latter when circumstances so dictate.[15] It especially has the ability to help spread Islamic values and lifestyle in majority Muslim societies, thus making them more receptive to the Islamists' political message. Barbara Metcalf has pointed out: "Tablighis share fundamental attitudes with the militants, not least their belief that Islam must be defended. They are also shaped by a commitment to individual action as effective in shaping the larger world, and they share the conviction that the faithful few, who act 'in the way of Allah,' can achieve far-reaching transformations. They also cultivate a cultural encapsulation that divides them starkly from a larger, evil, and threatening world."[16]

Is this correspondence in outlook and possible similarity in long-term goals between the TJ and Islamist movements, including the militant ones, enough to classify the TJ, as some analysts allege, as a transnational militant or extremist group on par with al-Qaeda and other comparable networks and organizations?[17] One must answer this question in the negative, for the simple reason that the vast majority of Islamist political formations, with whom the TJ may share its worldview, are themselves neither extremist nor violent. As has been pointed out time and again in this book and elsewhere, the large majority of Islamist formations work peacefully inside national boundaries, within the constitutional and political constraints imposed on them.

Even if one concedes that the TJ shares with mainstream Islamist groups the ultimate goal of Islamizing societies in order to pave the way for the establishment of Islamic states, its strategy for attaining this objective is far from violent. The TJ does not engage in violence or encourage its members to do so, for the simple reason that its leaders and rank and file realize that their immediate and overriding goal—namely, faith renewal—can never be achieved by the use of force. This conclusion holds true notwithstanding the fact that certain individual affiliates, whether members or former members of the TJ, may have gone down the violent, militant route. Some of them in fact left the TJ before turning to violence, because they were disappointed by the TJ's apolitical or insufficiently radical posture.[18] Furthermore, the very strong Wahhabi denunciation of the TJ (mentioned earlier) leads one to conclude that the leaders of al-Qaeda are likely to consider the TJ as anathema as well. It is improbable, therefore, that the TJ is ideologically linked to al-Qaeda (which is inspired by a mixture of Qutbist and Wahhabi ideologies) or that it colludes in or paves the way for the latter's terrorist activities.

Furthermore, although many of its members work across national boundaries, there is no evidence that the TJ's transnational activities are based on the premise that existing state frontiers are illegitimate and ought to be erased. Its conception of the Muslim *umma* is more spiritual than political. Unlike some other transnational Islamist movements, it is not focused on the re-creation of an ideal Islamic caliphate covering all or much of *dar al-Islam*. Its emphasis is on making individual Muslims better Muslims, not on the collective political deliverance of the *umma*. This characteristic distinguishes the transnational missionary Islamist movements, such as the TJ, from those movements—such as Hizb ut-Tahrir al-Islamiyya (literally, the Islamic Party of Liberation)—which espouse global political goals, with the reestablishment of an Islamic caliphate foremost among them.

Hizb-ut-Tahrir and the Revival of the Caliphate

Hizb ut-Tahrir (HT) is the prime example of a transnational Islamist political movement that aspires to achieve global objectives. Unlike the major national Islamist formations, such as the Muslim Brotherhood in Egypt and the Jamaat-i-Islami in Pakistan, it does not aim at transforming individual Muslim majority states into Islamic states where the sharia law is enforced or, at the very least, where the Islamic normative ethos permeates political life. The national Islamist parties accept the logic of the sovereign state system while attempting to change the character of individual states within which they operate. HT, in contrast, denies in theory the validity of the system of states, at least as it applies to the Muslim world.

HT was founded in 1952 in Jordanian-ruled East Jerusalem by the radical Palestinian Shaykh Taqiuddin al-Nabhani, a product of al-Azhar and a teacher and religious judge in Palestine under the British mandate and then under Jordanian rule. Al-Nabhani's ideas have become the core of HT ideology, and they reflect the unresolved tensions that have made the organization a marginal player in much of the Muslim world. On the one hand, al-Nabhani insisted on the immediate restoration of the caliphate. On the other, he "upheld peaceful politics and ideological subversion as the path to reinstating Islam through a popular Islamic revolution which would install a Caliph."[19] The peaceful restoration of an Islamic caliphate in a world of nation-states appeared and continues to appear too chimerical for it to have much political and ideological appeal. Al-Nabhani's objective regarding the caliphate isolated him and, later, HT from reformist Islamist political formations—such as the Muslim Brotherhood—who were committed to transforming existing nation-states into Islamic polities. His and HT's commitment to peaceful means meant that the militant national and transnational Islamists bent on using violence to attain their objectives would also have no truck with al-Nabhani's ideas or the organization he founded.

However, while HT's ultimate objective is to re-create a universal Islamic caliphate, it is not averse to beginning this venture by installing such caliphal rule in selected parts of the Muslim world that appear ripe for such a revolution. In fact, al-Nabhani himself first called for the establishment of the caliphate in the Arab world, before proceeding to extend its domain to non-Arab Muslim lands. Although HT's goal of reestablishing the caliphate is couched in universal, pan-Islamic terms, it limits its pursuit of the caliphate to particular countries or regions in its initial application. It is most active in Central Asia, although much of its global propaganda emanates from Britain, where it appeals to a small, articulate group of educated first- and second-generation Muslim immigrants primarily from South Asia. Although HT's highly secretive central leadership reportedly resides in Jordan, its overt center of operations that oversees its activities worldwide is located in London, and its most high-profile spokespersons operate from there. The choice of London is obviously dictated by the fact that HT can operate there relatively freely. It is harshly suppressed in the Middle East, in Central Asia, and in most other predominantly Muslim regions, where it challenges the legitimacy of existing states.

HT's even more radical offshoot al-Muhajiroun (AM; the name literally means "the Emigrants")—led until recently by the firebrand Syrian-born cleric Omar Bakri Muhammad, who was also based in Britain—broke away from HT because it considered it to be too gradualist in terms of the geographic scope of its activities that focus on one particular country or area at one time. Mandaville explains, "By contrast, al-Muhajiroun . . . works throughout the *ummah,* seeking *nussrah* [outside assistance] at all times"; furthermore, AM "criticizes HT's claim that *jihad* is an activity that can only be legitimately promulgated by a caliph and hence cannot be supported until such time as *khilafah* [caliphate] is reestablished."[20] Therefore, while not actively pursuing jihad itself, AM, unlike HT, believes that Muslims should support jihadi groups wherever they may be. AM can therefore be considered ideologically closer to the international jihadi networks, such as al-Qaeda, than to HT, which has major differences with al-Qaeda in terms of both ideology and strategy.

In terms of HT strategy, even one of its severest critics, Zeyno Baran, concedes, "Unlike most global jihadist groups, HT believes it can carry out the political revolution in a nonviolent manner, relying on the penetration of government institutions and the recruitment of key officials."[21] However, while Baran admits that "HT is not itself a terrorist organization," she argues that "it can usefully be thought of as a conveyor belt for terrorists."[22] This analogy, which ties HT to violent jihadi Islam of the type one identifies with al-Qaeda, is akin to the charge made against the TJ for preparing the ground for jihadists by Islamizing Muslim social behavior through its efforts. In the case of HT, the allegation relates to the propagation of an ideology that makes Muslims psychologically receptive to the jihadi message. According to Baran, HT is engaged in psychologically preparing Muslims to receive the jihadi idea by shifting "the terms of debate within the Muslim world": "Until a few years ago, most Islamist groups considered the notion of establishing a new caliphate a utopian goal. Now, an increasing number of people consider it a serious objective."[23] This last statement is not supported by evidence; in fact, it flies in the face of it. As has been stated repeatedly and supported by evidence in this book, not only most Muslims but also most Islamists are content working within the framework of the nation-state. The HT vision of a universal Islamic caliphate has the support of a very small minority, and outside of Central Asia, many of these are Muslim emigrants living in Britain. HT is therefore on the fringes of Islamist political activity, with very little impact on the day-to-day political and social struggles in the vast majority of Muslim countries.

There is another major internal inconsistency in Baran's criticism of HT. On the one hand, she accepts that "[s]ome radical groups, such as HT, believe that peaceful struggle suffices until a Caliph emerges to lead the *umma* to arms." This implies that HT does not accept armed struggle as legitimate until the reappearance of a caliph, because only the caliph can rightfully declare jihad on behalf of the *umma*. On the other hand, Baran argues in the same breath, "While al-Qaeda can be thought of as the overarching symbol representing militant, radical Islam, HT's global networks directly convey the radical Islamist message to Muslims on the ground."[24] One wonders if the messages delivered by al-Qaeda and HT are one and the same, since HT's strategy of "waiting for the caliph" is not only distinct from but directly opposed to al-Qaeda's strategy of jihad here and now that should also be declared by all and sundry whether or not they are qualified and authorized to do so within the bounds of Islamic doctrine. This disjuncture between HT and al-Qaeda's views deserves to be analyzed in greater detail by scholars of Islamist movements, because it pits HT's fundamental beliefs against those of al-Qaeda and does not appear to make the former the facilitator for the latter's activities. In fact, a report by the International Crisis Group asserts: "Little love is lost between Wahhabis [the ideological progenitors of al-Qaeda] in Central Asia and their HT 'brothers.' They reject each other as profoundly wrong on fundamental theological questions . . . [T]he main anti–Hizb ut-Tahrir website is Wahhabi-run, praises the Taliban, and rejects Hizb ut-Tahrir as 'secular modernists.'"[25]

It is obvious that HT, unlike the TJ, is fundamentally a political organization with political objectives—above all, the creation of what HT Web sites call a "caliphate state." It is this objective toward which the organization's energies are supposed to be directed. However, in practice, HT strategies adapt to and are determined by the different contexts in which they operate. For example, in Central Asia, especially in the demographically and geographically pivotal state of Uzbekistan, where HT has been the most active, the organization's "primary focus is devoted to socioeconomic and human rights issues."[26] It capitalizes on the corruption and repression endemic in Central Asian regimes, while providing sympathetic Uzbeks and others a link with the worldwide *umma*. The destruction of traditional Sufi Islam in Central Asia under Soviet rule—which led, after independence, to mass importation of religious books and preachers from more puritanical countries—has helped prepare fertile ground for the acceptance of HT's message. Above all, the repressive nature of regimes in Central Asia that have denuded the political landscape of secular and moderate Islamist opposition parties has provided opportunities for millenarian organizations, such as HT, and militant ones, such as the Islamic Movement of Uzbekistan, to present themselves as the only viable alternatives to existing oligarchies.[27]

There is, of course, a broader dimension to HT's activities in Central Asia, which it has chosen as an area of concentration and a major jumping-off point for its goal of a caliphate covering the entire Muslim world. Veteran journalist Ahmed Rashid observes: "The HT has a vision of uniting Central Asia, Xinjiang Province of China, and eventually the entire *umma* . . . under a *khilafat* . . . HT leaders believe that Central Asia has reached what they call a 'boiling point' and is ripe for takeover."[28] In HT perceptions, Central Asia forms a critical region where it can begin the implementation of its project for a caliphate state, possibly because of the hollowness of Central Asia's state structures, the artificiality of its Soviet-imposed state boundaries, and its cross-state tribal and kinship affinities.

However, there is little reason to believe that HT's appeal to most Central Asians goes beyond their disenchantment with local regimes to encompass HT's universal project. Rashid notes, "For the desperate youth of Central Asia, the HT's single-minded, incorruptible activists, to whom in better times they might not have given a second thought, now appear to be saviors."[29] The primary source of HT's popularity, therefore, are the unsavory regimes, not HT's ideological appeal, which is merely a dependent variable whose fortunes are likely to decline precipitously if Central Asian regimes undergo transformation and these polities move toward democratization. To conclude, HT's influence in Central Asia "should not be exaggerated"; in fact, "it has little public support in a region where there is limited appetite for political Islam."[30]

HT's other main arena of activity is Britain. But here it appears in the form of an organization catering to the psychological needs of a rootless group of educated immigrant Muslims. Since its appeal is limited to a small minority among immigrant Muslim communities, who themselves form a small minority in the country, its espousal of a universal caliphate through marches and demonstrations in London, Birmingham, and Bradford appears tragicomic. It may have some nuisance value and possibly aid in radicalizing a small minority of British Muslims, but its long-term impact on the British and wider European landscapes is likely to be minimal.

HT is plagued by a major ambivalence that may turn out to be its Achilles' heel. On the one hand, its ideal of creating a caliphate is by definition pan-Islamic, if not universal. On the other hand, it is willing to create a caliphate state in a part of the Muslim world and use it as the base to unify the Muslim world. The founding of such a state is likely to create its own dynamic that would lead the caliphate state to behave like any other sovereign state, making alliances with, waging wars against, and exchanging goods and money with its peers, Muslim and non-Muslim alike. It is likely to become a "normal" state, much like the former Soviet Union, which began its life as the standard-bearer of a universal mission but quickly turned into a conventional player of international politics committed to the rules of the game.

Eventually, caught in its own contradictions, HT is likely to be transformed beyond recognition or to wither away, especially if authoritarian regimes in Central Asia transition into more representative and responsive ones. This is especially likely to be the case since, in the words of one knowledgeable source, HT in Central Asia "is a relatively small, radical group, with little influence on wider society and almost none on opinion-makers in present political systems, whose ideas have gained little acceptance outside the ranks of marginalized young men."[31] The political impact of HT is therefore likely to be ephemeral as well as marginal as far as the vast majority of Muslim countries are concerned.

Al-Qaeda and the Transnational Jihadi Ideology

The fundamental difference between the transnational jihadi elements and other Islamist groups and parties, including those working transnationally, centers on the concept of jihad. The transnational jihadi groups have elevated jihad, in terms of its political and military dimension, to the status of one of the fundamental pillars of Islam, referring to it as the sixth pillar, in addition to the five commonly accepted by all Muslims—profession of faith, prayer, fasting, charity, and pilgrimage. They have also interpreted jihad as *fard ayn* (individual obligation) rather than *fard kifaya* (collective duty). The latter has been the traditional interpretation by Islamic religious authorities and entails the existence of a community of believers with a legitimate ruler who has the sole authority to declare jihad on behalf of the community.

As pointed out earlier, one of the major differences between HT and such groups as al-Qaeda revolves around whether jihad is perceived as an individual duty that is incumbent on every Muslim and that has to be undertaken by individual volition or as a collective duty to be determined by the *umma* and proclaimed on its behalf by the legitimate caliph. For HT, ordinary Muslims cannot declare jihad; it is the exclusive prerogative of the caliph. For al-Qaeda and its leader, Bin Laden, it is an individual obligation on par with prayer and fasting. As Gerges points out, for Bin Laden, jihad ranks second as a pillar of faith, after the profession of faith in God and his messenger.[32]

Al-Qaeda and like-minded jihadis have come upon this interpretation not from their reading of the classical texts of Islamic jurisprudence but against the dictates of the leading jurists of classical Islam. They have inherited the idea of jihad as "a perpetual war and a personal obligation"[33] from the Egyptian radical Islamist thinker Sayyid Qutb, the Muslim Brotherhood's chief ideologue in the 1950s and 1960s. Qutb's idea of jihad was both expansive and unapologetic. For him, interpreting jihad merely as defensive war did not make sense: "The Jihaad of Islam is to secure complete freedom for every man throughout the world by releasing him from servitude to other human beings so that he may serve his God, Who Is One and Who has no associates. This is in itself a sufficient reason for Jihaad . . . The reason for Jihaad exists in the nature of its message and in the actual conditions it finds in human societies, and not merely in the necessity for defense, which may be temporary and of limited extent . . . Those who say that Islamic Jihaad was merely for the defense of the 'homeland of Islam' diminish the greatness of the Islamic way of life and consider it less important than their 'homeland.'"[34] For Qutb and those he influenced, such as Osama bin Laden and Ayman al-Zawahiri, jihad is a "liberating" mission, not just a "defensive" one.

The concept of jihad as a perpetual duty of every individual Muslim is one that the transnational jihadis share with all jihadi groups, including those who are working within the confines of existing states and periodically attempt to overturn domestic regimes by force. This is their common inheritance from Sayyid Qutb. Where they part company is in the transnational jihadis' global orientation, a fundamental departure from the domestic preoccupation of almost all jihadi groups until the mid-1990s, when a major break took place between the national and the transnational jihadis.

The transnational orientation of al-Qaeda and like groups came through the conjunction of two major factors. The first was the launching and eventual success of the U.S.-supported Afghan "jihad" against Soviet military occupation. The second was the failure of militant Islamists to overthrow authoritarian and "un-Islamic" regimes in their home countries, principally Egypt and Algeria, despite an escalation of violence by extremist groups during the 1980s and the first half of the 1990s. These two experiences led some militant groups, such as the Egyptian Islamic Jihad and the coalition of factions that eventually came to be known as al-Qaeda, to come to two conclusions. The first was that they could defeat a superpower by sustained armed attacks. The second was that local regimes, the "near enemy," could not be overthrown until their external patrons, the "far enemy," are forced to withdraw their support from these regimes and stop meddling in the affairs of the Muslim world.

The stationing of American forces in Saudi Arabia during and after the Gulf War in 1990–91 provided the major incentive for the second conclusion. Despite Bin Laden's persistent efforts to prevent the deployment of American troops in Saudi Arabia, neither the Saudi regime nor the Wahhabi religious establishment showed any signs of taking his arguments seriously.[35] Operation Desert Storm demonstrated the extent to which Gulf Arab regimes, most particularly the House of Saud, had become dependent on the United States for their security. It was only logical that al-Qaeda and elements of related jihadi organizations that had these regimes in their crosshairs would soon come to the conclusion that the "near enemy" could not be dislodged without first expelling from *dar al-Islam* the United States, the lone superpower in the post–cold war world and the "far enemy" par excellence.

The transnationalization of jihad also took place as a result of disillusionment among some jihadi groups and general disarray among militant Islamist movements who had lost their sense of direction both because of their effective suppression at home (especially in Egypt and Algeria, where much of their fire had been concentrated) and because of the end of the Afghan jihad abroad. The former demonstrated the militant Islamists' political and military impotence domestically, and the latter led to the descent of Afghanistan into chaos and anarchy resulting from internecine warfare among the various Afghan jihadi groups, who split largely along ethnic lines. Consequently, leading national jihadi figures, such as Ayman al-Zawahiri of the Egyptian Islamic Jihad (who had moved to Afghanistan to participate in the war against the Soviets), and the transnational leaders of the Arab Afghans, such as Osama bin Laden, came to the conclusion that the jihadi movement needed a radical change of direction in order to keep itself alive.

It was in this context that the transnational jihadi strategy of targeting the "far enemy," the United States and its allies, was born. The conventional priority of targeting domestic regimes as the essential prerequisite for reducing Western influence in the Muslim world was reversed. The leaders of the Afghanistan-based jihadi movements, largely consisting of the Afghan Arabs and increasingly coalescing under the umbrella organization of al-Qaeda, decided that attacking American targets and thereby forcing the United States out of the Muslim world was the essential first step toward bringing down un-Islamic regimes in the Muslim world—especially in the Middle East—that were supported by Washington. American presence in the Muslim world thus became a prime justification for defining the United States as the logical major target of attack by the transnational jihadis. Attacks against U.S. embassies in East Africa and against the USS Cole off the port of Aden in Yemen were among the prelude to the attack against New York and Washington on 9/11.

According to Fawaz Gerges, the decision to globalize jihad was reached only in the latter half of the 1990s. It was reached as a result of intense internal debate among jihadi leaders. Gerges claims: "The globalization of jihadist tendencies and the road to September 11 were directly related to the internal upheaval within the jihadist movement as well as to changing regional and international conditions. Al Qaeda emerged as a direct result of the entropy of the jihadist movement in the late 1990s and as a desperate effort to alter the movement's route, if not its final destination, and to reverse its decline."[36] The failure of the jihadis to bring down the "near enemy" was the catalyst for al-Zawahiri, Bin Laden, and their colleagues in Afghanistan to settle on a strategy that would "drag the United States into a total confrontation with the ummah and wake Muslims from their political slumber."[37]

However, this did not mean that al-Qaeda came anywhere near representing the opinion of the majority of jihadis. In fact, most of the latter decided in the second half of the 1990s to make their peace with the local authorities and give up the strategy of terrorism and armed resistance. This was particularly true of the militant Islamists movements in Egypt and Algeria, which had been the major theaters of armed Islamist militancy during the first half of that decade. Most of the members of al-Zawahiri's own organization, the Egyptian Islamic Jihad, distanced themselves from al-Qaeda and its strategy of targeting the United States, believing that this strategy would further hurt the Islamist cause.

Al-Qaeda's Origins

Al-Qaeda's espousal of a global strategy aimed at the United States became clear with the attack on U.S. embassies in Tanzania and Kenya. This attack brought forth an equally fierce American response, under President Clinton's explicit instructions, and led to the bombing of suspected al-Qaeda bases in Afghanistan and Sudan. However, the American assault on al-Qaeda had deep ironies built into it. The American-supported and American-financed war against the Soviet Union and its client regime in Afghanistan during the 1980s was the crucial factor that made the transnational jihadi movement and its terror campaign against the United States possible in the late 1990s. It was the American-sponsored "jihad" against the Soviet Union in Afghanistan that provided fertile ground for the ingathering in Afghanistan of Islamist radicals from around the world, many of them actively recruited by the CIA and its local agents.

The subsequent collapse of the Afghan state, which was largely the result of vicious infighting among the various American-financed and American-supported mujahedin groups, provided al-Qaeda—whose leaders, including Osama bin Laden, were onetime favorites of the CIA—the space to organize itself to launch the global jihad against American interests. The Saudi regime and other conservative establishments in the Gulf contributed to this outcome in no small measure. Not only did they bankroll the Afghan jihad; they facilitated the passage of radical young men to Afghanistan to fight the Soviets. Fawaz Gerges has eloquently summed up the end result: "A new transnational generation of young warriors was born . . . Muslim men of various national and social backgrounds met on the battlefield and shed blood in defense of an imagined community . . . The old rules no longer applied or mattered to the new warriors, who viewed themselves as the vanguard of the ummah, not as citizens of separate countries."[38] It was from this pool of international warriors that al-Qaeda recruited its foot soldiers.

Founded by an amalgam of political radicals (principally from Egypt) and social and cultural conservatives (largely from the Arabian Peninsula), al-Qaeda was able to consolidate its base in Afghanistan thanks to the failure of the Afghan state. Afghanistan's descent into a bloody civil war following the withdrawal of Soviet troops created a political vacuum in the country that led to the emergence of the Pakistan-supported Taliban, with whom the al-Qaeda leadership established a working relationship. It was able to do so by bankrolling the Taliban regime, which was under stringent economic boycott thanks to the pressure of the American human rights lobby.

This combination of factors proved very conducive to al-Qaeda's plans to implement an international terrorist agenda. The Taliban–al-Qaeda nexus was full of irony. The Taliban's agenda was primarily domestic, rather than global, and their dependence on al-Qaeda eventually turned out to be a recipe for disaster as far as their own objective of "purifying" Afghan society was concerned. Nonetheless, this paradox does not detract from the fact that the American-supported "jihad" against godless communism and the consequent state failure in Afghanistan contributed not only to the creation of al-Qaeda but also to providing it a safe haven in that country.[39]

The ingathering of radical jihadis in Afghanistan also had ripple effects in far-flung parts of the Muslim world, such as Southeast Asia. Battle-hardened and ideologically indoctrinated jihadi elements, dispersed from Afghanistan after the expulsion of the Soviets, returned home burning with the desire to replicate their Afghan strategy in their own countries and regions. The International Crisis Group's report on the Southeast Asian Jemaah Islamiyah, accused of carrying out the Bali bombings of October 2002, has made this connection very clear.[40] Once again, despite the fact that Jemaah Islamiyah's following in Indonesia is minuscule compared to the huge numbers that adhere to mainstream Islamist organizations (e.g., the traditionalist Nahdlatul Ulama and the modernist Muhammadiyah), the former's dramatic acts of terror provide it with the sort of publicity that the latter have never enjoyed globally. This also has a psychological impact on the Muslim populations of Southeast Asia, raising the profile of transnational jihadists as forces of resistance—however misguided—to Western dominance.[41]

The Invasion of Iraq and the Spread of Transnational Jihadism

Just as the American-sponsored proxy war in Afghanistan created favorable conditions for the emergence of transnational jihadism in the form of al-Qaeda, the American-led invasion of Iraq created conditions for the ingathering of transnational jihadis in that country, the intensification of the insurgency in Iraq, and the emergence of the al-Zarqawi phenomenon. Much of this resulted from the collapse of the Iraqi state apparatus following the American invasion (especially the disbanding of the army) and from the inability of the occupation authorities to put a credible structure in its place. The consequent vacuum has provided the jihadis space to move in and set up shop without much let or hindrance. The collapse of the Iraqi state actually came as a great boon to the transnational jihadis, who were looking for a new base after the fall of the Taliban in Afghanistan and after the dispersal of the al-Qaeda leadership and rank and file following the American-led offensive against them. At the same time, it provided the transnational jihadis the opportunity to engage in ideological rethinking and reformulation of their strategy.[42]

The American invasion of Iraq was a godsend for the transnational jihadis in another sense as well. Daniel Benjamin and Steven Simon have stated: "By invading Iraq the United States provided the jihadists with the ideal opportunity to fulfill their obligations and drive an occupying army out of the lands of Islam . . . From the perspective of the jihadists, the targets were being delivered for the killing . . . They have been making the most of it through the insurgency, turning Iraq into an unrivaled theater of inspiration for the jihadi's drama of faith."[43] State collapse has also increased the salience of ethnic and religious fissures in Iraq: "Washington's conviction that the Ba'athist regime was essentially Sunni (it was not) and that large numbers of Sunni Arabs therefore were inherently opposed to its overthrow (they were not) became a self-fulfilling prophecy. Fearing resistance in Sunni Arab areas before it actually materialised, US forces treated them harshly. This helped heighten hostility from Sunni Arabs who increasingly, albeit reluctantly, identified themselves as such."[44] The consequent alienation of Sunni Arabs from the emerging post-Saddam structure helped create a hospitable environment for the transnational jihadis whose interests came to converge with those of Iraqi nationalists and former Baathists committed to driving the United States out of Iraq. It would be wrong to equate the Iraqi insurgency merely with transnational jihadi activities.[45] However, faulty American policies that alienated large segments of the Sunni Arab community provided crucial momentum and operating space to shadowy organizations, such as the al-Zarqawi led al-Qaeda in Mesopotamia, to prepare for and conduct acts of terror both within Iraq and in neighboring countries.[46]

The American invasion of Iraq so soon after its invasion of Afghanistan also played into the hands of transnational jihadis by demonstrating the validity of their argument that the United States is engaged in a war against Islam and Muslims and not just against al-Qaeda. The feeling of jubilation was summed up by Sami ul-Haq, director of the Haqqaniya Madrasa in Pakistan's North-

West Frontier Province, where much of the Taliban leadership, including Mullah Omar, had received their religious education. He told British journalist William Dalrymple in no uncertain terms: "We are in a good, strong position . . . Bush has woken the entire Islamic world. We are grateful to him."[47] The invasion of Iraq has to a significant extent replaced Palestine as the foremost grievance of the Muslim world against the West and has created a substantial reservoir of sympathy for the violent jihadi opposition to the American occupation and the successor regime in Baghdad. It is no coincidence that terrorists who have carried out strikes in such widely dispersed locales as Madrid, London, and Jakarta have justified their attacks in terms of retribution against the invasion and occupation of Iraq.

The blowback for America from the Iraq invasion is likely to be far greater than that from the American-supported war against the Soviets in Afghanistan in the 1980s: "Fighters in Iraq are more battle hardened than the Afghan Arabs, who fought demoralized Soviet army conscripts. They are testing themselves against arguably the best army in history, acquiring skills in their battles against coalition forces that will be far more useful for future terrorist operations than those their counterparts learned during the 1980s."[48] Just as many of the leading lights of the current generation of Islamist militants are veterans of the Afghan war, the insurgency in Iraq can be expected to produce the leadership for the next generation of jihadis, who are likely to pose major threats to Muslim regimes allied to the United States. According to Bergen and Reynolds, "the blowback from Iraq is likely to be as painful for Saudi Arabia as the blowback from Afghanistan was for Egypt and Algeria during the 1990s."[49]

Al-Qaeda: Network, Franchise, or Something More Nebulous?

That terrorist groups are carrying out similar attacks in Europe, in Indonesia, in Iraq, and elsewhere does not mean that they are part of a concerted effort controlled by a mastermind operating out of a global command center. Although many of these groups refer to themselves as al-Qaeda with appropriate regional suffixes (e.g., "in Europe," "in Mesopotamia," "in the Arabian Peninsula"), this results more from the appropriation of the name by diverse jihadi groups than from a devolution of regional responsibility to them by a single nerve center. It is not even an indication of the franchising of al-Qaeda activities; most of these groups arrogate the title to themselves before legitimacy is conferred on them ex post facto by al-Zawahiri or Bin Laden from their mountainous hideouts.

The freelance nature of transnational Islamist terrorism was evident in the case of the two most dramatic attacks in Europe, those in Madrid in March 2004 and London in July 2005. Two leading experts on terrorism contend: "[T]he Madrid bombings were not designed, funded, or executed by al Qaeda operatives . . . [T]he bloodshed in Spain was not the handiwork of Usama bin Laden. Instead, it was an homage—both honor and emulation—to him and his ideas . . . Madrid demonstrated the global reach of bin Laden's ideas, not his operations."[50] Much the same applied to the London bombings.

The independence of some terrorist groups also becomes clear from such communication as has come to light between the traditional leaders of al-Qaeda and their "deputies" around the globe. The former address the latter respectfully and give advice gingerly. This is particularly true in the case of al-Qaeda in Iraq, earlier known as *al-Tawhid wa al-Jihad* (Monotheism and Struggle), and its late leader, al-Zarqawi, who clearly seemed to be acting on his own, without directions from—and sometimes against the inclinations of—Bin Laden and his colleagues on the Afghanistan-Pakistan border. As observed in a report by the International Crisis Group, the fact that al-Zarqawi did not take orders from the nominal leaders of al-Qaeda is clearly demonstrated by "Zarqawi's willingness to attack other Muslims (especially the Shiites) and foment sectarian strife." The report continues, "Al-Qaeda, meanwhile, has emphasized that Muslims should stand united until their common enemies are defeated."[51] There is no indication that al-Zarqawi paid any heed to al-Qaeda's advice on this issue, although such advice was clearly proffered in al-Zawahiri's letter to al-Zarqawi made public by the Pentagon in October 2005.[52] This leads one to conclude, "If al-Qaeda is understood as a loose global network rather than a structured organization . . . its association with Zarqawi . . . [can be] more easily established."[53]

Looking to the Future

The Afghan and Iraqi cases demonstrate very clearly that transnational jihadism flourishes in those exceptional cases when states collapse and normal politics is suspended. Among other things, state evaporation makes national boundaries irrelevant, thereby allowing transnational movements to permeate the stateless country without much hindrance. This was clearly the case with the fall of the Saddam regime in Iraq in April 2003.

Fortunately, the vast majority of Muslim countries has not reached—and, in the short term, is unlikely to reach—the stage at which Iraq finds itself today and from which Afghanistan is still trying to emerge. This means that the arena of jihadi transnational activity in the Muslim world will be circumscribed. However, the problem with many Muslim states—Egypt, Syria, Jordan, and Algeria, to name a few—is that their regimes stand on very narrow and insecure foundations. At the same time, such regimes tenaciously refuse to open their systems to genuine political participation, thus allowing intense resentment to build underground. This resentment, often the product of a feeling of acute political impotence among the general public, is likely to provide the entry point for transnational jihadis and to help them put down roots in Muslim countries where their presence is currently shallow or nonexistent. This could especially be the case if Islamist national formations, such as the Muslim Brotherhood, fail to remove repressive regimes through peaceful action. Their failure to do so may detract from their credibility and open the way for greater inroads into Muslim polities by organizations of the al-Qaeda type.

Despite the possibility that transnational extremist movements may be able to exploit the democracy deficit in Muslim countries (especially in the Middle East), the domestic Islamist groups are currently the primary beneficiaries of regime repression, corruption, and inefficiency. Transnational jihadi groups, for all their dramatic acts of terror, so far have had little lasting impact on most Muslim societies, primarily because they lack genuine political agendas that are relevant to the needs and concerns of specific societies. As stated earlier, their impact is expected to be most visible in those cases where states have failed—as in Iraq—to perform their minimum functions of providing security and order to their populations.

In conclusion, transnational violent groups form only a small part of transnational Islamist activity, much of which is carried on peacefully and, as in the case of the TJ, in a deliberately nonpolitical manner. Al-Qaeda and similar organizations, such as Jemaah Islamiyah in Southeast Asia, therefore form a small part of a very small proportion of Islamist activity around the globe, activity that is peripheral to the concerns of the vast majority of peoples in predominantly Muslim societies. As earlier chapters in this book have demonstrated, most political activities undertaken in the name of Islam are carried on within discrete national boundaries and are both products of and respond to the contexts in which they operate.

CHAPTER 8

The Many Faces of Political Islam

This book has attempted, among other things, to address the potential of political Islam or Islamism to affect, in major ways, the future of major Muslim societies and polities around the world. It has done so primarily by examining manifestations of political Islam in several important Muslim countries where Islamist ideology and rhetoric has been used by parties and movements to further their political, economic, and social objectives in different and varied contexts. In the process, while making references to international factors in the first two chapters and more extensively in chapter 7, this study has so far largely concentrated on domestic variables to find explanations for the popularity and strength of Islamist parties and movements and for the weaknesses and contradictions that are inherent in Islamist mobilization. This focus has resulted from my convictions that political Islam in the contemporary era is by and large a national phenomenon and that its trajectories, while subject to international influence, are primarily determined by factors that are discrete to particular contexts.

International factors that have a major impact on the trajectory of political Islam in a particular context become salient when they are filtered through local conditions and concerns and interact with the latter in such a way that they augment trends already in existence because of domestic factors. As chapter 7 pointed out, international factors appear as major independent variables in determining the goals and strategies of transnational Islamist groups, especially those that take recourse to violence against countries they define as the "far enemy." Even here, as the discussion about the origins of al-Qaeda and its affiliates has clearly demonstrated, local factors, including state failure (in Afghanistan) and/or the inability of radical groups to successfully target local regimes (in Egypt, Algeria, and Saudi Arabia), played very important roles in the emergence of transnational Islamist extremism. Transnational jihadism was therefore as much a product of domestic as of global factors.

Additionally, such transnational groups form a very small minority among movements and parties defined as Islamist. The vast majority of Islamist formations are national in character, with their objectives confined to the territories of their nation-states. As chapter 7 has demonstrated, violent transnational jihadi groups form a small percentage even among transnational Islamist movements that include missionary and nonviolent political organizations as well. Thus, despite their dramatic acts of terror, their impact on Muslim societies is very limited, because they are marginal to the political and social struggles going on within predominantly Muslim countries and, unlike their national counterparts, do not have substantial support bases among the populations of predominantly Muslim societies.

Nonetheless, some international variables, especially American policies toward the Muslim world, deserve analysis, even if in abbreviated form, in this concluding chapter, because they can have major impact on the fortunes of political Islam within discrete societies when mediated though local concerns and domestic perceptions of the relationship between international and domestic factors. This applies especially to America's close relationship with several unrepresentative and authoritarian regimes in the Muslim world and to the general perception in Muslim countries that American policies are hostile to Muslim interests broadly defined. The impact of American policies in the Middle East on popular support for Islamist movements and parties clearly demonstrates the validity of this assertion. I shall return to this subject later in this chapter.

This book has argued—both in the introductory chapter and in the various case studies in the subsequent chapters—that it is only natural that political Islam is manifested largely as a national phenomenon. The discrete national manifestations of political Islam are due to the fact that there is wide diversity within the Muslim world in terms of socioeconomic characteristics, culture, political systems, and trajectories of intellectual development, making it extremely difficult, if not impossible, for the political expression of Islam developed in one context to be replicated in other locales. Moreover, as territorial boundaries of postcolonial nation-states have solidified and have come to be seen as legitimate and permanent, politics has become effectively circumscribed within national territorial limits. This is clearly demonstrated by the fact that the overwhelming majority of political actors in Muslim countries, Islamists and non-Islamists alike, has internalized the values of the nation-state system and is comfortable working within it rather than challenging its basic premise. Political Islam is therefore effectively nationalized in the contemporary era.

This is as true of self-proclaimed Islamic states, such as Saudi Arabia and Iran, as it is of those countries where Islamists are in opposition rather than in power. The tremendous differences in the ideologies and political systems of Iran and Saudi Arabia demonstrate that, despite all rhetoric to the contrary, there is no consensus on what constitutes an "Islamic state." As chapter 3 has shown clearly, both the Saudi and Iranian systems are products of their own historical, cultural, and political contexts and cannot be replicated elsewhere. Similarly, as successive chapters have demonstrated, Islamist movements, whether in Turkey, Egypt, Pakistan, or Indonesia, are all generated by their own milieus and specific to their geographic and cultural locales. This is also the case with Islamist national resistance movements, analyzed in chapter 6. The chief among them, Hamas and Hizbullah, are as much products of their own context as the Muslim Brotherhood and the Jamaat-i-Islami. Both seamlessly combine nationalism and Islamism in their ideologies and objectives. In fact, one could argue that the nationalism of Hizbullah and Hamas defines their Islamist agenda, rather than the other way around.

It is obvious, therefore, that political Islam comes in various shapes and sizes. Differences among Islamist groups can be clearly perceived not only among countries but within countries as well. The latter phenomenon is related to the fact that Islamists within specific countries are usually divided both ideologically and over objectives and strategies they seek to pursue in the political arena. The sometimes violent opposition to the Wahhabi Saudi regime from radical neo-Wahhabi elements within the kingdom is irrefutable proof of this phenomenon. Even this most "fundamentalist" of Muslim societies is torn by dissensions among self-proclaimed Islamists on very fundamental social and political issues.[1] As the chapters of this book have demonstrated, divisions abound among Islamist movements in countries of the Middle East and of South and Southeast Asia. There are, indeed, many faces of political Islam.

Regime Character and Political Islam

One thing this book has attempted to demonstrate is the increasing moderation over time of mainstream Islamist parties and their willingness and ability to work within constitutional restraints imposed on them by regimes that are normally unsympathetic to Islamist causes. Turkey, Egypt, and Pakistan are outstanding examples of this phenomenon. The transformation of Islamist parties in these countries into constitutional vehicles for political change is remarkable. As chapter 4 has demonstrated, the Muslim Brotherhood in Egypt and the Jamaat-i-Islami in Pakistan have made radical departures from their initially uncompromising and purist ideologies. Chapter 5 has revealed clearly the transformation of the AKP in Turkey into a conservative democratic party committed to "Muslimhood" in a way that may serve as a model for other Islamist political formations around the world.[2]

Some chapters in this book have also attempted to make projections about the likely course and the future of Islamist movements as Muslim polities democratize over time. One of the main arguments of this book is that the repressive and unrepresentative nature of many regimes in the Muslim world has both provided the political space for and augmented the popularity of Islamist political formations. It has done so by decimating much of the secular and non-Islamist opposition; by occasionally attempting to co-opt Islamist groups to use them to discredit secular opposition movements; and, often by default, by providing Islamist parties the opportunity to emerge as major avenues of opposition to authoritarian regimes, thus boosting their credibility and popularity among a generally disenchanted citizenry.

The nature of the political systems and of regimes in many Muslim countries have had and continue to have major impact on the growth of political Islam and the strategies adopted by Islamists in these countries. This variable is likely to influence the future trajectory of Islamism in substantial measure. Closed political systems and authoritarian regimes are standing invitations for the growth in the popularity of Islamist political formations and Islamist ideologies. Such regimes stifle political and intellectual debate and effectively decimate almost all secular opposition through the medium of the *mukhabarat* (intelligence/security) state, based on the effective penetration of their societies by the state's intelligence agencies with the sole objective of assuring the security and longevity of existing regimes. Paradoxically, these very regimes, by successfully eliminating secular opposition movements and parties and banishing normal politics, have created political and intellectual space for the Islamists to move in.

As has been repeatedly demonstrated in this book, the popularity of political Islam is to a substantial extent the result of the fact that even the most efficient and repressive regimes in the Muslim world are unable to fully suppress opposition expressed through the religious idiom. Unlike secular groups that can be neutralized by preventing them from speaking in public and from spreading their message through the media, Islamist political activity can never be effectively curbed, because of the vocabulary it uses and the institutions it can exploit. Islamic religious idiom, like the vocabulary of most other religions, has the potential of lending itself to political uses. At the same time, it can be made to appear politically innocuous and, therefore, immune to governmental retribution. Publishing houses that print religious literature, mosques and affiliated institutions that subtly disseminate Islamist propaganda, and religiously endowed charitable organizations sympathetic to Islamist causes can be used to send out political messages dressed up in religious garb and to build support for Islamist political activity.

The Islamic revolution in Iran is probably the leading example of this phenomenon. The shah's ruthless decimation of all opposition created the political vacuum into which the Islamists led by Ayatollah Khomeini moved in. This vacuum allowed the radical faction of the Shia clergy to portray itself as the primary, if not the only, avenue for opposition to the shah's repressive regime. The religious idiom used by the antishah *ulama* in their sermons—including elliptically portraying the shah as the twentieth-century incarnation of the usurper Caliph Yezid, on whose orders Imam Hussein, the grandson of the Prophet, was martyred in 680 CE—resonated with the Shia population of Iran. At the same time, the repressive agencies of the state were unable to respond adequately to the implicit political use of such imagery because it would have offended the religious sensibilities of the Iranian population and created further turmoil. This was borne out by the fact that the revolution was triggered by the shah's regime's decision in August and September 1978 to crack down on the radical clerics and to undertake a public campaign to discredit their leader, Ayatollah Khomeini. It was a strategy that backfired, with fatal consequences for the shah's rule.

Iran is not the only example of this phenomenon. The repressive policies of the regime of the National Liberation Front in Algeria gave tremendous fillip to the popularity of the Islamic Salvation Front (FIS) by decimating all its secular competitors. Similarly, successive Egyptian regimes so debilitated the secular opposition—ranging from the liberals through the Arab nationalists to the Communists—that they created a huge void that was filled by the Islamists. The current Pakistani regime's attempt to curtail the popularity of mainstream political parties has redounded to the benefit of Islamist formations by making the government dependent on their support while allowing them relative freedom to criticize official policies. This has provided substantial political clout to the Islamist formations in Pakistan, despite the secular pretensions of the Musharraf regime. One finds the same pattern repeated in country after Muslim country, especially in the broader Middle East.

Unrepresentative regimes, in addition to repressing political opposition ruthlessly, are usually corrupt and unresponsive to societal demands. Consequently, they fail to provide social services and a social safety net to the most vulnerable segments of their populations. As various case studies in this book have demonstrated, this is another void that Islamist groups, from the Muslim Brotherhood to Hizbullah and Hamas, move in to fill through charitable networks that are either affiliated to or set up as front organizations for Islamist political formations. Such charitable institutions fulfill the religiously enjoined duty of helping the needy by providing social services to the weakest sections of society. More important, they assist Islamist groups and movements in cultivating crucial constituencies, especially among underprivileged population segments that, already alienated from unresponsive and corrupt regimes, can be mobilized for political action. The close nexus between Islamist charitable networks and Islamist political formations from Turkey through Egypt to Pakistan and Indonesia has come to provide Islamist groups with great staying power in the face of state repression. It also provides an essential explanation for their growing popularity.

The nature of regimes in many Muslim countries, especially in the broader Middle East, is a crucial variable that explains the popularity of Islamist political formations. One can extrapolate from this analysis that as long as authoritarian and repressive regimes continue to rule Muslim countries, Islamism will continue to thrive as an ideology and political movement within those countries. It is true that the character of these regimes can be explained with reference to multiple factors operating in diverse mixes in different locales, but as far as political Islam is concerned, the outcome is similar in almost all contexts. The nature of regimes, one can argue, is a crucial factor that determines the degree of popularity political Islam is able to garner in widely divergent Muslim countries.

Democracy and Political Islam

The positive correlation between the authoritarian nature of regimes and the appeal of political Islam raises the important question whether Islamism will retain its current attraction once Muslim countries, especially in the Middle East, democratize to a significant extent. Political Islam has been an especially effective oppositional ideology in the context of autocratic rule. But once Islamists are allowed to become normal participants in the political process, with the prospect of achieving or sharing power, their oppositional rhetoric is no longer likely to suffice as a substitute for concrete policies; then, the Islamists' feet will also be held to the political fire. This book clearly demonstrates that this has been the case most clearly in Indonesia and Turkey, the two Muslim democracies that have been analyzed in considerable detail. It is also true in cases where closed polities have begun to liberalize in considerable measure. Millenarian ideologies lose a great deal of their shine when parties espousing such dogmas are unable to deliver on their political and economic promises to the electorate that has the power to remove them from office. One can argue, therefore, that democratization may be the ideal antidote to the appeal of Islamism and the rhetoric accompanying it.

Furthermore, acquiring and holding power necessitates compromises, induces pragmatism, and leads to moderation, defined as the willingness to accept democratic norms of political participation. These norms include nonviolent opposition, respect for the results of free and fair elections, and willingness to give up power if voted out of office. Such moderation should not be conflated with the term *moderation* as it is used in the Western media. The latter usage tends to suggest a foreign policy stance that is pro-Western—specifically, pro-American—and a willingness to accept Israel's legitimacy and work with the Jewish state. The combination of ideological moderation among Islamist parties and democratization of their states may in fact lead to hardening of their countries' positions on relations with the United States and Israel. These are issues on which authoritarian Muslim regimes, dependent as many of them are on American support, appear more "moderate" than their democratic counterparts are likely to be, especially because the latter will reflect popular opinion that is usually more anti-American and anti-Israeli than stances adopted by unrepresentative regimes.

The evidence regarding ideological moderation is not as conclusive in the case of the Arab world as it is with regard to Turkey and Indonesia, the two cases discussed at length in chapter 5. The primary reason for this is the highly restrictive nature of political systems in the Arab world that do not adequately reward moderation. Nevertheless, the route traveled by the Muslim Brotherhood in Egypt (detailed in chapter 4) is instructive in this regard. The party has clearly moved toward what Bruce Rutherford has termed "Islamic constitutionalism," even under the restrictions imposed on it by the authoritarian Egyptian regime. According to Rutherford, "this distinctively Islamic conception of constitutionalism . . . legitimates many of the key goals of liberal governance, including constraints on state power, governmental accountability, and protection of some civil and political rights."[3] While this conception of constitutionalism differs significantly from its liberal equivalent, especially on the issue of the moral purpose of the state, it nevertheless appears to be a significant improvement over the existing authoritarian orders in much of the Middle East.

However, one can postulate that if Egypt moves toward becoming a genuine democracy, significantly improving the chances of the Muslim Brotherhood acquiring or sharing power through democratic means, the party can be expected to moderate further. This is likely to be the case because ideological and political compromises are imperatives necessary to forge a governing coalition, as the example of the AKP in Turkey demonstrates so clearly. The Muslim Brotherhood, in fact, already has a record of cooperation with secular, liberal, and leftist parties in Egypt, having, among other things, run candidates under the banner of some of these parties. This tendency toward cooperation is likely to accelerate if the system democratizes and if the rewards of cooperation become clearly apparent.

The Islamic Action Front (IAF), the Muslim Brotherhood's political front in Jordan, has established a record of cooperation with secular and liberal opposition elements since the mid-1990s and "points to the fact that it coordinates deals and 'shakes hands' with secularists as evidence of the Party's moderation." It has done so under the semiopen conditions prevailing in Jordan. However, that the IAF cooperates only selectively and on issues (usually related to foreign policy) that do not contravene its conception of the sharia brings into doubt its much-touted moderation. According to Janine Clark, "This does not mean that cooperative arrangements . . . are not evidence of moderation or that moderation does or will not occur, but it does suggest we need to rethink the presumed causal link within the democratization literature between cooperation and ideological moderation."[4] This is a very useful warning, but a major study of the IAF in Jordan suggests that its moderation may have gone further than Clark gives it credit for.[5] Taken as a whole, the trajectories of Islamist parties that have attained or seem close to attaining or sharing power suggest that while ideological moderation should not be presumed to be the inevitable outcome of democratization, the causal link between the two phenomena is stronger than its critics suggest.

That political openness encourages the appearance of several Islamist tendencies within individual countries has been proven in various contexts in the Muslim world. The Turkish case demonstrates the capacity of democratic systems to fracture the Islamist base. The AKP arose out of a division within the erstwhile Islamist formation—which had operated under different names, such as Refah (Welfare) and Fazilet (Virtue)—based partially on ideology and partially on differences in terms of political strategy both at home and abroad. The rump of the conservative Islamists under the banner of the Saadet (Felicity) Party—led by the doyen of Turkish Islamists, Necmettin Erbakan—performed very poorly in the 2002 elections that the AKP won so handsomely.

Indonesia and Pakistan are also good examples of this phenomenon. In the former, the split between the modernist Muhammadiya and the traditionalist Nahdlatul Ulama (NU) has been a fixture of social and political life and is now manifested in a number of Islamically inclined parties, some inside the present government and others opposed to it. In Pakistan, the *ulama*-based parties—such as the Jamiat-ul-Ulema-i-Islam and the Jamiat-ul-Ulema-i-Pakistan, the former espousing a more strict interpretation of Hanafi *fiqh* than the latter—have competed not only against each other but also against the lay Jamaat-i-Islami, thus dividing Islamist votes and demonstrating that political Islam is no monolith. Islamism has found multiple manifestations even in the Islamic Republic of Iran, which, as chapter 3 has demonstrated, is replete with cross-cutting political and economic cleavages. Consequently, one finds political formations competing in the Iranian political arena that range from the liberal and reformist to hard-line conservatives, all swearing fealty to Islam and to the ideas of Ayatollah Khomeini.

Democracy, even when practiced imperfectly, creates political space for Islamist parties, in the truly plural sense of the term. By splitting the Islamist base within polities and cutting individual Islamist political formations down to size, democracy neutralizes the possibility that a unified Islamist bloc will take and hold power. Democracy in action truly shows the many faces of political Islam within each individual Muslim country. This makes Islamists appear less of a threat to their secular counterparts and more as normal players of the political game. The future of political Islam is therefore intimately tied, in more than one way, to the future of democracy in the Muslim world. This interrelationship applies with special force to the Middle East and Central Asia, which have been the slowest among predominantly Muslim regions in moving toward genuine democratic change.

International Factors and Political Islam

The various manifestations of political Islam do not operate in an environment insulated from broader international currents. A major international factor that has been discussed only tangentially so far possesses considerable relevance to the future of political Islam and needs to be analyzed in some detail in this concluding chapter. This variable is related to the international power structure, especially in terms of policies followed by the major powers toward issues of genuine concern for much of the Muslim world. It applies with particular force in the post–cold war era to the United States' unrivaled power and the policies that flow from it.

It goes without saying that the current distribution of political, economic, and military power in the international system is heavily tilted against Muslim countries. This is in large part the result of the colonial process and the policies followed by the dominant powers in the postcolonial period to solidify and extend the strategic and economic gains they had achieved during the colonial era. Such policies of direct and indirect domination have left an indelible mark on the psyche of most politically conscious Muslims. This is a mind-set that Islamists are in a good position to exploit, for a number of reasons.

The first such reason is that they have a simple and apparently coherent explanation for Muslim political decline. As stated earlier in this book, Islamists argue that Muslim societies declined the more they moved away from the model of the golden age that Islamists depict in their romanticized version of the early years of Islam. They argue further that if Muslims are able to re-create a true and pure Islamic society, they will be able to reattain their former glory or at least compete with the West on a basis of equality. Their slogan "Islam is the solution" emanates from this interlocking set of arguments. In theory, their prescription is simple, although it undergoes significant mutation when they attempt to put it into practice in individual countries. As stated earlier in this book, this Islamist prescription has found great resonance in widely diverse Muslim societies because the secular, nationalist project in the immediate postcolonial decades was unable to provide dignity, freedom, power, or wealth to most Muslims around the world.

American Policies and Political Islam

The major powers and their policies are perceived by most Muslims as being largely responsible for keeping Muslim societies in the sad plight they are in today. This applies with particular force to American policies in the current era. In much of the Muslim world, American policies are seen as akin to those followed by the erstwhile European colonial powers, aimed principally at preventing any challenge to Western domination arising from Muslim countries.

This argument finds great resonance among politically conscious Muslims because it does correspond to reality in significant measure. The policies of erstwhile colonial powers in the 1950s and the 1960s, especially in the Middle East, bore adequate testimony to the fact that they were committed to maintaining their control over strategically important parts of the Muslim world despite the formal end of colonialism. Such policies ranged from the overthrow of the democratically elected Iranian prime minister Mohammad Mossadegh in 1953 after he had nationalized the Anglo-Iranian Oil Company in 1951 to the Anglo-French-Israeli invasion of Egypt following President Nasser's nationalization of the Suez Canal in 1956.

The bloody war of independence forced on the Algerians by France's intransigent insistence that Algeria was a part of France and, therefore, inalienable territory augmented the feeling among many Muslims that European powers were bent on the subjugation of Muslim lands even after colonialism had become discredited both as ideology and as a form of governance. Since the major European colonial powers were important allies of the United States and since the latter collaborated with Britain in the covert operation in Iran in 1953 and turned a blind eyed toward French brutality in Algeria, the opprobrium heaped on the former colonial powers rubbed off on America as well.

The hostile Muslim perception of the United States was augmented by the cold war strategies adopted by Washington and by its proclivity to step into the European powers' imperial shoes in the Middle East, ostensibly to contain Soviet expansion. Although American opposition to Arab nationalism and to the emergence of independent centers of power in the Middle East was the result largely of cold war considerations, it confirmed for most Muslims that American policy was basically a continuation of the colonial policies of the previous era. America's current military occupation of Iraq has further convinced most Muslims that the United States is working within the same imperialist paradigm used in the Middle East by the British and the French.[6] Washington's unqualified support for Israel is also seen as a part of America's strategy to create and strengthen proxies so as to better control the resource-rich Middle East.[7]

Furthermore, the support that Western powers—above all, the United States—have extended to authoritarian and repressive regimes in the Muslim world during the cold war and after has alienated the Muslim masses from the West in general and from the United States in particular. Support extended to the shah of Iran forms the quintessential example of this policy but is not the only one of its kind. Propping up regimes like those of Presidents Sadat and

Mubarak in Egypt and Kings Hussein and Abdullah in Jordan and collaborating with Saddam Hussein of Iraq to check the growing influence of revolutionary Iran in the 1980s are part of anti-American folklore not only in the Middle East but also throughout the Muslim world. All this augments the image Muslim populations have of America as a global power bent on supporting repressive client regimes to further its own strategic and economic objectives in Muslim countries.

America, Israel, and Political Islam

Above all, it is the unstinted and unquestioning American support to Israel, especially to its policy of continued occupation of and settlement within Palestinian lands conquered in 1967, that demonstrates to politically conscious Muslims that the United States is committed to treating Muslims and Arabs not only with insensitivity but with utter contempt. The American policy of vetoing or threatening to veto UN Security Council resolutions condemning Israeli policies provides to most Muslims proof beyond doubt of American-Israeli collusion to dominate the Muslim Middle East politically and militarily. America's insistence that Middle Eastern countries from Iraq to Iran to Lebanon abide by UN Security Council resolutions while it supports repeated Israeli defiance of a much larger number of resolutions passed by the same body further strengthens the feeling in the Muslim world that the United States unabashedly uses double standards when it comes to Israeli defiance of international opinion.[8] American insistence that Iran give up its nuclear option while America condones—indeed, connives at—the Israeli possession of nuclear weapons and sophisticated delivery systems augments the double standards argument as far as most Muslims are concerned.

Many Muslims perceive America's discriminatory policies aimed against Muslim countries as violation of their dignity, a variable often overlooked by most Western political analysts of the Muslim world. For most Muslims, the antipathy toward America is not based on opposition to American values of democracy and freedom, as some superficial analysts pronounce. It is fundamentally grounded in their opposition to particular aspects of American foreign policy, especially the perception of the blatant use of double standards by Washington in relation to the Muslim Middle East.[9]

Several of the Muslims' concerns relating to dignity come together on the issue of Palestine. Palestine has therefore become the Muslim grievance par excellence. Many politically conscious Muslims believe that all Muslims are potential "Palestinians," the ultimate outsiders, who can be dispossessed and dishonored with impunity and the justice of whose cause will always be dismissed by the West—particularly by the United States—as irrational fanaticism. The American occupation of Iraq has further fueled Muslim anger against the United States, since it is seen as a ploy to fragment a major Arab and Muslim country, to control the oil wealth of the Middle East, and to consolidate Israeli hegemony in the region.[10]

The American endorsement of the Israeli policy of inflicting highly disproportionate damage on Lebanon in July and August 2006 in retaliation for Hizbullah's kidnapping of two Israeli soldiers has added to the long list of Muslim grievances against the United States and further fueled Muslim anger against Washington and its allies. As a leading scholar of Islamist politics pointed out, "Far from weakening Hezbollah, Israel's military onslaught increased the group's popularity throughout the Muslim world." Furthermore, it has "made Hezbollah into the new vanguard of armed resistance to Israel and America in the eyes of tens of millions of Arabs and Muslims."[11] America's support for Israel has worked to the advantage of Islamist political formations, Sunni and Shia alike, especially in the Middle East. The increasing support for Hamas in occupied Palestine and for Hizbullah in Lebanon is in substantial part a reaction to perceived injustices inflicted on Muslim populations because of America's collusion with Israel, including the resupply of arms to Israel during its invasion of Lebanon in 2006. In the Muslim world, Islamism thrives to a considerable degree on anti-Americanism.

America and Transnational Islamist Extremism

Many people do not realize that the United States has had a long history of flirting with political Islam, going back at least to the 1950s. Then, Washington encouraged Saudi Arabia, the "fundamentalist" kingdom par excellence, to use its Islamic credentials as the keeper of Islam's holiest places and the repository of conservative Islamic values to counter the rising tide of Arab nationalism as the unifying force in the Arab world. American policy makers perceived Arab nationalist regimes, such as Egypt, Syria, and Iraq, to be allied to the Soviet Union and therefore inimical to American interests. The United States looked kindly on and covertly supported the anti-Nasser activities of the Egyptian Muslim Brotherhood, because of its animosity toward an Egyptian leader who had come to symbolize Arab nationalism and the dream of Arab unity. It is ironic that the ideology espoused by the current jihadi radicals who target the

United States is a combination of Wahhabi religious doctrines dominant in Saudi Arabia and the radical political ideas espoused by Sayyid Qutb, the ideologue of the Egyptian Muslim Brotherhood in the 1950s and 1960s, who spent many years in Nasser's prison before he was executed in 1966. America's erstwhile favorites in the Middle East have spawned tendencies highly inimical to American interests and objectives in that strategically important region.

As has been pointed out in chapter 7, the rise of transnational militant Islam in its current embodiment owes a great deal to American policy during the 1980s, when the United States funneled massive resources, including funds and weaponry, in collaboration with Saudi Arabia and Pakistan, to fuel the Islamist insurgency against the Soviet military presence in Afghanistan. Al-Qaeda would not have emerged as the threat it is seen to be today had it not been for the American policy that encouraged and facilitated the ingathering in Afghanistan of radical Islamist youth from all parts of the Muslim world in order to further America's own cold war ends. Following this policy created a failed state in Afghanistan that became a safe haven for Osama bin Laden and his ilk.[12] American support to variants of political Islam in the 1950s and 1960s and in the 1980s has therefore had major unintended consequences and tremendous blowback that was not anticipated by successive generations of policy makers in Washington.

As has been argued in chapter 7, the American invasion of Iraq in 2003 has turned out to be a great boon for transnational extremists. The collapse of the Iraqi state following the invasion provided jihadist elements a new safe haven just as they were being deprived of their bases in Afghanistan by another American-led military operation. More important, the invasion of Iraq confirmed the argument made by Osama bin Laden and like-minded elements that the United States, the leader of the "Christian-Zionist" alliance, was bent on waging war on the world of Islam and that it was the duty of all Muslims to resist American "aggression" and engage in "jihad" against it. Consequently, the invasion of Iraq led to increased recruitment of Muslim youth, including a considerable number from Europe, for the transnational jihadist cause.

This conclusion is confirmed by the U.S. National Intelligence Estimate titled "Trends in Global Terrorism: Implications for the United States" and completed in April 2006. According to the *New York Times,* the estimate represents a consensus view of the sixteen disparate spy services inside the American government. The estimate "asserts that Islamic radicalism, rather than being in retreat, has metastasized and spread across the globe . . . [and] that the Iraq war has made the overall terrorism problem worse." The *New York Times* reported,

"The estimate concludes that the radical Islamic movement has expanded from a core of Qaeda operatives and affiliated groups to include a new class of 'self-generating' cells inspired by Al Qaeda's leadership but without any direct connection to Osama bin Laden or his top lieutenants." Furthermore, the estimate "mentions the possibility that Islamic militants who fought in Iraq could return to their home countries, 'exacerbating domestic conflicts or fomenting radical ideologies.'"[13]

In the context of Washington's perceived support for Israel (whether against the Palestinians, the Lebanese, or Arabs and Muslims in general), the American invasion of Iraq has both augmented and further radicalized Islamist forces in the Middle East. This has increased the Islamist threat to secular regimes, both those friendly to the West and those, such as Syria, whose relations with Washington remain tense, if not actually hostile.[14] It may also have helped move mainstream Islamist opinion closer to that held by the transnational extremists. While these may be unintended consequences of Washington's decision to eliminate the Saddam regime, American decision makers cannot escape blame for providing Islamist extremists with a cause when they were running out of steam, thus augmenting their capacity to resuscitate themselves politically and militarily and to broaden their constituency. The impact of the American decision to invade Iraq is likely to haunt Washington and its allies for a long time to come. The monumental mismanagement of the occupation has further added to America's woes not only in Iraq but in the rest of the Muslim world as well.[15] This is particularly the case as the country slips into unmitigated chaos while sectarian strife escalates out of control. This outcome, as Toby Dodge points out convincingly, "is not the result of resurgent primordial antipathies or an indication of the unsustainability of Iraq as a united country." Dodge claims, "Instead, the collapse of the Iraqi state and the failure to resurrect it are a direct result of the US invasion of 2003 and a series of profound policy mistakes made by both the US government and the CPA in its aftermath."[16]

Unfortunately for the United States, both its support—for instrumental reasons—for certain forms of Islamic radicalism (seen as benign by American policy makers in the past) and the overall thrust of American policy, which most Muslims perceive as antithetical to their own interests, have combined to create in Muslim countries a high degree of disillusionment with and resentment toward the United States. Islamists of all varieties manipulate this general sense of disenchantment and anger to advance their own agendas against American-supported regimes in the Muslim world. When and where the sense of impotence becomes very acute, it provides extremist elements the opportunity to exploit the prevailing climate of despair in order to launch terrorist attacks, including suicide bombings. Extremist groups, which attempt to arrogate the right to speak in the name of "Islam," justify terrorism as the only way to overcome the asymmetry in power between the "Muslims" and the "West." They see global terrorism as the only strategy that can wrest the initiative from the hands of the much stronger Western powers and those perceived to be their surrogates in the Muslim world. However ill-conceived such a strategy may be, it appeals to those radical elements that view America and the world of Islam as being engaged in an apocalyptic war, a perception strengthened by Washington's recent actions in the Middle East.

The Interweaving of Domestic and External Factors

While the transnational violent jihadi formations continue to remain a very small minority among Islamists across the Muslim world, it is clear that American policies, especially those relating to the Middle East, have of late become a major factor in promoting the overall popularity of Islamists among ordinary Muslims who cannot be described as Islamists by any stretch of imagination. American policies do so by facilitating the interweaving of domestic grievances against repressive regimes with international grievances against the general thrust of U.S. policies toward the Middle East in particular and the Muslim world in general. Several of the authoritarian regimes in the Muslim world, including those ruling Morocco, Egypt, Jordan, Saudi Arabia, and Pakistan, are allies or clients of the United States whose security is guaranteed to a substantial extent by Washington. They therefore dare not oppose—except very feebly—American policies in the Muslim world in general and the Middle East in particular, for fear that the United States may withdraw its support to them, with consequences likely to be deleterious for their regimes. This was driven home dramatically during the Israeli invasion of Lebanon in July and August 2006, when most Muslim leaders remained silent spectators of America's one-sided policy on the issue, which resulted in their being castigated as "half men" in much of the Muslim world.[17]

Islamists, in contrast, have no compunction in opposing American policies very vocally and virulently and in rebuking their regimes for collaborating with the United States to promote the latter's designs, seen as anti-Muslim by large segments of populations in many Muslim countries. This augments the Islamists' political appeal, because they articulate opinions widely held by Muslim populations around the world. They therefore come to be seen as the primary vehicle for the expression of most Muslims' genuine grievances, both domestically and internationally. This gives Islamists the appearance of being larger than life-size within Muslim societies, because, in stark contrast to Muslim regimes, they speak to the concerns of large numbers of Muslims, Islamists and non-Islamists alike.

It would be irresponsible to ignore that American policy toward issues considered both substantively and symbolically important by most Muslims has made a crucial contribution to the growth in Islamism's popular appeal. While American policies are perceived through filters provided by domestic contexts within discrete Muslim countries, the close relationship between Washington and several unsavory and repressive regimes in the Muslim world strengthens the feeling that the United States is a party to the suppression and oppression of Muslim populations. This perception is further augmented by America's unqualified support for Israel and its use of double standards in the Middle East. Consequently, a symbiotic relationship has developed between the nature of regimes in Muslim countries and American policies toward the Muslim world, with both reinforcing hostile perceptions simultaneously toward local regimes and the United States among large segments of populations in Muslim countries. It is no wonder that anti-Americanism is highest in those Muslim countries whose regimes are most closely allied with the United States.[18]

Current American rhetoric about democracy promotion in the Middle East is perceived in much of the Muslim world as a blatantly hypocritical afterthought to justify the invasion of Iraq after Washington failed to discover weapons of mass destruction or to establish a link between al-Qaeda and the Saddam regime. It is also seen as a veneer for the promotion of other objectives and as an exercise in dishonesty, especially since the United States has clearly demonstrated its unwillingness to accept democratic outcomes of which it does not approve. As chapter 6 has pointed out, the American refusal to deal with a democratically elected Hamas government in occupied Palestine and the imposition of economic sanctions on the Palestinian Authority following the Hamas victory has immeasurably strengthened the perception in the Muslim world that America's commitment to democracy in the Middle East is but skin-deep.

All this seems to have redounded greatly to the benefit of Islamist parties and movements, because of their clear-cut opposition both to the United States and to the authoritarian excesses of domestic regimes. It would therefore not be wrong to argue that unless both these crucial variables—the character of domestic regimes and the general trajectory of American policy—undergo fundamental change, political Islam will continue to attract a significant amount of support among Muslim populations, and Islamism's political appeal will continue to reach beyond the committed devotees of that ideology. The popularity of political Islam is in significant part the result of a unique interplay of domestic and international factors that continuously reinforce each other. This is a nexus not easy to break unless domestic political systems and major ingredients of American policy undergo substantial transformation. Democratization must go hand in hand with a major reorientation of American policy toward the Muslim world in general and the Middle East in particular in order to curb the appeal of political Islam.

However, when all is said and done, it still remains true that the potency of political Islam rests in large measure on very distinct domestic contexts in the various Muslim countries. External factors, such as American policies, are filtered through domestic concerns and popular emotions, thus affecting the future of political Islam in discrete locales through a complex interplay of international and domestic variables. International factors have the ability to reinforce domestic trends and opinions, but they cannot (except in rare cases) create such trends and opinions in the absence of local conditions conducive to their growth. The future of political Islam in distinct contexts is subject to the same logic of the primacy of the domestic concerns over external variables.

Nonetheless, it needs to be understood that while the domestic context usually matters more than the international context, the latter's importance should not be ignored, especially in the present circumstances of unipolarity, when an unrivaled global power has tremendous capacity that it can use for good or ill. Unfortunately for the United States, the overwhelming perception as far as Muslim peoples, especially those in the Middle East, are concerned is that Washington has most of the time used its might for ill rather than for good in Muslim countries. It cannot be denied that this perception is relevant to the discussion of the future trajectory of Islamist movements and parties in the Muslim world. But this is a subject that deserves independent treatment and must await the publication of another book as a sequel to this one.

Notes

CHAPTER 1

1. Graham Fuller, *The Future of Political Islam* (New York: Palgrave Macmillan, 2003), xi.

2. Greg Barton, *Jemaah Islamiyah: Radical Islamism in Indonesia* (Singapore: Ridge Books, 2005), 28.

3. Guilain Denoeux, "The Forgotten Swamp: Navigating Political Islam," *Middle East Policy* 9, no. 2 (2002): 61

4. For a discussion regarding inventing tradition, see the collection of essays in Eric Hobsbawm and Terence Ranger, eds., *The Invention of Tradition* (New York: Cambridge University Press, 1983).

5. Patricia Crone, *God's Rule: Government and Islam* (New York: Columbia University Press, 2004), 318.

6. The consensus in the majority branch of Sunni Islam over the theory of the four caliphs evolved over the first couple of centuries of Islam. Early on, there was a great deal of contention over the respective claims particularly of the third and fourth caliphs, Uthman and Ali. The minority Shiites do not accept the idea of the four righteously guided caliphs. For them the fourth caliph, Ali, should have succeeded the Prophet as the political head of the community but was denied the right to do so by the machinations of his rivals, especially Abu Bakr and Umar, who became the first and second caliphs, respectively. Patricia Crone (*God's Rule*, 135) dates the consensus among the majority Sunnis that the first four caliphs were all "righteously guided" to the ninth century CE.

7. L. Carl Brown, *Religion and State: The Muslim Approach to Politics* (New York: Columbia University Press, 2000), 50.

8. For a discussion of Kharijites, Ismailis, and other smalls sects of Islam, see Crone, *God's Rule*, especially chaps. 5, 9, and 15.

9. For a discussion of Imami, or Twelver Shiite, beliefs, see ibid., chap. 10.

10. For a discussion of "hydraulic society" and its implications for imperial rule in the classical age of Islam, see L. Brown, *Religion and State,* 64–67.

11. Quran 4:59.

12. L. Brown, *Religion and State,* 54.

13. Crone, *God's Rule,* 21–22.

14. For a discussion of Al-Ghazali's innovative political theories, see ibid., 243–49.

15. Albert Hourani, *Arabic Thought in the Liberal Age, 1798–1939* (New York: Cambridge University Press, 1983), 19 (the quote is from Ibn Taymiyya).

16. Ibid., 148.

17. Malcolm H. Kerr, *Islamic Reform: The Political and Legal Theories of Muhammad 'Abduh and Rashid Rida* (Berkeley: University of California Press, 1966), 155.

18. H. A. R. Gibb, *Modern Trends in Islam* (Chicago: University of Chicago Press, 1947), 34.

19. Rudolph Peters, who has done extensive work on the subject of jihad, explains: "[T]o the best of my knowledge the word *watan* [homeland] was first used in combination with jihad during the 'Urabi revolt [in the 1880s in Egypt]. Many preachers that backed 'Urabi's cause, coupled the concept of defence of the fatherland with that of defence of religion" (*Islam and Colonialism: The Doctrine of Jihad in Modern History* [New York: Mouton, 1979], 196 n. 72).

20. Ibid., 152.

21. Robert W. Hefner, "Introduction: Modernity and the Remaking of Muslim Politics," in *Remaking Muslim Politics: Pluralism, Contestation, Democratization,* ed. Robert W. Hefner (Princeton: Princeton University Press, 2005), 23.

22. Fouad Ajami, *The Arab Predicament,* updated ed. (New York: Cambridge University Press, 1992), 242.

23. L. Brown, *Religion and State,* especially chaps. 3–7.

24. Mohammed Ayoob, "Turkey's Multiple Paradoxes," *Orbis* 48, no. 3 (2004): 457.

25. For a discussion of the rise and decline of the Mughal Empire in India, see John F. Richards, *The Mughal Empire* (Cambridge: Cambridge University Press, 1996).

26. John S. Habib, *Ibn Saud's Warriors of Islam: The Ikhwan of Najd and Their Role in the Creation of the Saudi Kingdom, 1910–1930* (Leiden: E. J. Brill, 1978).

27. The term *Islamdom,* analogous to the term *Christendom,* was introduced by the late Marshall G. S. Hodgson to describe predominantly Muslim societies. It helps mitigate the confusion that usually arises when, as is common in Western writings, "Islam" is juxtaposed against Christendom or the West or Europe. Hodgson explained: "'Islamdom' . . . is the society in which the Muslims and their faith are recognized as prevalent and socially dominant, in one sense or another—a society in which, of course, non-Muslims have always formed an integral, if subordinate, element, as have Jews in Christendom. It does not refer to an area as such, but to *a complex of social relations,* which, to be sure, is territorially more or less well-defined" (*The Venture of Islam,* vol. 1, *The Classical Age of Islam* [Chicago: University of Chicago Press, 1974], 58).

28. Wael Hallaq, *The Origins and Evolution of Islamic Law* (New York: Cambridge University Press, 2005), 204.

29. Graham Fuller, "The Future of Political Islam," *Foreign Affairs* 81, no. 2 (2002): 48–60.

30. Olivier Roy, *The Failure of Political Islam* (Cambridge, MA: Harvard University Press, 1996), vii.

31. Dale F. Eickelman and James Piscatori, *Muslim Politics* (Princeton: Princeton University Press, 1996), 4.

32. Adeed Dawisha, *Arab Nationalism in the Twentieth Century: From Triumph to Despair* (Princeton: Princeton University Press, 2002); Malik Mufti, *Sovereign Creations: Pan-Arabism and Political Order in Syria and Iraq* (Ithaca: Cornell University Press, 1996).

33. For an analysis of the process of state building in the postcolonial world, including its Muslim components, see Mohammed Ayoob, *The Third World Security Predicament: State Making, Regional Conflict, and the International System* (Boulder: Lynne Rienner, 1995), chap. 2.

34. Fawaz Gerges, *The Far Enemy: Why Jihad Went Global* (New York: Cambridge University Press, 2005).

35. See Carrie Rosefksy Wickham, *Mobilizing Islam: Religion, Activism, and Political Change in Egypt* (New York: Columbia University Press, 2002); Vali Nasr, *The Vanguard of the Islamic Revolution: The Jama'at-I-Islami of Pakistan* (Berkeley: University of California Press, 1994).

36. Gerges, *Far Enemy.*

37. Judith Palmer Harik, *Hezbollah: The Changing Face of Terrorism* (New York: I. B. Tauris, 2004).

38. Khalil Shikaki, "Palestinians Divided," *Foreign Affairs* 81, no. 1 (2002): 89–105.

39. Two Israeli analysts argue: "A close scrutiny of Hamas's roots and its record . . . reveals that . . . it is essentially a social movement . . . Hamas has directed its energies and resources primarily toward providing services to the community, especially responding to its immediate hardships and concerns . . . Hamas is deeply rooted in the Palestinian society . . . and thus is aware of the society's anxieties, sharing its concerns, expressing its aspirations, and tending to its needs and difficulties" (Shaul Mishal and Avraham Sela, *The Palestinian Hamas* [New York: Columbia University Press, 2000], vii).

40. For al-Qaeda, see Jason Burke, *Al-Qaeda: Casting a Shadow of Terror* (New York: I. B. Tauris, 2004); for Jemaah Islamiyah, see Barton, *Jemaah Islamiyah.*

41. Sami Zubaida, "Islam and Nationalism: Continuities and Contradictions," *Nations and Nationalism* 10, no. 4 (2004): 407–20.

42. International Crisis Group, *Understanding Islamism,* Middle East/North Africa Report No. 37, March 2005, 18.

43. Augustus Richard Norton, "Thwarted Politics: The Case of Egypt's Hizb Al-Wasat," in *Remaking Muslim Politics: Pluralism, Contestation, Democratization,* ed. Robert W. Hefner (Princeton: Princeton University Press, 2005), 133–60.

CHAPTER 2

1. See, for example, Bernard Lewis, "Roots of Muslim Rage," *Atlantic Monthly* 266, no. 3 (1990): 47–60; Samuel Huntington, *The Clash of Civilizations and the Remaking of World Order* (New York: Simon and Schuster, 1996).

2. For an insightful discussion of their arguments justifying the killing of civilians, see Quintan Wiktorowicz, "A Genealogy of Radical Islam," *Studies in Conflict and Terrorism* 28, no. 2 (2005): 86–92.

3. Hefner, "Introduction," 6.

4. Hamid Enayat, *Modern Islamic Political Thought* (Austin: University of Texas Press, 1982), 162.

5. Nikki Keddie, *Modern Iran: Roots and Results of Revolution* (New Haven: Yale University Press, 2003), 146.

6. L. Brown, *Religion and State*, 164.

7. Philip Kennicott, "The Religious Face of Iraq," *Washington Post,* February 18, 2005.

8. Crone, *God's Rule*, 220.

9. For a convincing argument that this has been the case, see Muhammad Qasim Zaman, "Pluralism, Democracy, and the 'Ulama," in *Remaking Muslim Politics: Pluralism, Contestation, Democratization,* ed. Robert W. Hefner (Princeton: Princeton University Press, 2005), 60–86.

10. For commonalities between the Christian Reformation and the proto-Reformation in Islam, see L. Brown, *Religion and State*, 136–39.

11. For details of this argument, see Carl W. Ernst, *Following Muhammad: Rethinking Islam in the Contemporary World* (Chapel Hill: University of North Carolina Press, 2003), 66–67; Richard W. Bulliet, "The Crisis within Islam," *Wilson Quarterly* 26, no. 1 (2002): 11–19.

12. Saeed Abdullah, "The Official Ulama and the Religious Legitimacy of the Modern Nation State," in *Islam and Political Legitimacy*, ed. Shahram Akbarzadeh and Abdullah Saeed (New York: Routledge Curzon, 2003), 14–15.

13. Seyyed Vali Reza Nasr, "Mawdudi and the Jamat-I-Islami," in *Pioneers of Islamic Revival*, ed. Ali Rahnema (London: Zed Books, 1994), 105.

14. Charles Tripp, "Sayyid Qutb: The Political Vision," in *Pioneers of Islamic Revival,* ed. Ali Rahnema (London: Zed Books, 1994), 178.

15. Incidentally, the same is true of Osama bin Laden, who studied management and economics, and of his deputy, Ayman al-Zawahiri, who was trained as a physician.

16. For analyses of Sayyid Qutb's ideas, see Yvonne Haddad, "Sayyid Qutb: Ideologue of Islamic Revival," in *Voices of Resurgent Islam,* ed. John L. Esposito (New York: Oxford University Press, 1983), 67–98; Tripp, "Sayyid Qutb."

17. Crone, *God's Rule*, 386.

18. For Saudi Arabia, see Gilles Kepel, *The War for Muslim Minds: Islam and the West* (Cambridge, MA: Belknap, 2004), chap.5; for Pakistan, see Vali Nasr, "Military Rule, Islamism, and Democracy in Pakistan," *Middle East Journal* 58, no. 2 (2004): 195–209.

19. See Daniel Brumberg, *Reinventing Khomeini: The Struggle for Reform in Iran* (Chicago: University of Chicago Press, 2001).

20. Keddie, *Modern Iran,* chaps. 9–10.

21. See Muhammad Qasim Zaman, *The Ulama in Contemporary Islam: Custodians of Change* (Princeton: Princeton University Press, 2002).

22. The phrase "new religious intellectuals" is borrowed from Eickelman and Piscatori, *Muslim Politics,* 44.

23. L. Brown, *Religion and State,* 112.

24. This was argued eloquently two decades ago in James Piscatori, *Islam in a World of Nation-States* (New York: Cambridge University Press, 1986).

25. Mark Sedgwick, "Is There a Church in Islam?" *ISIM Newsletter,* December 2003, 41. The International Institute for the Study of Islam in the Modern World (ISIM) is situated in Leiden in the Netherlands.

26. Daniel Brown, *Rethinking Tradition in Modern Islamic Thought* (New York: Cambridge University Press, 1999), 112.

27. See Wickham, *Mobilizing Islam,* on Egypt; Nasr, *Vanguard of the Islamic Revolution,* on Pakistan.

28. Roy, *Failure of Political Islam,* 26.

29. Mohammed Ayoob, "The Future of Political Islam: The Importance of External Variables," *International Affairs* 81, no. 5 (2005): 951–61.

30. Reuel Marc Gerecht, *The Islamic Paradox: Shiite Clerics, Sunni Fundamentalists, and the Coming of Arab Democracy* (Washington, DC: AEI Press, 2004).

31. International Crisis Group, *Understanding Islamism,* 6–7.

32. Wiktorowicz, "Genealogy of Radical Islam," 94.

33. For the impact of the Internet on Islamist activities, see Gary R. Bunt, *Islam in the Digital Age: E-Jihad, Online Fatwas, and Cyber Islamic Environments* (London: Pluto, 2003).

34. The phrase "network of networks" is borrowed from Burke, *Al-Qaeda,* 16.

35. Kepel, *War for Muslim Minds,* 6, 112.

36. Mahmood Mamdani, *Good Muslim, Bad Muslim* (New York: Pantheon Books, 2004).

37. Hourani, *Arabic Thought in the Liberal Age,* 130.

38. L. Brown, *Religion and State,* 95.

39. Christian W. Troll, *Sayyid Ahmad Khan: A Reinterpretation of Muslim Theology* (New Delhi: Vikas, 1978).

40. Knut S. Vickor, "The Development of Ijtihad and Islamic Reform, 1750–1850" (paper presented at the Third Nordic Conference on Middle Eastern Studies, Joensuu, Finland, June 19—-22, 1995).

41. Suha Taji-Farouki, introduction to *Modern Muslim Intellectuals and the Qu'ran,* ed. Suha Taji-Farouki (New York: Oxford University Press, 2004), 2. For selections of writings of some of the reformist scholars mentioned in text, see Charles Kurzman, *Liberal Islam: A Source Book* (New York: Oxford University Press, 1998).

42. Daniel Brumberg, "Islam Is Not the Solution (or the Problem)," *Washington Quarterly* 29, no. 1 (2005): 100–101.

43. For Fazlur Rahman's ideas, see his *Revival and Reform in Islam: A Study of Islamic Fundamentalism,* ed. Ebrahim Moosa (Oxford: Oneworld Publications, 1999). For a study of Nurcholish Madjid's ideas, see Greg Barton, *Liberal Islamic Ideas: A Study of the Writing of Nurcholish Madjid* (Jakarta: Pustaka Antara/Paramadina/Yayasan Adikarya IKAPI, 1999); Anthony H. Johns and Abdullah Saeed, "Nurcholish Madjid and the Interpretation of the Qur'an: Religious Pluralism and Tolerance," in *Modern Muslim Intellectuals and the Qu'ran,* ed. Suha Taji-Farouki (New York: Oxford University Press, 2004), 67–96.

44. For Tariq Ramadan's ideas, see his *Western Muslims and the Future of Islam* (New York: Oxford University Press, 2003).

45. Peter Mandaville, "Sufis and Salafis: The Political Discourse of Transnational

Islam," in *Remaking Muslim Politics: Pluralism, Contestation, Democratization,* ed. Robert W. Hefner (Princeton: Princeton University Press, 2005), 320.

CHAPTER 3

1. Madawi Al-Rasheed, *A History of Saudi Arabia* (New York: Cambridge University Press, 2002), 1, 3.

2. Quoted in ibid., 17.

3. Natana J. Delong-Bas, *Wahhabi Islam: From Revival and Reform to Global Jihad* (New York: Oxford University Press, 2004), chap. 5.

4. Hamid Algar, *Wahhabism: A Critical Essay* (Oneonta, NY: Islamic Publications International, 2002).

5. Michael Cook, *Commanding Right and Forbidding Wrong in Islamic Thought* (New York: Cambridge University Press, 2000), 174–75.

6. For details of the ebb and flow of Saudi power during the eighteenth and nineteenth centuries, see Alexei Vassiliev, *The History of Saudi Arabia* (New York: New York University Press, 2000).

7. According to John S. Habib, the Ikhwan were "those Bedouins who accepted the fundamentals of orthodox Islam of the Hanbali school as preached by 'Abd-al-Wahhab which their fathers and forefathers had forgotten or had perverted, and who, through the persuasion of the religious missionaries and with the material assistance of Ibn Sa'ud, abandoned their nomadic life to live in the *hujar* which were built by him for them" (*Ibn Saud's Warriors of Islam: The Ikhwan of Najd and Their Role in the Creation of the Saudi Kingdom, 1910–1930* [Leiden: E. J. Brill, 1978], 16–17). A major grievance for the Ikhwan against Ibn Saud was that he allowed the use of "automobiles, telegraph, wireless, and telephones, all of which were Christian innovations, and inventions of the devil" (ibid., 122). One wonders if the contemporary Wahhabis and neo-Wahhabis would have been as successful in spreading their message as they have been without the use of such "inventions of the devil."

8. For British support to Ibn Saud's expansionist project and the suppression of the Ikhwan, see Joseph Kostiner, *The Making of Saudi Arabia, 1916–1936: From Chieftancy to Monarchical State* (New York: Oxford University Press, 1993).

9. Al-Rasheed, *History of Saudi Arabia,* 70.

10. For the Hijazi reaction to political marginalization, see Mai Yamani, *Cradle of Islam: The Hijaz and the Quest for an Arabian Identity* (London: I. B. Tauris, 2004). Yamani asserts that the "urban Hijazi elites have sought not only to preserve but also to accentuate a distinct cultural identity . . . that serves to bolster a sense of cultural superiority and to counter their political and economic subordination to the country's Najdi rulers" (12). For the plight of the Saudi Shia, see International Crisis Group, *The Shiite Question in Saudi Arabia,* Middle East Report No. 45, September 2005.

11. Al-Rasheed, *History of Saudi Arabia,* 68.

12. Ervand Abrahamian, *Iran between Two Revolutions* (Princeton: Princeton University Press, 1982), 41.

13. Nikki Keddie, "Religion and Irreligion in Early Iranian Nationalism," *Comparative Studies in Society and History* 4, no. 3 (1962): 290.

14. Abrahamian, *Iran between Two Revolutions,* 40.

15. The major exception to this rule occurred in the period between 1951 and 1953 when some senior clerics first supported Prime Minister Mossadeq against the shah but later backed off in fear of Communist and secularist influences in Mossadeq's government and contributed to its downfall. See Keddie, *Modern Iran,* 146.

16. For details, see Said Amir Arjomand, *The Turban for the Crown: The Islamic Revolution in Iran* (New York: Oxford University Press, 1988); Misagh Parsa, *Social Origins of the Iranian Revolution* (New Brunswick: Rutgers University Press, 1989).

17. There is not space enough in this chapter to go into the details of the causes and consequences of the Iranian revolution. Interested readers can find incisive analyses in books by Abrahmian, Keddie, Arjomand, and Parsa referenced in this chapter.

18. See Martin Wight, *Systems of States* (Leicester: Leicester University Press, 1977); Charles Tilly, *Coercion, Capital, and European States, AD 990–1990* (Cambridge: Blackwell, 1990); Hendrik Spruyt, *The Sovereign State and Its Competitors* (Princeton: Princeton University Press, 1994).

19. For details of this argument, see Ayoob, *Third World Security Predicament,* chap. 3.

20. The text of the Saudi Basic Law is available on the Internet at http://www .oefre.unibe.ch/law/icl/sa00000_.html.

21. International Crisis Group, *Saudi Arabia Backgrounder: Who Are the Islamists?* Middle East Report No. 31, September 2004, 4.

22. The tensions within Khomeini's ideas, the impact they had on the fashioning of the postrevolutionary system in Iran, and their continuing relevance to contemporary debates between reformists and hard-liners in Iran are discussed insightfully in Brumberg, *Reinventing Khomeini.*

23. For a concise analysis of this revolution, see A. K. S. Lambton, "The Persian Constitutional Revolution of 1905–6," in *Revolution in the Middle East, and Other Case Studies,* ed. P. J. Vatikiotis (London: Allen and Unwin, 1972), 173–82.

24. For details, see Abrahamian, *Iran between Two Revolutions.*

25. Ibid., 90.

26. For details, see the text of the constitution on the Internet at http://www.iranonline.com/iran/iran-info/Government/constitution-3.html.

27. International Crisis Group, *Iran: What Does Ahmadi-Nejad's Victory Mean?* Middle East Briefing No. 18, August 2005.

28. See http://www.iranonline.com/iran/iran-info/Government/constitution-6-2 .html.

29. Brumberg, *Reinventing Khomeini,* 140.

30. Ray Takeyh and Nikolas K. Gvosdev, "Pragmatism in the Midst of Iranian Turmoil," *Washington Quarterly* 27, no. 4 (2004): 33–56; see also Bahram Rajaee, "Deciphering Iran: The Political Evolution of the Islamic Republic and U.S. Foreign Policy after September 11," *Comparative Studies of South Asia* 24, no. 1 (2004): 159–72.

31. For two articles that unravel the complexities of Iranian politics, see Ali M. Ansari, "Continuous Regime Change from Within," *Washington Quarterly* 26, no. 4 (2003): 53–67; Mahmood Sariolghalam, "Understanding Iran: Getting Past Stereotypes and Mythology," *Washington Quarterly* 26, no. 4 (2003): 69–82.

32. See chapter 1.

33. For an eloquent case for a Hijazi identity that is very distinct from the Najdi/Saudi identity that dominates the Saudi landscape today, see Yamani, *Cradle of Islam.*

34. For a very thoughtful analysis of U.S.-Saudi relations and the role of religion in complicating this relationship, see Rachel Bronson, "Rethinking Religion: The Legacy of the U.S.-Saudi Relationship," *Washington Quarterly* 28, no. 4 (2005): 121–37.

35. Article 5 of the Iranian constitution states, "During the Occultation of the Wali al-Asr (may God hasten his reappearance), the wilayah and leadership of the Ummah devolve upon the just ['adil] and pious [muttaqi] faqih, who is fully aware of the circumstances of his age; courageous, resourceful, and possessed of administrative ability, he will assume the responsibilities of this office in accordance with Article 107" (http://www.iranonline.com/iran/iran-info/Government/constitution-1.html). Articles 107–12 lay out the qualifications, functions, and responsibilities of the supreme jurist and the Council of the Guardian (http://www.iranonline.com/iran/iran-info/Government/constitution-8.html).

36. Ruhollah Khomeini, *Islamic Government,* trans. Joint Publications Research Service (New York: Manor Books, 1979); *Islam and Revolution: Writings and Declarations of Imam Khomeini,* trans. Hamid Algar (Berkeley: Mizan, 1981).

37. Hamid Enayat, "Khumayni's Concept of the 'Guardianship of the Jurisconsult,'" in *Islam in the Political Process,* ed. James P. Piscatori (New York: Cambridge University Press, 1983), 174.

38. See H. E. Chehabi, "Religion and Politics in Iran," *Daedalus* 120, no. 3 (1991): 69–91.

39. Grand Ayatollah Hossein Ali Montazeri, at one time anointed to succeed Ayatollah Khomeini as the supreme jurist but removed from his position because of his differences with Khomeini regarding the role of the clergy in governance, is the most vocal exponent of such views. He has even gone to the extent of calling the present system in Iran "a monarchical setup," an obvious reference to the powers of the supreme jurist. For more on Montazeri's views, see Christopher de Bellaigue, "Who Rules Iran?" *New York Review of Books* 49, no. 11 (2002): 17–19.

40. Rajaee, "Deciphering Iran," 161.

41. Enayat, "Khumayni's Concept of the 'Guardianship of the Jurisconsult,'" 174.

42. The late Grand Ayatollah Mohammed Kazem Shariatmadari, then under house arrest for opposing Khomeini's ideas about how Iran ought to be governed, said as much to me in an interview in Qom in March 1981, just two years after the revolution. According to him, Khomeini's ideas were more akin to the Sunni concept of the caliphate, with which, he thought, the *vilayat-i faqih* had substantial similarities, than to the Shia concept of the imamate, which was based on extraordinary spiritual attributes rather than temporal power. He more than implied that Khomeini was more a Sunni than a Shia, a damning indictment of the supreme leader of the (Shia) Islamic revolution of Iran, who had declared himself the *rahbar* (supreme leader) under the postrevolution constitution. Ayatollah Shariatmadari emphasized his point by telling me, "He [Khomeini] is closer to you [a Sunni] than he is to me [a Shia]."

43. Richard Dekmejian, "The Liberal Impulse in Saudi Arabia," *Middle East Journal* 57, no. 3 (2003): 400–413.

44. Gwenn Okruhlik, "Empowering Civility through Nationalism: Reformist Islam and Belonging in Saudi Arabia," in *Remaking Muslim Politics: Pluralism, Contestation, Democratization,* ed. Robert W. Hefner (Princeton: Princeton University Press, 2005), 209.

45. For the most comprehensive analysis of the religious-based opposition to the Saudi regime, see Mamoun Fandy, *Saudi Arabia and the Politics of Dissent* (New York: Palgrave Macmillan, 1999).

46. Eric Rouleau, "Trouble in the Kingdom," *Foreign Affairs* 81, no. 4 (2002): 79.

47. For analyses of Sayyid Qutb's ideas, see Yvonne Haddad, "Sayyid Qutb: Ideologue of Islamic Revival," in *Voices of Resurgent Islam,* ed. John L. Esposito (New York: Oxford University Press, 1983), 67–98; Tripp, "Sayyid Qutb."

48. Al-Rasheed, *History of Saudi Arabia,* 154.

49. For details of the *sahwa,* their views, and differences among them, see International Crisis Group, *Saudi Arabia Backgrounder.*

50. Bronson, "Rethinking Religion," 127.

51. Toby Craig Jones, "The Clerics, the Sahwa, and the Saudi State," *Strategic Insights* 4, no. 3 (2005), http://www.ccc.nps.navy.mil/si/2005/Mar/jonesMar05.pdf.

52. International Crisis Group, *Saudi Arabia Backgrounder,* 7.

53. Mohammad Khatami, *Islam, Liberty, and Development* (Binghamton: Global Academic Publishing, 1998).

54. Christopher de Bellaigue, "New Man in Iran," *New York Review of Books* 52, no. 13 (2005): 22.

55. For Abdolkarim Soroush's ideas, see his *Reason, Freedom, and Democracy in Islam: Essential Writings of Abdolkarim Soroush,* Ed. and trans. Mahmoud Sadri and Ahmad Sadri (New York: Oxford University Press, 2000); for Akbar Ganji, see Azar Nafisi, "The Voice of Akbar Ganji," *Journal of Democracy* 16, no. 4 (2005): 35–37.

56. Mahmoud Sadri and Ahmad Sadri, *Reason, Freedom, and Democracy in Islam: Essential Writings of Abdolkarim Soroush* (New York: Oxford University Press, 2000), xviii.

57. Rajaee, "Deciphering Iran," 161.

58. Ibid., 159–60.

59. John R. Bradley, "Al Qaeda and the House of Saud: Eternal Enemies or Secret Bedfellows?" *Washington Quarterly* 28, no. 4 (2005): 150.

60. Gawdat Bahgat, "The War on Terrorism: The Mujahedeen E-Khalk Saga," *Studies in Conflict and Terrorism* 27, no. 5 (2004): 377–85.

61. For external factors aiding the creation of Saudi Arabia, see Kostiner, *Making of Saudi Arabia.*

CHAPTER 4

1. For details of the struggle for the political soul of Pakistan during its formative years, see Khalid B. Sayeed, *The Political System of Pakistan* (Boston: Houghton Mifflin, 1967).

2. Richard P. Mitchell, *The Society of the Muslim Brothers* (New York: Oxford University Press, 1969), 33.

3. Nasr, *Vanguard of the Islamic Revolution,* 7, 21.

4. L. Brown, *Religion and State,* 147–48.

5. Mitchell, *Society of the Muslim Brothers,* 232.

6. Seyyed Vali Reza Nasr, *Mawdudi and the Making of Islamic Revivalism* (New York: Oxford University Press, 1996), 59.

7. Charles J. Adams, "Mawdudi and the Islamic State," in *Voices of Resurgent Islam,* ed. John L. Esposito (New York: Oxford University Press, 1983), 116.

8. Ibid., 119.

9. See discussion about Iran in chapter 3.

10. Nasr, *Mawdudi and the Making of Islamic Revivalism,* 83.

11. Ibid., 60.

12. Nasr, *Vanguard of the Islamic Revolution,* 8–9.

13. Nasr, *Mawdudi and the Making of Islamic Revivalism,* 77.

14. Nasr, *Vanguard of the Islamic Revolution,* 120.

15. Nasr, *Mawdudi and the Making of Islamic Revivalism,* 74.

16. L. Brown, *Religion and State,* 146.

17. Mitchell, *Society of the Muslim Brothers,* 103.

18. Ibid., 235.

19. Ibid., 246–47.

20. Ibid., 237.

21. For Mawdudi's views on the *ulama,* see Nasr, *Mawdudi and the Making of Islamic Revivalism,* 110–22.

22. See chapter 2.

23. Mitchell, *Society of the Muslim Brothers,* 211–12.

24. L. Brown, *Religion and State,* 156.

25. Ibid.

26. Nasr, *Mawdudi and the Making of Islamic Revivalism,* 68.

27. For details of Qutb's ideas and comparisons with the ideas of Mawdudi, see Gilles Kepel, *The Prophet and the Pharaoh: Muslim Extremism in Egypt* (London: Saqi Books, 1985); Ahmad S. Moussalli, *Radical Islamic Fundamentalism: The Ideological and Political Discourse of Sayyid Qutb* (Beirut: University of Beirut, 1992).

28. Lisa Anderson, "Fulfilling Prophecies: State Policy and Islamist Radicalism," in *Political Islam: Revolution, Radicalism, or Reform?* ed. John L. Esposito (Boulder: Lynne Rienner, 1997), 18–19.

29. Maye Kassem, *Egyptian Politics: The Dynamics of Authoritarian Rule* (Boulder: Lynne Rienner, 2004), 137–38.

30. Nasr, *Vanguard of the Islamic Revolution,* 148.

31. For a detailed account of the relationship between the MB and the Mubarak regime and of their attempts to use each other to attain greater legitimacy, see Hesham Al-Awadi, *In Pursuit of Legitimacy: The Muslim Brothers and Mubarak, 1982–2000* (New York: Tauris Academic Studies, 2000); "Mubarak and the Islamists: Why Did the 'Honeymoon' End?" *Middle East Journal* 59, no. 1 (2005): 62–80. See also Wickham, *Mobilizing Islam.*

32. Michael Slackman, "Egyptians Rue Election Day Gone Awry," *New York Times,* December 8, 2005.

33. Nasr, *Vanguard of the Islamic Revolution,* 148–49.

34. Ibid., 149.

35. Ibid., 195.

36. Kepel, *The Prophet and the Pharaoh,* 62.

37. Ibid., 63.

38. Carrie Rosefsky Wickham, "The Path to Moderation: Strategy and Learning in the Formation of Egypt's Wasat Party," *Comparative Politics* 36, no. 2 (2004): 206.

39. For an incisive analysis of the emergence and importance of the centrist tendency represented by al-Wasat, see ibid.

40. Norton, "Thwarted Politics," 157–58.

41. For details of the MB leadership's criticism of the al-Wasat faction, see ibid., 151–54.

42. The MB had put up only 130 candidates for the 454-member National Assembly, so as not to alarm both Egyptians and outsiders that it was bent on capturing power by itself.

43. Khairat el-Shatir, "No Need to be Afraid of Us," *Guardian,* November 23, 2005.

44. Issandr El Amrani, "Controlled Reform in Egypt: Neither Reformist nor Controlled," *Middle East Report Online,* 2005, http://www.merip.org/mero/mero 121505.html.

45. International Crisis Group, *Islamism in North Africa II: Egypt's Opportunity,* Middle East/North Africa Briefing No. 13, April 2004, 2–3.

46. For a discussion of the Islamization of Pashtun nationalism, see Nasr, "Military Rule," 205.

47. For details of Pakistan's election results, see the statistical data compiled by the Election Commission of Pakistan, accessible on the Internet at http://www.ecp.gov.pk/content/docs/STATS.pdf.

48. For an incisive analysis of these interrelated phenomena, see Bassma Kodmani, *The Dangers of Political Exclusion: Egypt's Islamist Problem,* Carnegie Paper No. 63 (Washington, DC: Carnegie Endowment for International Peace, 2005).

49. Kassem, *Egyptian Politics,* 145

50. Ibid., 156.

51. For details, see Gerges, *Far Enemy.*

52. For details, see Hassan Abbas, *Pakistan's Drift into Extremism: Allah, the Army, and America's War on Terror* (Armonk, NY: M. E. Sharpe, 2005).

53. Aqil Shah, "Pakistan's 'Armored' Democracy," *Journal of Democracy* 14, no. 4 (2003): 33

54. For a succinct but incisive discussion of the relationship between the military and Islamist groups, both moderate and extremist, see Frederic Grare, *Pakistan: The Myth of an Islamist Peril,* Policy Brief No. 45 (Washington, DC: Carnegie Endowment for International Peace, 2006). See also Stephen Philip Cohen, "The Jihadist Threat to Pakistan," *Washington Quarterly* 26, no. 3 (2003): 7–25.

55. Nasr, "Military Rule," 209.

CHAPTER 5

1. For the impact of liberal ideas on the Muslim world, especially the Arab/Muslim world, see Hourani's classical study *Arabic Thought in the Liberal Age.*

2. For details, see Mohammed Ayoob, "The Muslim World's Poor Record of Modernization and Democratization: The Interplay of External and Internal Factors," in *Modernization, Democracy, and Islam,* ed. Shireen T. Hunter and Huma Malik (Westport: Praeger; Washington, DC: Center for Strategic and International Studies, 2005).

3. Charles Tilly, "Reflections on the History of European State-Making," in *The Formation of National States in Western Europe,* ed. Charles Tilly (Princeton: Princeton University Press, 1975), 3–83.

4. Cornelia Navari, "The Origins of the Nation-State," in *The Nation-State: The Formation of Modern Politics,* ed. Leonard Tivey (Oxford: Martin Robertson, 1981), 34.

5. Talal Asad, "Religion, Nation-State, Secularism," in *Nation and Religion: Perspectives on Europe and Asia,* ed. Peter van der Veer and Hartmut Lehmann (Princeton: Princeton University Press, 1999), 178, 184.

6. Anthony W. Marx, "The Nation-State and Its Exclusions," *Political Science Quarterly* 117, no. 1 (2002): 116.

7. For details of this argument, see Ayoob, *Third World Security Predicament.*

8. Robert W. Hefner, *Civil Islam: Muslims and Democratization in Indonesia* (Princeton: Princeton University Press, 2000), 12.

9. Vali Nasr, "The Rise Of 'Muslim Democracy,'" *Journal of Democracy* 16, no. 2 (2005): 15.

10. Through the "soft coup," the military succeeded in ousting the coalition government, of which the Islamist Refah Party was the senior partner, by sending clear signals to Turkey's political actors that it would no longer tolerate a civilian government composed of Refah members. The coup is called "soft" because the political class caved in and did the military's bidding without the latter having had to take recourse to its "hard" power, as it had done in 1960 and 1980. The 1997 coup was similar to the 1971 coup in that it was a coup by memorandum, leading to the formation of an interim government from within the parliament rather than a direct military takeover. In 1971, Prime Minister Demirel resigned upon receiving a letter of memorandum signed by the chief of staff; in 1997, Prime Minister Erbakan did the same when faced with pressure from the military top brass. For the "soft coup" of 1997, see Metin Heper and Aylin Guney, "The Military and the Consolidation of Democracy: The Recent Turkish Experience," *Armed Forces and Society* 26, no. 4 (2000): 635–57.

11. Mohammed Ayoob, "Who's Afraid of a Head Scarf?" YaleGlobal, May 10, 2007, http://yaleglobal.yale.edu/display.article?id_9165. See also Gamze Cavdar, "Behind Turkey's Presidential Battle," *Middle East Report Online,* May 7, 2007, http://www.merip.org/mero/mero050707.html.

12. Bahtiar Effendy, *Islam and the State in Indonesia* (Athens: Ohio University Press, 2003).

13. Barton, *Jemaah Islamiyah,* 45.

14. For the importance of the 2002 elections, see Soli Ozel, "Turkey at the Polls: After the Tsunami," *Journal of Democracy* 14, no. 2 (2003): 80–94.

15. Omer Taspinar explains: "Kemalism refers to the sacrosanct character of the Turkish republic as a unitary and secular nation-state. Therefore, any deviation from the Turkish character of the nation-state and the secular framework of the republic presents a challenge to Kemalist identity. It is primarily within Turkey's military circles that this Kemalist identity and reaction is most discernible" (*Kurdish Nationalism and Political Islam in Turkey: Kemalist Identity in Transition* [New York: Routledge, 2005], x).

16. Brumberg, "Islam Is Not the Solution," 109.

17. Yesim Arat, *Rethinking Islam and Liberal Democracy: Islamist Women in Turkish Politics* (New York: State University of New York Press, 2005), 4.

18. See Effendy, *Islam and the State in Indonesia,* 73.

19. Clifford Geertz, *Islam Observed: Religious Development in Morocco and Indonesia* (Chicago: University of Chicago Press, 1971), 73.

20. For details, see Effendy, *Islam and the State in Indonesia* ; B. J. Boland, *The Struggle of Islam in Modern Indonesia* (The Hague: Martinus Nijhoff, 1982).

21. Ziya Onis, "The Political Economy of Islam and Democracy in Turkey: From the Welfare Party to the AKP," in *Democratization and Development: New Political Strategies for the Middle East,* ed. Dietrich Jung (New York: Palgrave Macmillan, 2006), 103.

22. For the role of the provincial bourgeoisie in increasing the salience of Islam in Turkish social and political life in recent decades, see M. Hakan Yavuz, "The Role of the New Bourgeoisie in the Transformation of the Turkish Islamic Movement," in *The Emergence of a New Turkey: Democracy and the AK Parti,* ed. M. Hakan Yavuz (Salt Lake City: University of Utah Press, 2006), 1–19.

23. Taspinar, *Kurdish Nationalism and Political Islam,* 115

24. Hefner, *Civil Islam,* 39.

25. Boland, *Struggle of Islam,* 126.

26. For details, see ibid.

27. Hefner, *Civil Islam,* 58–59.

28. Ibid., 59. The Soeharto regime's experience with Islam has an uncanny resemblance to the experience of the Egyptian regime under Sadat and Mubarak. Promoting piety and Islamic social mores while restricting Islamist political participation helps Islamize society in ways that, in the long run, are likely to redound to the benefit of Islamist political movements.

29. Ibid., 97.

30. Jenny B. White, "The End of Islamism? Turkey's Muslimhood Model," in *Remaking Muslim Politics: Pluralism, Contestation, Democratization,* ed. Robert W. Hefner (Princeton: Princeton University Press, 2004), 87–111.

31. For the Turkish case, see Ihsan D. Dagi, "Transformation of Islamic Political Identity in Turkey: Rethinking the West and Westernization," *Turkish Studies* 6, no. 1 (2005): 21–37. For the Indonesian case, see Hefner, *Civil Islam.*

32. For details, see Yavuz, "Role of the New Bourgeoisie"; Onis, "Political Economy of Islam."

33. Hasan Kosebalaban, "The Impact of Globalization on Islamic Political Identity," *World Affairs* 168, no. 1 (2005): 27–37.

34. For the NSC and the military's role in politics, see Heper and Guney, "The Military and the Consolidation of Democracy."

35. For details of the Indonesian military's role in politics before the transition to democracy, see Harold Crouch, *The Army and Politics in Indonesia* (Ithaca: Cornell University Press, 1988); Terence Lee, "The Nature and Future of Civil-Military Relations in Indonesia," *Asian Survey* 40, no. 4 (2000): 692–706.

36. For a discussion of "authoritarian secularism" in the case of Turkey, see Omer Taspinar, *An Uneven Fit? The "Turkish Model" and the Arab World*, U.S. Relations with the Islamic World, Analysis Paper No. 5 (Washington, DC: Brookings Institution, 2003).

37. Taspinar, *Kurdish Nationalism and Political Islam*, 115.

38. Ibid., 138.

39. A recent report explains: "[R]ogue members of the security forces . . . secretly armed the fighters of the 'Kurdish Hizbullah' movement throughout the separatist war of the 1990s. Kurdish Hizbullah—which has no links to its Lebanese namesake—was once considered useful to Turkey's authorities because it fought the PKK. When the PKK called off its insurgency after the capture of its leader, Abdullah Ocalan, in 1999, security forces raided Hizbullah cells across the country and killed the group's leader in an Istanbul shootout" (Turkey's Kurds: "The Real Challenge to Secular Turkey," *Economist*, September 2, 2006, 33–34).

40. R. William Liddle and Saiful Mujani, "Indonesia in 2005: A New Multiparty Presidential Democracy," *Asian Survey* 46, no. 1 (2006): 132–39.

41. Nasr, "Rise Of 'Muslim Democracy,'" 18.

42. For an incisive discussion of these issues, see Onis, "Political Economy of Islam."

43. Yavuz, "Role of the New Bourgeoisie," 2–3.

44. White, "End of Islamism?" 109.

45. Anies Rasyid Baswedan, "Political Islam in Indonesia: Present and Future Trajectory," *Asian Survey* 44, no. 5 (2004): 674–75, 78.

46. Muhammad Qodari, "Indonesia's Quest for Accountable Governance," *Journal of Democracy* 16, no. 2 (2005): 80.

47. Ibid., 79.

48. For a comprehensive account of *Jemaah Islamiyah*, see Barton, *Jemaah Islamiyah*.

CHAPTER 6

1. David Rudge, "Hizbullah Defiant in Face of US Criticism," *Jerusalem Post*, September 10, 2002.

2. For a comparison of Islamist national resistance movements and transnational Islamist movements, such as al-Qaeda, see Anders Strindberg and Mats Warn, "Realities of Resistance: Hizballah, the Palestinian Rejectionists, and Al-Qa'ida Compared," *Journal of Palestine Studies* 34, no. 3 (2005): 23–41.

3. In the first chapter of this book, I elaborated on the point that resistance against non-Muslim foreign domination and encroachment, whether direct or indirect, became the paradigmatic jihad of modern times as a result of the colonial experience. For details, see Peters, *Islam and Colonialism*.

4. For example, see Article 15 of the Hamas Charter, which states, "When an enemy usurps a Muslim land, then a jihad is an individual religious duty on every Muslim; and

in confronting the unlawful seizure of Palestine by the Jews, it is necessary to raise the banner of jihad." The charter is reproduced as document number 2 in the appendix of Khaled Hroub, *Hamas: Political Thought and Practice* (Washington, DC: Institute for Palestine Studies, 2000); the quote can be found on p. 276.

5. Robert Pape, "What We Still Don't Understand about Hizbollah," *Observer* (London), August 6, 2006, http://www.guardian.co.uk/commentisfree/story/0,,1838214,00.html.

6. Francois Burgat, *Face to Face with Political Islam* (New York: I. B. Tauris, 2003), xiv.

7. For more on Musa al-Sadr, see Fouad Ajami, *The Vanished Imam: Musa Al Sadr and the Shia of Lebanon* (Reprint, Ithaca: Cornell University Press, 1992).

8. Naim Qassem, *Hizbullah: The Story from Within* (London: Saqi Books, 2005).

9. Ibid., 56–57.

10. Augustus Richard Norton, "Hizballah: From Radicalism to Pragmatism?" *Middle East Policy* 5, no. 4 (1998): 152.

11. For details of Hamas's ideological origins, see Andrea Nusse, *Muslim Palestine: The Ideology of Hamas* (Abingdon, UK: Routledge Curzon, 2004).

12. Ziad Abu-Amr, *Islamic Fundamentalism in the West Bank and Gaza: Muslim Brotherhood and Islamic Jihad* (Bloomington: Indiana University Press, 1994), xiii–xiv.

13. Nusse, *Muslim Palestine*, 2.

14. Quoted in ibid., 49.

15. Hroub, *Hamas*, 11. The continuities among various phases of Palestinian nationalism have been charted in Helga Baumgarten, "The Three Faces/Phases of Palestinian Nationalism, 1948–2005," *Journal of Palestine Studies* 34, no. 4 (2005): 25–48.

16. Hroub, *Hamas*, 45–48.

17. Ibid.

18. For a succinct account of Hizbullah's origins, see Lara Deeb, "Hizballah: A Primer," *Middle East Report Online*, 2006, http://www.merip.org/mero/mero073106.html.

19. Augustus Richard Norton, "Hizballah and the Israeli Withdrawal from Southern Lebanon," *Journal of Palestine Studies* 30, no. 1 (2000): 27.

20. Ibid., 26.

21. Nusse, *Muslim Palestine*, 16.

22. Harik, *Hezbollah*.

23. Deeb, "Hizballah."

24. Oussama Safa, "Getting to Arab Democracy: Lebanon Springs Forward," *Journal of Democracy* 17, no. 1 (2006): 28.

25. Ahmad Nizar Hamzeh, *In the Path of Hizbullah* (Syracuse: Syracuse University Press, 2004), 1.

26. "Letting Lebanon Burn," *Middle East Report Online*, 2006, http://www.merip.org/mero/mero072106.html.

27. Rami G. Khouri, "Now Comes the Next War," *Newsweek*, August 14, 2006, international edition, http://www.msnbc.msn.com/id/14207059.

28. Ibid.

29. Personal conversation between author and Hassan Ezzeddin, chief spokesman of Hizbullah and member of its Supreme Council, Beirut, August 2003.

30. Qassem, *Hizbullah,* 31.

31. Tamar Hausman, "U.S. Ambassador says 'Israel encouraged Islamists in bid to dampen Palestinian nationalism,'" *Ha'aretz,* December 21, 2001.

32. Hroub, *Hamas,* 253.

33. Ibid., 2.

34. Ibid., 44.

35. Hamas leaders, including Sheikh Yassin and Abdul Aziz al-Rantisi, both assassinated by Israel, had expressed these views since the 1990s. For details, see ibid., 73–86.

36. Mousa Abu Marzook, "What Hamas Is Seeking," *Washington Post,* January 31, 2006.

37. For an authoritative study of Palestinian public opinion that has come to this conclusion, see Khalil Shikaki, *Willing to Compromise: Palestinian Public Opinion and the Peace Process,* Special Report No. 158 (Washington, DC: United States Institute of Peace, 2006).

38. For example, see "Hamas 'Ready to Talk to Israel,'" interview of Khaled Meshaal, February 8, 2006, http://news.bbc.co.uk/2/hi/middle_east/4692114.stm; "Hamas Leader Sets Conditions for Truce," interview of Mahmooud al-Zahar, January 29, 2006, http://www.cnn.com/2006/WORLD/meast/01/29/hamas.interview (accessed March 6, 2006).

39. Mahmoud al-Zahar, "Hamas Leader Sets Conditions for Truce," January 29, 2006, http://www.cnn.com/2006/WORLD/meast/01/29/hamas.interview (accessed March 6, 2006).

40. Greg Myre, "Israel and Palestinians Reach Truce after Months of Fighting in Gaza," *New York Times,* November 26, 2006.

41. Craig S. Smith, "Despite Ties to Hamas, Militants Aren't Following Political Leaders," *New York Times,* July 21, 2006.

42. Tariq Ali, "A Protracted Colonial War," *Guardian,* July 20, 2006.

CHAPTER 7

1. Mandaville, "Sufis and Salafis," 321.

2. Gerges, *Far Enemy,* 3.

3. Kepel, *War for Muslim Minds,* chap. 3.

4. Bruce Lawrence, *Messages to the World: The Statements of Osama Bin Laden* (New York: Verso, 2005), 61.

5. Aziz Ahmad, "Sayyid Ahmad Khan, Jamal Al-Din Al-Afghani, and Muslim India," *Studia Islamica* 13 (1960): 55–78.

6. For a detailed study of al-Afghanis ideas and activities, see Nikki Keddie, *Sayyid Jamal Ad-Din Al-Afghani: A Political Biography* (Los Angeles: University of California Press, 1972).

7. Hourani, *Arabic Thought in the Liberal Age,* 116.

8. Gerges, *Far Enemy,* chap. 1.

9. For details, see Muhammad Khalid Masud, *Travellers in Faith: Studies of the Tab-*

lighi Jama'at as a Transnational Islamic Movement for Faith Renewal (Leiden: E. J. Brill, 2000); Yoginder Sikand, *The Origins and Development of the Tablighi Jamaat (1920–2000): A Cross-Country Comparative Study* (New Delhi: Orient Longman, 2002).

10. Barbara Metcalf, "Travelers' Tales in the Tablighi Jama'at," *Annals of the American Academy of Political and Social Science* 588, no. 1 (2003): 136–48.

11. For the Deoband movement and the origins of the Deobandi school, see Barbara Daly Metcalf, *Islamic Revival in British India: Deoband, 1860–1900* (New York: Oxford University Press, 2004).

12. Sayyid Athar Abbas Rizvi, *Shah Wali-Allah and His Times: A Study of Eighteenth Century Islam, Politics, and Society in India* (Canberra: Maarifat Publishing, 1980).

13. Bin Baaz's fatwa on the TJ is cited in Yoginder Sikand, "A Critique of the 'Tablighi-As-Terrorist Thesis,'" http://www.uvm.edu/~envprog/madrassah/TablighiCritique.htm (accessed December 2, 2006).

14. For example, see Yoginder S. Sikand, "The Origins and Growth of the Tablighi Jamaat in Britain," *Islam and Christian-Muslim Relations* 9, no. 2 (1998): 171–92.

15. Yoginder Sikand, "The Tablighi Jama'at and Politics: A Critical Reappraisal," *Muslim World* 96, no. 1 (2006): 175–95.

16. Metcalf, "Travelers' Tales in the Tablighi Jama'at," 146.

17. Alex Alexiev, "Tablighi Jamaat: Jihad's Stealthy Legions," *Middle East Quarterly* 12, no. 1 (2005), accessed at www.meforum.org/article/686.

18. Yoginder Sikand, "A Critique of the 'Tablighi-As-Terrorist Thesis,'" http://www.uvm.edu/~envprog/madrassah/TablighiCritique.htm (accessed December 2, 2006).

19. Suha Taji-Farouki, *A Fundamental Quest: Hizb Al-Tahrir and the Search for the Islamic Caliphate* (London: Grey Seal, 1996), 190.

20. Mandaville, "Sufis and Salafis," 311.

21. Zeyno Baran, "Fighting the War of Ideas," *Foreign Affairs* 84, no. 6 (2005): 72.

22. Ibid., 68.

23. Ibid., 69.

24. Zeyno Baran, *Hizb Ut-Tahrir: Islam's Political Insurgency* (Washington, DC: Nixon Center, 2004), 12–13.

25. International Crisis Group, *Radical Islam in Central Asia: Responding to Hizb Ut-Tahrir,* Asia Report No. 63, June 2003, 31.

26. Baran, *Hizb Ut-Tahrir,* 81.

27. Ahmed Rashid, *Jihad: The Rise of Militant Islam in Central Asia* (New Haven: Yale University Press, 2002).

28. Ibid., 115–16.

29. Ibid., 135.

30. International Crisis Group, *Radical Islam in Central Asia,* i.

31. Ibid., 33.

32. Gerges, *Far Enemy,* 3.

33. Ibid., 6.

34. Sayyid Qutb, *Milestones,* chap. 4, "Jihaad in the Cause of God," http://www.youngmuslims.ca/online_library/books/milestones/hold/chapter_4.asp

(accessed June 25, 2007). For an incisive analysis of Qutb's ideas, see Kepel, *The Prophet and the Pharaoh*, chap. 2.

35. Jonathan Randal, *Osama: The Making of a Terrorist* (New York: Alfred A. Knopf, 2004), 104–05.

36. Gerges, *Far Enemy*, 24.

37. Ibid., 160.

38. Ibid., 62–63.

39. For a polemical but nonetheless convincing analysis of the American contribution to the emergence of transnational jihadis from the killing fields of Afghanistan, see Mamdani, *Good Muslim, Bad Muslim.*

40. International Crisis Group, *Jemaah Islamiyah in Southeast Asia: Damaged but Still Dangerous*, Asia Report No. 63, August 2003.

41. For further details on *Jemaah Islamiyah* and its connections with al-Qaeda, see Zachary Abuza, *Militant Islam in Southeast Asia: Crucible of Terror* (Boulder: Lynne Rienner, 2003); Barton, *Jemaah Islamiyah.*

42. For details of ideological rethinking and strategic reformulation among transnational jihadis, see Thomas Hegghammer, "Global Jihadism after the Iraq War," *Middle East Journal* 60, no. 1 (2006): 11–32.

43. Daniel Benjamin and Steven Simon, *The Next Attack: The Failure of the War on Terror and the Strategy of Getting It Right* (New York: Times Books, 2005), 34.

44. Robert Malley and Peter Harling, "A Counter-Intuitive Strategy For Iraq," *Financial Times*, November 22, 2005.

45. For the complex nature of the Iraqi insurgency, see Ahmed S. Hashim, "Iraq: From Insurgency to Civil War?" *Current History* 104, no. 678 (2005): 10–18.

46. A number of stringent critiques of the American invasion of Iraq, the subsequent failure in putting together a viable system in the country, and the impact of both these factors on the war against terrorism have been published. Among the best are George Packer's *The Assassin's Gate: America in Iraq* (New York: Farrar, Straus and Giroux, 2005) and Larry Diamond's *Squandered Victory: The American Occupation and the Bungled Effort to Bring Democracy to Iraq* (New York: Times Books, 2005).

47. William Dalrymple, "Inside the Madrasas," *New York Review of Books* 52, no. 19 (2005): 16–20.

48. Peter Bergen and Alec Reynolds, "Blowback Revisited: Today's Insurgents in Iraq Are Tomorrow's Terrorists," *Foreign Affairs* 84, no. 6 (2005): 4.

49. Ibid., 6.

50. Benjamin and Simon, *Next Attack*, 6.

51. International Crisis Group, *Jordan's 9/11: Dealing with Jihadi Islamism*, Middle East Report No. 47, November 2005, 12 n. 93.

52. A letter from al-Zawahiri to al-Zarqawi dated July 9, 2005, was reportedly discovered by U.S. forces and was released by the Pentagon in October 2005. Although suspicions persist about the authenticity of the letter, several analysts seem to be in favor of accepting its authenticity in at least some limited fashion. For a perceptive commentary on the content of the letter, see the analysis put out by Strategic Forecasting, Inc. (Stratfor), "The Al-Zawahiri Letter: Insights into the Jihadist Movement," October 19, 2005,

http://biz.stratfor.com/products/premium/read_article.php?selected=Terrorism%20B
rief&id=257 342 (subscription required).

53. International Crisis Group, *Jordan's 9/11,* 12 n. 93.

CHAPTER 8

1. For details of the multiple manifestations of Islamism in Saudi Arabia, see International Crisis Group, *Saudi Arabia Backgrounder.*

2. White, "End of Islamism?"

3. Bruce K. Rutherford, "What Do Egypt's Islamists Want? Moderate Islam and the Rise of Islamic Constitutionalism," *Middle East Journal* 60, no. 4 (2006): 707.

4. Janine A. Clark, "The Conditions of Islamist Moderation: Unpacking Cross-Ideological Cooperation in Jordan," *International Journal of Middle East Studies* 38, no. 4 (2006): 539–40.

5. Jillian Schwedler, *Faith in Moderation: Islamist Parties in Jordan and Yemen* (New York: Cambridge University Press, 2006).

6. This point has been eloquently argued in Rashid Khalidi, *Resurrecting Empire: Western Footprints and America's Perilous Path in the Middle East* (Boston: Beacon, 2004).

7. Shibley Telhami, *The Stakes: America in the Middle East* (Boulder: Westview, 2002), chap. 4.

8. Two leading American scholars of international relations, both from the realist school, have cogently made the argument that America's unquestioning support for Israel, in substantial part the result of the strength of the Israeli lobby in Washington, is highly counterproductive from the perspective of American national interest in the Middle East. See John Mearsheimer and Stephen Walt, "The Israel Lobby," *London Review of Books* 28, no. 6 (2006): 3–12. For an expanded version of the article that provides meticulous documentation, see John Mearsheimer and Stephen Walt, "The Israel Lobby and U.S. Foreign Policy," *Middle East Policy* 13, no. 3 (2006): 29–87.

9. For a cogent and detailed argument on these lines, see Fawaz Gerges, *America and Political Islam: Clash of Cultures or Clash of Interests?* (Cambridge: Cambridge University Press, 1999).

10. Mohammed Ayoob, "The War against Iraq: Normative and Strategic Implications," in *The Wars on Terrorism and Iraq: Human Rights, Unilateralism, and U.S. Foreign Policy,* ed. Thomas G. Weiss, Margaret Crahan, and John Goering (New York: Routledge, 2004), 27–39.

11. Fawaz Gerges, "Gauging Terror—Part I, Lebanon," *YaleGlobal Online,* August 15, 2006, http://yaleglobal.yale.edu/display.article?id=7996.

12. For details, see Barnett R. Rubin, *The Fragmentation of Afghanistan: State Formation and Collapse in the International System,* 2nd ed. (New Haven: Yale University Press, 2002); Ahmed Rashid, *Taliban: Militant Islam, Oil, and Fundamentalism in Central Asia* (New Haven: Yale University Press, 2001).

13. Mark Mazetti, "Spy Agencies Say Iraq War Worsens Terror Threat," *New York Times,* September 24, 2006.

14. Michael Slackman, "Islamists' Rise Imperils Mideast's Order," *New York Times,* September 18, 2006.

15. For a detailed eyewitness recounting of American mismanagement in Iraq, see the account by long-serving former *Washington Post* bureau chief in Baghdad Rajiv Chandrasekaran, entitled *Imperial Life in the Emerald City: Inside Iraq's Green Zone* (New York: Alfred A. Knopf, 2006).

16. Toby Dodge, "How Iraq Was Lost," *Survival* 48, no. 4 (2006), 169.

17. The term "half men" was first used by President Bashar Assad of Syria to characterize those elements in the Arab world that refused to support Hizbullah against Israel (Michael Slackman, "Islamists' Rise Imperils Mideast's Order," *New York Times,* September 18, 2006). Although the Syrian government clarified that President Assad did not use the term to refer to Arab leaders, the appellation seems to have stuck to them in the Arab street. See "Lebanon and Regional Diplomacy: Arab Neighbours Thinking Ahead," *Economist,* August 24, 2006.

18. Polls conducted under the auspices of the Pew Global Attitudes Project confirm these findings. Polls conducted in 2006 showed that favorable opinion of the United States in Jordan, Turkey, and Pakistan stood at 15, 12, and 27 percent, respectively (http://pewglobal.org/reports/display.php?ReportID=252). The findings were released in June 2006, ahead of the Israeli invasion of Lebanon and American replenishment of the Israeli military arsenal during the invasion. One can reasonably expect that favorable ratings for the United States would have gone down further following the Israel-Hizbullah conflict. The finding is corroborated by a poll taken in October 2005 in six Arab countries whose regimes have close ties with the United States—Jordan, Lebanon, Morocco, Saudi Arabia, Egypt, and the United Arab Emirates. Sixty-three percent of the respondents saw the United States as one of the two major threats to their countries, with Israel ranking at 70 percent, slightly above America. Eighty percent identified American policies, rather than values, as the reason for their negative attitude toward the United States. The poll was conducted jointly by the Anwar Sadat Chair for Peace and Development at the University of Maryland and the polling firm Zogby International. Details are available at http://www.bsos.umd.edu/SADAT/PUB/Arab-attitudes-2005.htm.

Glossary of Terms

dar al-Islam. Literally, "the abode of Islam"; territories in which Islamic law is, in theory, applicable. The opposite of *dar al-Harb* (literally, "the land of war"), which refers to all territories in which Islamic law is not applied and/or Muslims are not in political control. *Dar al-Islam* is differentiated from *umma*, which refers to the community of Muslims. *Dar al-Islam* refers to territories under Muslim political control. "Islamdom" is a good equivalent in English.

dawa. Literally, "call," that is, inviting others to Islam; the act of educating non-Muslims about Islam. Also used to invite Muslims to become better practicing Muslims.

fatwa. A legal pronouncement made by a scholar capable of issuing judgments on Islamic law.

fiqh. Islamic jurisprudence, which covers all aspects of life. In Sunni Islam, disagreement on authenticity of hadith to use as sources to arrive at a verdict on a particular issue has led to the emergence of several schools of jurisprudence. The four most prominent are Hanafi, Shafi'i, Maliki, and Hanbali, named after their most prominent founders. Unlike the Sunni-Shia division, these schools do not transform into social and political identities. Most Shia follow the Ja'afri school of jurisprudence, named after their sixth Imam, himself a great jurist.

fitna. Mischief, dissension, and conflict within the *umma*.

hadith. Words and deeds of Prophet Muhammad. Collected and verified meticulously, they form the source for determining the sunna, the way of the Prophet.

hudna. Truce, armistice, or cease-fire. In Western parlance, the term is most frequently used in reference to an Israeli-Palestinian truce, particularly one that would involve such organizations as Hamas.

ijtihad. Derived from *jahada*, which means to struggle to attain an objective. The process of arriving at an Islamic legal decision through independent reasoning and interpretation of basic sources, such as the Quran and the sunna. The opposite of *taqlid*, or following precedent or existing practice without questioning it. A person who has the scholarly credentials to conduct *ijtihad* is called a *mujtahid*.

imam. Literally, "leader." In everyday usage, a prayer leader. In the Sunni tradition, a recognized religious leader or teacher. In Shia Islam, a descendant of the Prophet through his daughter Fatima and son-in-law Ali. These descendants were recognized as spiritual leaders of the community. According to Shia belief, the twelfth imam went into occultation and will return at the end of time to inaugurate an era of absolute justice in the world. The Shias believe that all government is illegitimate pending the return of the Mahdi, the twelfth imam.

intifada. Palestinian uprising to free the West Bank and Gaza from the Israeli occupation begun in 1967. The first intifada began in 1987, the second in 2000.

jahiliyya. Literally, "state of ignorance." Refers specifically to the state of being ignorant of Islam, the condition in which Arabs found themselves in Arabian society prior to Islam. Modern Islamist scholars, such as Qutb and Mawdudi, used this term to describe Muslim societies where Islamic law did not prevail.

jihad. Literally, "effort" or "struggle." The term has been conventionally interpreted as armed struggle by Muslims to defend or advance Islam against unbelievers. After a saying of the Prophet, some traditions emphasize "greater jihad," which means struggle against one's inner temptations, as opposed to "lesser jihad," which connotes armed struggle.

jihadis. Muslim militants who favor and adopt violence as a means to achieve political ends, often in a transnational context.

madrassa. School; more specifically, schools in which religious instruction is offered.

Mahdi. The prophesied redeemer of Islam, who will change the world into a perfect Islamic society alongside the Prophet Jesus before the Day of the Resurrection. The belief in Mahdi is shared by both Sunnis and Shiites; however, Twelver Shiites believe that the twelfth imam is the Mahdi and will reappear from his hiding.

muhajir. Muslim refugee or immigrant who flees his/her homeland due to oppression and persecution. The term was initially applied to the Muslims of Mecca who migrated to Medina with the Prophet in 622 CE. Several groups in the past have also been referred to as *muhajirs*, including Muslim refugees from India who settled in Pakistan after independence in 1947.

Salafis. Members of the Sunni puritanical movement of *salafiyya*. Salafis favor a return to the practice of the *salaf al-salih* (the "righteous ancestors"), the first three generations of Muslims. Salafis are known by their strict interpretation of the Quran and the sunna and their strong opposition to traditional and Sufi practices. In addition, salafis are known for their strong anti-Shia discourse.

sharia. Literally "the way"; the body of Islamic law that governs individual and social aspects of Muslim life. The two basic sources of sharia are the Quran and the hadith. In the Muslim historical context, the term often refers more to rule of law than to a particular legal system.

Sheikh al-Islam (Şeyhül slam in Turkish). Highest authority on religious issues in the Sunni political tradition. Title given to the highest Ottoman religious authority, in contrast to the political position of the sultan-caliph.

Shia. One of the two major sects in Islam. Cf. **Sunnis.** The Shia view is that succession had to come from the family of the Prophet (Ahl al-Bayt); hence, Ali bin Abi Talib, son-in-law of the Prophet, had to be the first legitimate successor. Shia's believe that Imams are infallible spiritual guides.

shura. Literally, "consultation." Muslim movements argue that Islam requires consultation as a decision-making principle, allowing for a synthesis of Islam and representative democracy.

sunna. The deeds, sayings, and approvals of Prophet Muhammad and, according to the Shia, those of the twelve Imams.

Sunnis. One of the two major sects in Islam. Cf. **Shia.** Sunnis accept election or selection by the leaders of the community as the means of choosing the caliph. They regard the first four caliphs—Abu Bakr, Umar, Uthman, and Ali—as "rightly guided." Other than the question of succession, there are theological differences between the two. Sunnis regard caliphs as fallible political leaders.

takfir. The practice of denouncing as an apostate an individual who identifies himself or herself as Muslim. In classical Muslim scholarship, conditions of *takfir* are extensively discussed. In modern context, marginal and extremist groups accuse entire Muslim societies of being apostates.

taqlid. The opposite of *ijtihad;* implies total acceptance of previous scholarly opinions on religious and daily matters without demanding a detailed justification of them.

ulama (pl. of *alim*). Religious-legal scholars of Islam.

umma. The worldwide Muslim community, including majority and minority Muslim populations.

vilayat-i faqih. Guardianship of the jurisconsult. The concept establishes the authority of the *faqih,* or expert in *fiqh* (jurisprudence), over religious as well as political matters. It was first developed by Ayatollah Khomeini in 1963 and incorporated into Iran's constitutional system in 1979, establishing him as the highest authority in the country.

Wahhabism. An Islamic puritanical doctrine of reform and renewal attributed to Muhammad ibn Abdul Wahhab (1703–87), who allied himself with the House of Saud. Wahhabism has served as the official ideology of the Saudi regime. The term was coined by ibn Abdul Wahhab's opponents; his followers prefer to call themselves Muwahhidun (Unitarians).

Bibliography

Abbas, Hassan. *Pakistan's Drift into Extremism: Allah, the Army, and America's War on Terror.* Armonk, NY: M. E. Sharpe, 2005.

Abdullah, Saeed. "The Official Ulama and the Religious Legitimacy of the Modern Nation State." In *Islam and Political Legitimacy,* ed. Shahram Akbarzadeh and Abdullah Saeed, 14–28. New York: Routledge Curzon, 2003.

Abrahamian, Ervand. *Iran between Two Revolutions.* Princeton: Princeton University Press, 1982.

Abu-Amr, Ziad. *Islamic Fundamentalism in the West Bank and Gaza: Muslim Brotherhood and Islamic Jihad.* Bloomington: Indiana University Press, 1994.

Abuza, Zachary. *Militant Islam in Southeast Asia: Crucible of Terror.* Boulder: Lynne Rienner, 2003.

Adams, Charles J. "Mawdudi and the Islamic State." In *Voices of Resurgent Islam,* ed. John L. Esposito, 99–103. New York: Oxford University Press, 1983.

Ahmad, Aziz. "Sayyid Ahmad Khan, Jamal Al-Din Al-Afghani, and Muslim India." *Studia Islamica* 13 (1960): 55–78.

Ajami, Fouad. *The Arab Predicament.* Updated ed. New York: Cambridge University Press, 1992.

Ajami, Fouad. *The Vanished Imam: Musa Al Sadr and the Shia of Lebanon.* Reprint, Ithaca: Cornell University Press, 1992.

Al-Awadi, Hesham. *In Pursuit of Legitimacy: The Muslim Brothers and Mubarak, 1982–2000.* New York: Tauris Academic Studies, 2000.

Al-Awadi, Hesham. "Mubarak and the Islamists: Why Did the 'Honeymoon' End?" *Middle East Journal* 59, no. 1 (2005): 62–80.

Alexiev, Alex. "Tablighi Jamaat: Jihad's Stealthy Legions." *Middle East Quarterly* 12, no. 1 (2005).

Algar, Hamid. *Wahhabism: A Critical Essay.* Oneonta, NY: Islamic Publications International, 2002.

Al-Rasheed, Madawi. *A History of Saudi Arabia.* New York: Cambridge University Press, 2002.

Anderson, Lisa. "Fulfilling Prophecies: State Policy and Islamist Radicalism." In *Politi-*

cal Islam: Revolution, Radicalism, or Reform? ed. John L. Esposito, 17–31. Boulder: Lynne Rienner, 1997.

Ansari, Ali M. "Continuous Regime Change from Within." *Washington Quarterly* 26, no. 4 (2003): 53–67.

Arat, Yesim. *Rethinking Islam and Liberal Democracy: Islamist Women in Turkish Politics.* New York: State University of New York Press, 2005.

Arjomand, Said Amir. *The Turban for the Crown: The Islamic Revolution in Iran.* New York: Oxford University Press, 1988.

Asad, Talal. "Religion, Nation-State, Secularism." In *Nation and Religion: Perspectives on Europe and Asia,* ed. Peter van der Veer and Hartmut Lehmann, 178–96. Princeton: Princeton University Press, 1999.

Ayoob, Mohammed. "The Future of Political Islam: The Importance of External Variables." *International Affairs* 81, no. 5 (2005): 951–61.

Ayoob, Mohammed. "The Muslim World's Poor Record of Modernization and Democratization: The Interplay of External and Internal Factors." In *Modernization, Democracy, and Islam,* ed. Shireen T. Hunter and Huma Malik, 186–202. Westport: Praeger; Washington, DC: Center for Strategic and International Studies, 2005.

Ayoob, Mohammed. *The Third World Security Predicament: State Making, Regional Conflict, and the International System.* Boulder: Lynne Rienner, 1995.

Ayoob, Mohammed. "Turkey's Multiple Paradoxes." *Orbis* 48, no. 3 (2004): 451–63.

Ayoob, Mohammed. "The War against Iraq: Normative and Strategic Implications." In *The Wars on Terrorism and Iraq: Human Rights, Unilateralism, and U.S. Foreign Policy,* ed. Thomas G. Weiss, Margaret Crahan, and John Goering, 27–39. New York: Routledge, 2004.

Bahgat, Gawdat. "The War on Terrorism: The Mujahedeen E-Khalk Saga." *Studies in Conflict and Terrorism* 27, no. 5 (2004): 377–85.

Baran, Zeyno. "Fighting the War of Ideas." *Foreign Affairs* 84, no. 6 (2005): 68–78.

Baran, Zeyno. *Hizb Ut-Tahrir: Islam's Political Insurgency.* Washington, DC: Nixon Center, 2004.

Barton, Greg. *Jemaah Islamiyah: Radical Islamism in Indonesia.* Singapore: Ridge Books, 2005.

Barton, Greg. *Liberal Islamic Ideas: A Study of the Writing of Nurcholish Madjid.* Jakarta: Pustaka Antara/Paramadina/Yayasan Adikarya IKAPI, 1999.

Baswedan, Anies Rasyid. "Political Islam in Indonesia: Present and Future Trajectory." *Asian Survey* 44, no. 5 (2004): 669–90.

Baumgarten, Helga. "The Three Faces/Phases of Palestinian Nationalism, 1948–2005." *Journal of Palestine Studies* 34, no. 4 (2005): 25–48.

Bellaigue, Christopher de. "New Man in Iran." *New York Review of Books* 52, no. 13 (2005): 19–22.

Benjamin, Daniel, and Steven Simon. *The Next Attack: The Failure of the War on Terror and the Strategy of Getting It Right.* New York: Times Books, 2005.

Bergen, Peter, and Alec Reynolds. "Blowback Revisited: Today's Insurgents in Iraq Are Tomorrow's Terrorists." *Foreign Affairs* 84, no. 6 (2005): 2–6.

Blecher, Robert. "Converging upon War." *Middle East Report Online,* 2006, http://www.merip.org/mero/mero071806.html.

Boland, B. J. *The Struggle of Islam in Modern Indonesia.* The Hague: Martinus Nijhoff, 1982.

Bradley, John R. "Al Qaeda and the House of Saud: Eternal Enemies or Secret Bedfellows?" *Washington Quarterly* 28, no. 4 (2005): 139–52.

Bronson, Rachel. "Rethinking Religion: The Legacy of the U.S.-Saudi Relationship." *Washington Quarterly* 28, no. 4 (2005): 121–37.

Brown, Daniel. *Rethinking Tradition in Modern Islamic Thought.* New York: Cambridge University Press, 1999.

Brown, L. Carl. *Religion and State: The Muslim Approach to Politics.* New York: Columbia University Press, 2000.

Brumberg, Daniel. "Islam Is Not the Solution (or the Problem)." *Washington Quarterly* 29, no. 1 (2005): 97–116.

Brumberg, Daniel. *Reinventing Khomeini: The Struggle for Reform in Iran.* Chicago: University of Chicago Press, 2001.

Bulliet, Richard W. "The Crisis within Islam." *Wilson Quarterly* 26, no. 1 (2002): 11–19.

Bunt, Gary R. *Islam in the Digital Age: E-Jihad, Online Fatwas, and Cyber Islamic Environments.* London: Pluto, 2003.

Burgat, Francois. *Face to Face with Political Islam.* New York: I. B. Tauris, 2003.

Burke, Jason. *Al-Qaeda: Casting a Shadow of Terror.* New York: I. B. Tauris, 2004.

Chandrasekaran, Rajiv. *Imperial Life in the Emerald City: Inside Iraq's Green Zone.* New York: Alfred A. Knopf, 2006.

Chehabi, H. E. "Religion and Politics in Iran." *Daedalus* 120, no. 3 (1991): 69–91.

Clark, Janine A. "The Conditions of Islamist Moderation: Unpacking Cross-Ideological Cooperation in Jordan." *International Journal of Middle East Studies* 38, no. 4 (2006): 539–60.

Cohen, Stephen Philip. " The Jihadist Threat to Pakistan." *Washington Quarterly* 26, no. 3 (2003): 7–25.

Cook, Michael. *Commanding Right and Forbidding Wrong in Islamic Thought.* New York: Cambridge University Press, 2000.

Crone, Patricia. *God's Rule: Government and Islam.* New York: Columbia University Press, 2004.

Crouch, Harold. *The Army and Politics in Indonesia.* Ithaca: Cornell University Press, 1988.

Dagi, Ihsan D. "Transformation of Islamic Political Identity in Turkey: Rethinking the West and Westernization." *Turkish Studies* 6, no. 1 (2005): 21–37.

Dalrymple, William. "Inside the Madrasas." *New York Review of Books* 52, no. 19 (2005): 16–20.

Dawisha, Adeed. *Arab Nationalism in the Twentieth Century: From Triumph to Despair.* Princeton: Princeton University Press, 2002.

de Bellaigue, Christopher. "Who Rules Iran?" *New York Review of Books* 49, no. 11 (2002): 17–19.

Deeb, Lara. "Hizballah: A Primer." *Middle East Report Online,* 2006, http://www.merip.org/mero/mero073106.html.

Dekmejian, Richard. "The Liberal Impulse in Saudi Arabia." *Middle East Journal* 57, no. 3 (2003): 400–413.

Delong-Bas, Natana J. *Wahhabi Islam: From Revival and Reform to Global Jihad.* New York: Oxford University Press, 2004.

Denoeux, Guilain. "The Forgotten Swamp: Navigating Political Islam." *Middle East Policy* 9, no. 2 (2002): 56–81.

Diamond, Larry. *Squandered Victory: The American Occupation and the Bungled Effort to Bring Democracy to Iraq.* New York: Times Books, 2005.

Dodge, Toby. "How Iraq Was Lost." *Survival* 48, no. 4 (2006): 157–72.

Effendy, Bahtiar. *Islam and the State in Indonesia.* Athens: Ohio University Press, 2003.

Eickelman, Dale F., and James Piscatori. *Muslim Politics.* Princeton: Princeton University Press, 1996.

El Amrani, Issandr. "Controlled Reform in Egypt: Neither Reformist nor Controlled." *Middle East Report Online,* 2005, http://www.merip.org/mero/mero121505.html.

Enayat, Hamid. "Khumayni's Concept of the 'Guardianship of the Jurisconsult.'" In *Islam in the Political Process,* ed. James P. Piscatori, 160–80. New York: Cambridge University Press, 1983.

Enayat, Hamid. *Modern Islamic Political Thought.* Austin: University of Texas Press, 1982.

Ernst, Carl W. *Following Muhammad: Rethinking Islam in the Contemporary World.* Chapel Hill: University of North Carolina Press, 2003.

Fandy, Mamoun. *Saudi Arabia and the Politics of Dissent.* New York: Palgrave Macmillan, 1999.

Fuller, Graham. "The Future of Political Islam." *Foreign Affairs* 81, no. 2 (2002): 48–60.

Fuller, Graham. *The Future of Political Islam.* New York: Palgrave Macmillan, 2003.

Geertz, Clifford. *Islam Observed: Religious Development in Morocco and Indonesia.* Chicago: University of Chicago Press, 1971.

Gerecht, Reuel Marc. *The Islamic Paradox: Shiite Clerics, Sunni Fundamentalists, and the Coming of Arab Democracy.* Washington, DC: AEI Press, 2004.

Gerges, Fawaz. *America and Political Islam: Clash of Cultures or Clash of Interests?* Cambridge: Cambridge University Press, 1999.

Gerges, Fawaz. *The Far Enemy: Why Jihad Went Global.* New York: Cambridge University Press, 2005.

Gibb, H. A. R. *Modern Trends in Islam.* Chicago: University of Chicago Press, 1947.

Grare, Frederic. *Pakistan: The Myth of an Islamist Peril.* Policy Brief No. 45. Washington, DC: Carnegie Endowment for International Peace, 2006.

Habib, John S. *Ibn Saud's Warriors of Islam: The Ikhwan of Najd and Their Role in the Creation of the Saudi Kingdom, 1910–1930.* Leiden: E. J. Brill, 1978.

Haddad, Yvonne. "Sayyid Qutb: Ideologue of Islamic Revival." In *Voices of Resurgent Islam,* ed. John L. Esposito, 67–98. New York: Oxford University Press, 1983.

Hamzeh, Ahmad Nizar. *In the Path of Hizbullah.* Syracuse: Syracuse University Press, 2004.

Harik, Judith Palmer. *Hezbollah: The Changing Face of Terrorism.* New York: I. B. Tauris, 2004.

Hashim, Ahmed S. "Iraq: From Insurgency to Civil War?" *Current History* 104, no. 678 (2005): 10–18.

Hefner, Robert W. *Civil Islam: Muslims and Democratization in Indonesia.* Princeton: Princeton University Press, 2000.

Hefner, Robert W. "Introduction: Modernity and the Remaking of Muslim Politics." In *Remaking Muslim Politics: Pluralism, Contestation, Democratization,* ed. Robert W. Hefner, 1–36. Princeton: Princeton University Press, 2005.

Hegghammer, Thomas. "Global Jihadism after the Iraq War." *Middle East Journal* 60, no. 1 (2006): 11–32.

Heper, Metin, and Aylin Guney. "The Military and the Consolidation of Democracy: The Recent Turkish Experience." *Armed Forces and Society* 26, no. 4 (2000): 635–57.

Hobsbawm, Eric, and Terence Ranger, eds. *The Invention of Tradition.* New York: Cambridge University Press, 1983.

Hodgson, Marshall G. S. *The Venture of Islam.* Vol. 1, *The Classical Age of Islam.* Chicago: University of Chicago Press, 1974.

Hourani, Albert. *Arabic Thought in the Liberal Age, 1798–1939.* New York: Cambridge University Press, 1983.

Hroub, Khaled. *Hamas: Political Thought and Practice.* Washington, DC: Institute for Palestine Studies, 2000.

Huntington, Samuel. *The Clash of Civilizations and the Remaking of World Order.* New York: Simon and Schuster, 1996.

International Crisis Group. *Iran: What Does Ahmadi-Nejad's Victory Mean?* Middle East Briefing No. 18, August 2005.

International Crisis Group. *Islamism in North Africa II: Egypt's Opportunity.* Middle East/North Africa Briefing No. 13, April 2004.

International Crisis Group. *Jemaah Islamiyah in Southeast Asia: Damaged but Still Dangerous.* Asia Report No. 63, August 2003.

International Crisis Group. *Jordan's 9/11: Dealing with Jihadi Islamism.* Middle East Report No. 47, November 2005.

International Crisis Group. *Radical Islam in Central Asia: Responding to Hizb Ut-Tahrir.* Asia Report No. 58, June 2003.

International Crisis Group. *Saudi Arabia Backgrounder: Who Are the Islamists?* Middle East Report No. 31, September 2004.

International Crisis Group. *The Shiite Question in Saudi Arabia.* Middle East Report No. 45, September 2005.

International Crisis Group. *Understanding Islamism.* Middle East/North Africa Report No. 37, March 2005.

Johns, Anthony H., and Abdullah Saeed. "Nurcholish Madjid and the Interpretation of the Qur'an: Religious Pluralism and Tolerance." In *Modern Muslim Intellectuals and the Qu'ran,* ed. Suha Taji-Farouki, 67–96. New York: Oxford University Press, 2004.

Jones, Toby Craig. "The Clerics, the Sahwa, and the Saudi State." *Strategic Insights* 4, no. 3 (2005), http://www.ccc.nps.navy.mil/si/2005/Mar/jonesMar05.pdf.

Kassem, Maye. *Egyptian Politics: The Dynamics of Authoritarian Rule.* Boulder: Lynne Rienner, 2004.

Keddie, Nikki. *Modern Iran: Roots and Results of Revolution.* New Haven: Yale University Press, 2003.

Keddie, Nikki. "Religion and Irreligion in Early Iranian Nationalism." *Comparative Studies in Society and History* 4, no. 3 (1962): 265–95.

Keddie, Nikki. *Sayyid Jamal Ad-Din Al-Afghani: A Political Biography.* Los Angeles: University of California Press, 1972.

Kepel, Gilles. *The Prophet and the Pharaoh: Muslim Extremism in Egypt.* London: Saqi Books, 1985.

Kepel, Gilles. *The War for Muslim Minds: Islam and the West.* Cambridge, MA: Belknap, 2004.

Kerr, Malcolm H. *Islamic Reform: The Political and Legal Theories of Muhammad 'Abduh and Rashid Rida.* Berkeley: University of California Press, 1966.

Khalidi, Rashid. *Resurrecting Empire: Western Footprints and America's Perilous Path in the Middle East.* Boston: Beacon, 2004.

Khatami, Mohammad. *Islam, Liberty, and Development.* Binghamton: Global Academic Publishing, 1998.

Khomeini, Ruhollah. *Islam and Revolution: Writings and Declarations of Imam Khomeini.* Trans. Hamid Algar. Berkeley: Mizan, 1981.

Khomeini, Ruhollah. *Islamic Government.* Trans. Joint Publications Research Service. New York: Manor Books, 1979.

Kodmani, Bassma. *The Dangers of Political Exclusion: Egypt's Islamist Problem.* Carnegie Paper No. 63. Washington, DC: Carnegie Endowment for International Peace, 2005.

Kosebalaban, Hasan. "The Impact of Globalization on Islamic Political Identity." *World Affairs* 168, no. 1 (2005): 27–37.

Kostiner, Joseph. *The Making of Saudi Arabia, 1916–1936: From Chieftancy to Monarchical State.* New York: Oxford University Press, 1993.

Kurzman, Charles. *Liberal Islam: A Source Book.* New York: Oxford University Press, 1998.

Lambton, A. K. S. "The Persian Constitutional Revolution of 1905–6." In *Revolution in the Middle East, and Other Case Studies,* ed. P. J. Vatikiotis, 173–82. London: Allen and Unwin, 1972.

Lawrence, Bruce. *Messages to the World: The Statements of Osama Bin Laden.* New York: Verso, 2005.

Lee, Terence. "The Nature and Future of Civil-Military Relations in Indonesia." *Asian Survey* 40, no. 4 (2000): 692–706.

Lewis, Bernard. "Roots of Muslim Rage." *Atlantic Monthly* 266, no. 3 (1990): 47–60.

Liddle, R. William, and Saiful Mujani. "Indonesia in 2005: A New Multiparty Presidential Democracy." *Asian Survey* 46, no. 1 (2006): 132–39.

Mamdani, Mahmood. *Good Muslim, Bad Muslim.* New York: Pantheon Books, 2004.

Mandaville, Peter. "Sufis and Salafis: The Political Discourse of Transnational Islam." In *Remaking Muslim Politics: Pluralism, Contestation, Democratization,* ed. Robert W. Hefner, 302–25. Princeton: Princeton University Press, 2005.

Marx, Anthony W. "The Nation-State and Its Exclusions." *Political Science Quarterly* 117, no. 1 (2002): 103–26.

Masud, Muhammad Khalid. *Travellers in Faith: Studies of the Tablighi Jama'at as a Transnational Islamic Movement for Faith Renewal.* Leiden: E. J. Brill, 2000.

Mearsheimer, John, and Stephen Walt. "The Israel Lobby." *London Review of Books* 28, no. 6 (2006): 3–12.

Mearsheimer, John, and Stephen Walt. "The Israel Lobby and U.S. Foreign Policy." *Middle East Policy* 13, no. 3 (2006): 29–87.

Metcalf, Barbara Daly. *Islamic Revival in British India: Deoband, 1860–1900.* New York: Oxford University Press, 2004.

Metcalf, Barbara. "Travelers' Tales in the Tablighi Jama'at." *Annals of the American Academy of Political and Social Science* 588, no. 1 (2003): 136–48.

Mishal, Shaul, and Avraham Sela. *The Palestinian Hamas.* New York: Columbia University Press, 2000.

Mitchell, Richard P. *The Society of the Muslim Brothers.* New York: Oxford University Press, 1969.

Moussalli, Ahmad S. *Radical Islamic Fundamentalism: The Ideological and Political Discourse of Sayyid Qutb.* Beirut: University of Beirut, 1992.

Mufti, Malik. *Sovereign Creations: Pan-Arabism and Political Order in Syria and Iraq.* Ithaca: Cornell University Press, 1996.

Nafisi, Azar. "The Voice of Akbar Ganji." *Journal of Democracy* 16, no. 4 (2005): 35–37.

Nasr, Seyyed Vali Reza. "Mawdudi and the Jamat-I-Islami." In *Pioneers of Islamic Revival,* ed. Ali Rahnema, 98–124. London: Zed Books, 1994.

Nasr, Seyyed Vali Reza. *The Vanguard of the Islamic Revolution: The Jama'at-I-Islami of Pakistan.* Berkeley: University of California Press, 1994.

Nasr, Seyyed Vali Reza. *Mawdudi and the Making of Islamic Revivalism.* New York: Oxford University Press, 1996.

Nasr, Vali. "Military Rule, Islamism, and Democracy in Pakistan." *Middle East Journal* 58, no. 2 (2004): 195–209.

Nasr, Vali. "The Rise Of 'Muslim Democracy.'" *Journal of Democracy* 16, no. 2 (2005): 13–27.

Navari, Cornelia. "The Origins of the Nation-State." In *The Nation-State: The Formation of Modern Politics,* ed. Leonard Tivey, 13–38. Oxford: Martin Robertson, 1981.

Norton, Augustus Richard. "Hizballah and the Israeli Withdrawal from Southern Lebanon." *Journal of Palestine Studies* 30, no. 1 (2000): 22–35.

Norton, Augustus Richard. "Hizballah: From Radicalism to Pragmatism?" *Middle East Policy* 5, no. 4 (1998): 147–58.

Norton, Augustus Richard. "Thwarted Politics: The Case of Egypt's Hizb Al-Wasat." In *Remaking Muslim Politics: Pluralism, Contestation, Democratization,* ed. Robert W. Hefner, 133–60. Princeton: Princeton University Press, 2005.

Nusse, Andrea. *Muslim Palestine: The Ideology of Hamas.* Abingdon, UK: Routledge Curzon, 2004.

Okruhlik, Gwenn. "Empowering Civility through Nationalism: Reformist Islam and Belonging in Saudi Arabia." In *Remaking Muslim Politics: Pluralism, Contestation, Democratization,* ed. Robert W. Hefner, 189–212. Princeton: Princeton University Press, 2005.

Onis, Ziya. "The Political Economy of Islam and Democracy in Turkey: From the Welfare Party to the AKP." In *Democratization and Development: New Political Strategies for the Middle East,* ed. Dietrich Jung, 103–28. New York: Palgrave Macmillan, 2006.

Ozel, Soli. "Turkey at the Polls: After the Tsunami." *Journal of Democracy* 14, no. 2 (2003): 80–94.

Packer, George. *The Assassin's Gate: America in Iraq.* New York: Farrar, Straus and Giroux, 2005.

Parsa, Misagh. *Social Origins of the Iranian Revolution.* New Brunswick: Rutgers University Press, 1989.

Peters, Rudolph. *Islam and Colonialism: The Doctrine of Jihad in Modern History.* New York: Mouton, 1979.

Piscatori, James *Islam in a World of Nation-States.* New York: Cambridge University Press, 1986.

Qassem, Naim. *Hizbullah: The Story from Within.* London: Saqi Books, 2005.

Qodari, Muhammad. "Indonesia's Quest for Accountable Governance." *Journal of Democracy* 16, no. 2 (2005): 73–87.

Rahman, Fazlur. *Revival and Reform in Islam: A Study of Islamic Fundamentalism.* Ed. Ebrahim Moosa. Oxford: Oneworld Publications, 1999.

Rajaee, Bahram. "Deciphering Iran: The Political Evolution of the Islamic Republic and U.S. Foreign Policy after September 11." *Comparative Studies of South Asia* 24, no. 1 (2004): 159–72.

Ramadan, Tariq. *Western Muslims and the Future of Islam.* New York: Oxford University Press, 2003.

Randal, Jonathan. *Osama: The Making of a Terrorist.* New York: Alfred A. Knopf, 2004.

Rashid, Ahmed. *Jihad: The Rise of Militant Islam in Central Asia.* New Haven: Yale University Press, 2002.

Rashid, Ahmed. *Taliban: Militant Islam, Oil, and Fundamentalism in Central Asia.* New Haven: Yale University Press, 2001.

Richards, John F. *The Mughal Empire.* Cambridge: Cambridge University Press, 1996.

Rizvi, Sayyid Athar Abbas. *Shah Wali-Allah and His Times: A Study of Eighteenth Century Islam, Politics, and Society in India.* Canberra: Maarifat Publishing, 1980.

Rouleau, Eric. "Trouble in the Kingdom." *Foreign Affairs* 81, no. 4 (2002): 75–89.

Roy, Olivier. *The Failure of Political Islam.* Cambridge, MA: Harvard University Press, 1996.

Rubin, Barnett R. *The Fragmentation of Afghanistan: State Formation and Collapse in the International System.* 2nd ed. New Haven: Yale University Press, 2002.

Rutherford, Bruce K. "What Do Egypt's Islamists Want? Moderate Islam and the Rise of Islamic Constitutionalism." *Middle East Journal* 60, no. 4 (2006): 707–31.

Safa, Oussama. "Getting to Arab Democracy: Lebanon Springs Forward." *Journal of Democracy* 17, no. 1 (2006): 22–37.

Sariolghalam, Mahmood. "Understanding Iran: Getting Past Stereotypes and Mythology." *Washington Quarterly* 26, no. 4 (2003): 69–82.

Sayeed, Khalid B. *The Political System of Pakistan.* Boston: Houghton Mifflin, 1967.

Schwedler, Jillian. *Faith in Moderation: Islamist Parties in Jordan and Yemen.* New York: Cambridge University Press, 2006.

Sedgwick, Mark. "Is There a Church in Islam?" *ISIM Newsletter*, December 2003, 40–41.

Shah, Aqil. "Pakistan's 'Armored' Democracy." *Journal of Democracy* 14, no. 4 (2003): 15–40.

Shikaki, Khalil. "Palestinians Divided." *Foreign Affairs* 81, no. 1 (2002): 89–105.

Shikaki, Khalil. *Willing to Compromise: Palestinian Public Opinion and the Peace Process.* Special Report No. 158. Washington, DC: United States Institute of Peace, 2006.

Sikand, Yoginder. *The Origins and Development of the Tablighi Jamaat (1920–2000): A Cross-Country Comparative Study.* New Delhi: Orient Longman, 2002.

Sikand, Yoginder. "The Origins and Growth of the Tablighi Jamaat in Britain." *Islam and Christian-Muslim Relations* 9, no. 2 (1998): 171–92.

Sikand, Yoginder. "The Tablighi Jama'at and Politics: A Critical Reappraisal." *Muslim World* 96, no. 1 (2006): 175–95.

Soroush, Abdolkarim. *Reason, Freedom, and Democracy in Islam: Essential Writings of Abdolkarim Soroush.* Ed. and trans. Mahmoud Sadri and Ahmad Sadri. New York: Oxford University Press, 2000.

Spruyt, Hendrik. *The Sovereign State and Its Competitors.* Princeton: Princeton University Press, 1994.

Strindberg, Anders, and Mats Warn. "Realities of Resistance: Hizballah, the Palestinian Rejectionists, and Al-Qa'ida Compared." *Journal of Palestine Studies* 34, no. 3 (2005): 23–41.

Taji-Farouki, Suha. *A Fundamental Quest: Hizb Al-Tahrir and the Search for the Islamic Caliphate.* London: Grey Seal, 1996.

Taji-Farouki, Suha. Introduction to *Modern Muslim Intellectuals and the Qu'ran*, ed. Suha Taji-Farouki. New York: Oxford University Press, 2004.

Takeyh, Ray, and Nikolas K. Gvosdev. "Pragmatism in the Midst of Iranian Turmoil." *Washington Quarterly* 27, no. 4 (2004): 33–56.

Taspinar, Omer. *Kurdish Nationalism and Political Islam in Turkey: Kemalist Identity in Transition.* New York: Routledge, 2005.

Taspinar, Omer. *An Uneven Fit? The "Turkish Model" and the Arab World.* U.S. Relations with the Islamic World, Analysis Paper No. 5. Washington, DC: Brooking Institution, 2003.

Telhami, Shibley. *The Stakes: America in the Middle East.* Boulder: Westview, 2002.

Tilly, Charles. *Coercion, Capital, and European States, AD 990–1990.* Cambridge: Blackwell, 1990.

Tilly, Charles. "Reflections on the History of European State-Making." In *The Formation of National States in Western Europe*, ed. Charles Tilly, 3–83. Princeton: Princeton University Press, 1975.

Tripp, Charles. "Sayyid Qutb: The Political Vision." In *Pioneers of Islamic Revival*, ed. Ali Rahnema, 154–83. London: Zed Books, 1994.

Troll, Christian W. *Sayyid Ahmad Khan: A Reinterpretation of Muslim Theology.* New Delhi: Vikas, 1978.

Vassiliev, Alexei. *The History of Saudi Arabia.* New York: New York University Press, 2000.

Vickor, Knut S. "The Development of Ijtihad and Islamic Reform, 1750–1850." Paper presented at the Third Nordic Conference on Middle Eastern Studies, Joensuu, Finland, June 19–22, 1995.

White, Jenny B. "The End of Islamism? Turkey's Muslimhood Model." In *Remaking Muslim Politics: Pluralism, Contestation, Democratization,* ed. Robert W. Hefner, 87–111. Princeton: Princeton University Press, 2004.

Wickham, Carrie Rosefksy. *Mobilizing Islam: Religion, Activism, and Political Change in Egypt.* New York: Columbia University Press, 2002.

Wickham, Carrie Rosefsky. "The Path to Moderation: Strategy and Learning in the Formation of Egypt's Wasat Party." *Comparative Politics* 36, no. 2 (2004): 205–28.

Wight, Martin. *Systems of States.* Leicester: Leicester University Press, 1977.

Wiktorowicz, Quintan. "A Genealogy of Radical Islam." *Studies in Conflict and Terrorism* 28, no. 2 (2005): 75–97.

Yamani, Mai. *Cradle of Islam: The Hijaz and the Quest for an Arabian Identity.* London: I. B. Tauris, 2004.

Yavuz, M. Hakan. "The Role of the New Bourgeoisie in the Transformation of the Turkish Islamic Movement." In *The Emergence of a New Turkey: Democracy and the AK Parti,* ed. M. Hakan Yavuz, 1–19. Salt Lake City: University of Utah Press, 2006.

Zaman, Muhammad Qasim. "Pluralism, Democracy, and the 'Ulama." In *Remaking Muslim Politics: Pluralism, Contestation, Democratization,* ed. Robert W. Hefner, 60–86. Princeton: Princeton University Press, 2005.

Zaman, Muhammad Qasim. *The Ulama in Contemporary Islam: Custodians of Change.* Princeton: Princeton University Press, 2002.

Zubaida, Sami. "Islam and Nationalism: Continuities and Contradictions." *Nations and Nationalism* 10, no. 4 (2004): 407–20.

Index